f15

WITH A TWINKLE IN MY EYE

THE AUTHOR

CLARKSON ROSE

WITH A TWINKLE IN MY EYE

Foreword by
SIR BARRY JACKSON, M.A.

Preface by
COLLIE KNOX

Introduction by
GEORGE F. REYNOLDS

MUSEUM PRESS LIMITED
63 Old Brompton Road London S.W.7

FIRST PUBLISHED 1951

PRINTED IN GREAT BRITAIN BY J. AND J. GRAY, EDINBURGH

"All the world's a stage,
And all the men and women merely players:
They have their exits and their entrances;
And one man in his time plays many parts. . . ."

WILLIAM SHAKESPEARE:

As You Like it.
Act II, Scene 7

For

OLIVE

Because she has helped me not to be frightened of fear.
Because she taught me that honesty should not be
merely a policy

ILLUSTRATIONS

FOREWORD

by

SIR BARRY JACKSON, M.A.

"HE shouldn't act in straight plays. He should be a music-hall comedian. Whatever he does or attempts to do, he makes us laugh all the time."

This was the type of remark passed to me, either by word of mouth or by letter, about Clarkson Rose when he was a member of the Birmingham Repertory Theatre Company during the First World War. I am said to have given him similar advice, but be it far from me to claim that I helped him to become a famous comedian. He was a natural comic from the very start; hard work and sheer ability have done the rest.

More often than not I am disappointed by what I find in records—Press or otherwise—for they convey little or nothing of the personality that makes an artiste beloved of his audience. I find that young Clarkson Rose played Oliver in "As You Like It" for me at Birmingham. I have no recollection of that performance, no doubt due to the fact that the Royal Navy was by way of occupying my attention at the time, but though Clarkson Rose's technical skill may have made gigantic strides since those days, I should much liked to have heard him, even then, describing himself as " . . . A wretched man, o'er-grown with hair. . . ." It is more than possible that a tiny, tiny twinkle of humour shook the semi-serious fairy-tale speech to the foundation. Yes—he would be more at home with Kastril, the angry boy in "The Alchemist", for parts of this variety are solid meat for natural and gifted comedians.

Clarkson Rose has scintillated in all branches of theatrical humour, but it is as the Dame in that most peculiarly British institution, Pantomime, that he shines at his brightest—be "she" an angular spinster, an old

Widow Twankey of a crone, or a voluptuous Nelly Gwyn-cum-"Forever Amber" creation. He is alert and observant, and much of what he sees around him goes into his self-carved characters. Now, not having seen the content of his autobiography at the time of writing, I cannot give even the vaguest idea of what it contains. I can only be sure that the sparkle that is in his show, "Twinkle", will be present in no small measure, for if Clarkson Rose puts as much of his personality on to the written page as he has done, and is doing, on our stage, then happy hours lie ahead for his readers.

IT would not be unduly difficult for me to pen many beautiful and resounding phrases to laud—albeit with sincerity—the talents of my good friends Clarkson Rose and Olive Fox. They have brought to their life partnership the same qualities of heart and character that have won for them so assured a position in their professional calling. But I will not embarrass them with verbal bouquets. The highest compliment I could pay them—and one which they themselves would appreciate—is to describe them as two "magnificent troupers". In the theatrical world, to be a good trouper is to have risen from small beginnings to the top of the bill without losing a sense of proportion or succumbing to self-glory. It means that those who have won this accolade have known hard struggles and bitter disappointment, that no matter how hopeless the journey may have seemed at times, they have unfailingly kept their heads high, and their eyes fixed on the hills. When at last they emerged into the sunlight, they never forgot the lessons of their darker hours or those less fortunate than themselves. I feel that the tribute "He was a good trouper" is the finest epitaph that could be paid to a man in any walk of life—statesman, actor, author, artist, tinker, tailor, or candlestick-maker. It is simple. It is definite. It is all-embracing.

Clarkie has been on the stage for more than forty years, and during that period he has played an astonishing variety of roles. He is a brilliant comedian, and to be of the elect it is necessary also to be a very good actor. This Clarkie assuredly is. The inspired clown is he who is not only, as was Shakespeare's "Yorick", a "fellow of infinite jest of most excellent fancy", but he who can move an audience to tears as easily as he can woo them to laughter. There are but a few who are sufficiently masters of their art to achieve this feat. Clarkson Rose ranks high amongst them. I meet, in the course of my own professional life, large numbers of stage folk. Mostly they are splendid people, and many of them I like greatly and are valued friends of mine. A few I dislike more than I can express. Into the last category fall the vain and the spoiled—those who are for ever acting a part even when the house lights are out and the curtain is down—and, in particular, those who rave about "My public" and posture interminably. Why I hold both Clarkie and Olive in such esteem is that there is no humbug about them. They are downright and forthright. They have none of that *folie de grandeur* which usually conceals—and not very cleverly—limited talent and unlimited conceit. They have no soul-searing "Message" to deliver to a panting posterity. They have a job to do, and they spare no pains to do it to the utmost of their ability. The public pay good money to see them, and their company perform. Thus, the public must get full money's worth in both performance and production. Dame Marie Tempest once said to me, "I am the servant of the public." And meant it. Clarkson Rose would say the same and mean it.

After a year of experience at the Birmingham Repertory Theatre under the now Sir Barry Jackson, he transferred his allegiance to variety . . . and was a double turn with Olive Fox for several years. Later he became a single act, and after constantly 'headlining' at the Alhambra and the London Coliseum, appeared at the Royal Variety Performance in London in 1928. Then he co-starred with the glamorous Shirley Kellogg in the "Happy Hours" revue, the biggest touring revue ever to be sent on the road at that time. There is a tide in the affairs of man which, taken at the flood, leads on to—"Twinkle". In 1921 Clarkie had a brain-wave. He devised, arranged, and produced his soon to be famous summer show, "Twinkle", in which he and Olive played the leads—

and thus created a pleasant old age pension for them both, to which delighted and packed audiences at East-bourne, Hastings, Bognor, Bath, Stratford-on-Avon, Cardiff, Brighton and other coastal resorts still continue to subscribe. In 1933 he toured the show in all the principal theatres in Australia. "Twinkle" was the first seaside production to be broadcast for a whole hour, from Westcliff-on-Sea in 1926, thus welcoming to its arms new devotees. "Twinkle" is always bright, entertaining, sparkling, and the perfect family entertainment. It is a model of its kind.

Clarkson Rose each Christmas adorns the stage as a "dame" in pantomime, and is, to my mind, a "dame" to end all "dames". Dressed in ravishing creations, immense, staggeringly dignified, this First Lady of Pantomime land is unique of 'her' kind. "She" has to be seen to be disbelieved, and long may "she" reign over us.

Clarkie has the courage to strike a blow on behalf of his fellow artistes. He has little patience with cranks and killjoys. In September 1948, along with other members of the Blackpool studio audience at a Sunday night recording of the Henry Hall Guest Night, I witnessed a whacking smack in the eye delivered to the ridiculous and antiquated law that bans Sunday performances with artistes in 'make-up'. Wilfred Pickles and others had been forced to cancel bookings. Clarkie was booked as guest-artiste, and proclaimed, "I shall broadcast in full 'dame' regalia." The B.B.C. North Region lost its nerve and banned him. But, just before the recording, Clarkie told me that the B.B.C. in London had upheld him, and had said, "Go ahead. Wear the kitchen stove if you like. We will take full legal responsibility." So, before our delighted eyes, on he strode, magnificent to behold. I wondered what the morning would bring forth. But the law could not do a thing about it, as the audience had not paid to come in. Clarkie's resolute action helped to prove the utter fatuity of a law which, while allowing a Marx Brothers film at the local cinema on Sundays, debars artistes from giving Sunday shows—even for charity—should they dare to wear a hat or a false eyebrow or two.

This book tells the story of a man who has climbed the ladder of ambition but has never let ambition o'er-reach itself. It is the record of a "good trouper" and of a sensitive, kindly human being. Truly a Rose without a thorn.

INTRODUCTION

by

GEORGE F. REYNOLDS

*General Manager at the Alhambra, Leicester Square,
from 1920 until 1937*

I FIRST met Clarkson Rose when, in 1915, he and a
lady partner did an audition for me at the Manchester
Hippodrome, which I was then managing. He had
dashed over from where he was appearing with the
Birmingham Repertory Theatre Company, and, indeed,
had badgered me until I gave him this audition.

My verdict on his double-act was that it was good, but
that he should exploit his obvious comic singing abilities
in a single-act.

He didn't listen to me then, but instead prepared an
excellent act, known as "Fox and Rose", which several
times played successfully at theatres under my charge.

It was an accident to Miss Fox at the Bristol Hippodrome that turned Clarkson Rose into a comic singing
star almost overnight. Reports from the Bristol management were so good that Sir Oswald Stoll immediately
booked him for the Alhambra.

When he first appeared at the Alhambra he was in very
small type on the bills, and in the rather unenviable
position of second turn on the programme.

His success was phenomenal. He was, as that great
variety critic, Buchanan Taylor, described him in *Town
Topics*, "Young, lively, cheerful and distinct. He had
none of the extraneous aids of the regulation comedian;
his pants were not baggy, his nose was not red, his face
was not disfigured, and his enunciation was so distinct
that he might have been heard from one end of Olympia
to the other."

Shortly afterwards, "Clarkie" (as I always knew him) returned to my theatre as one of the headliners, and more than justified his proud position.

I have never seen an artiste more completely 'stop' the programme as Clarkson Rose did during those glorious few years of variety revival at the Alhambra. He appeared frequently, several times a year, and his audience could not have enough of him. Time and again he would have to make a speech before the next turn could follow on. What contributed to his success, I am convinced, was that he had clear enunciation, a fine singing voice, and did not require that horrible "mike".

Rose had some wonderful songs, and he was fortunate that he was able to write for himself. His *Back I went to the Ministry of Labour* goes easily into the gallery of music-hall classics, and it was, in my opinion, this song that established him in stardom. Then his Victorian study as *A Girl of the Old Brigade* ran it very close. Rose never made the mistake of singing one of his successful songs too long, he always brought something fresh.

It was shrewd Sir Oswald Stoll who nursed him to stardom, and in him Sir Oswald took a personal interest. Rose was always a favourite of his and Lady Stoll's. Other managers followed Sir Oswald's lead, and soon Rose was in great demand all over the country.

It was, in a way, a puzzle to me that in the height of his success he would suddenly turn down attractive engagements and return to what he would call his Pierrot troupe at the seaside.

I used to remonstrate with him and point out what he was throwing away. Yet I suppose I had a secret sympathy for him, because, at one time, I too was a member of a happy band of seaside troubadours, and I know the fascination, the charm, and the intimate personal enjoyment one can have in such engagements.

As an instance of this attitude, one particular night three famous managers were in the theatre at the same

time. They all made "Clarkie" attractive offers, which
he told me about. "Well, what are you going to do?" I
said. "These are great opportunities, you know, my boy."

He replied, "Well, I'm afraid I can't accept any of them
because it will interfere with my summer season in the
Isle of Wight."

Whether he was right or wrong is not my business, but
what has been the music-hall's loss has certainly been the
seaside's gain, for he has now made his intimate musical
"Twinkle" an institution in our coastal and spa towns.
And just to keep his hand in, so to speak, he still returns
to the music-halls for odd weeks, and is as big a success
as ever. Each Christmas, of course, he appears in pantomime, in which his "dame" study, which he hall-marked
for so many years at the old Lyceum Theatre, London,
is considered to be one of the best in the profession.

In a recent letter to me he tells me that one of his
cherished mementoes is the Alhambra Souvenir, which
was published to mark the tenth anniversary of the new
variety regime there, and in which Sir Oswald Stoll paid
him the tribute of placing the photograph of Clarkson
Rose alongside those of Marie Lloyd and Will Fyffe, and
referred to them as three of the stars who had kept the
variety flag flying at the Alhambra.

I can understand that feeling, for the Alhambra was
to me the theatre that was responsible for putting real
variety back on the West End map, and Rose was certainly,
with Marie Lloyd, Will Fyffe, Lily Morris—and a few
others—in the vanguard of stars who helped Sir Oswald
in this enterprise.

In late middle-age he still remains young and enthusiastic in thought—maybe there's "something in the
seaside air"—as Whit Cunliffe used to sing!

CHAPTER ONE

SHORTLY after I made my first entrance, on 8th December 1890, Dame Fortune, so far as my family was concerned, made her exit.

Goldthorne Court, Wolverhampton, and Ednam House, Dudley, Worcs., were considered two of "the stately homes" of that part of England, and they were my ancestral homes. But all that I ever knew of them were the reminiscences of my mother and father and other relations. And occasional visits when, as children, we were taken to stand outside the gates and gaze at the family's "lost splendour".

When I was due to make my first appearance in "The Comedy of Life" my parents were living in a semi-detached villa. But my mother, doubtless feeling that I ought to be born in the shade of Ednam House, arranged to present me to the world in a house called "The Cedars", to which my grandmother had moved, and which, standing in Ednam Road, was but the proverbial stone's-throw from Ednam House.

"You were a miserable little thing," my grandmother used to say. "When you were born, we could have bathed you in a quart jug. I just don't know how you were ever reared."

Nevertheless, reared I was, and by parents who had to face and endure comparative poverty in their middle-age. Whereas ease and luxury had been, until then, their lot.

That big rambling villa is still very clear in my mind. The dining-room, with its sombre mahogany furniture and its pictures of Bettws-y-Coed, the large photograph of Queen Victoria, another of Mr. Gladstone, and, when the Boer War came, of course one of Sir Redvers Buller and another of Lord Roberts.

Then there was the drawing-room with too much delicate furniture, an upright piano with a curtained front, dozens of little tables which would have rocked if breathed on, bulrushes in a pot in one corner, whatnots and knick-knacks and cupboards with glass and china displayed therein.

There was a large kitchen in which I spent a great deal of time on baking-days. And there was a pleasant garden with a load of sand spread for the children in one corner, so that we could pretend that we were at the seaside even when we could not afford to go there.

At the top of the house, on the fifth floor, was the large nursery and various bedrooms. One of the largest rooms in the house was the bathroom in which the bath was raised on a wooden platform and almost hidden by a wooden casement.

Father would have his cold bath in the morning—and then he would see that all us kids followed suit. The bathroom was also the room in which we were chastised or caned.

I was about ten years old when I first made up my mind definitely to go on the stage. The germ had taken root when I was given a toy theatre. Not until the cardboard and wood of the structure, and the figures of the players, were alike battered and bent beyond recognition, was this wonderful toy theatre discarded.

The Boer War was in full swing when I reached the age of ten. I knew the words of Kipling's *Tommy Atkins*—*Good-bye, Dolly, I must leave you*—*Farewell my Bluebell*—and, of course, *The Soldiers of the Queen*. But the *pièce de résistance* of my repertoire was undoubtedly a chorus which I had heard sung when on holiday at Rhyl.

"The baby's name was Kitchener, Carrington,
  Methuen, Kekewich, White,
  Cronje, Kruger, Powell, Majuba,
  Gatacre, Warren, Colenso, Joubert,
  Capetown, Mafeking, French,
  Kimberley, Ladysmith, Bobs,
  Union Jack, Fighting Mac,
  Lyddite, Pretoria Blobbs."

This was always the finish of "my act" in those days.

When Mother had callers—for this was the era of "at home days"—I was taken to the bathroom by my nurse, washed with thoroughness and care, and then taken into the drawing-room to do my "party piece".

If, by any chance, Mrs. Thompson, Mrs. Price, Mrs. Newey, Mrs. Shelley, or any of the other august-looking ladies who sat round eating cakes the size of postage stamps, drinking tea from the tiniest of cups, and looking most peculiar with their veils raised and supported on their noses, were so forgetful as *not* to ask me to do my "turn", then I promptly reminded them myself, and did it without further invitation.

"There's a clever boy"—"Hasn't he got a good memory"—"Where does he get it from?"—these were the comments of these kindly "critics". But an end was put to these recitals when, one day, I added an encore the words of which, doubtless, I had picked up from *The Pink 'Un* or the *Winning Post*. The encore went thus:

> "There was a young lady named Fanny,
> Whose methods were rather uncanny.
> She went out late at night
> In the shades of moonlight,
> And made her poor mother a granny."

Of course I did not realise the implications of this limerick. But I was not allowed to appear at any more of my mother's "at home days". (Incidentally, my immediate reaction on being sent from the room after delivering it was to sweep all the carefully laid cards from the silver salver in the hall on to the floor.)

Later I prepared another "entertainment", in which I would take out a lamp-glass, announce that I was going to give an imitation of a phonograph, disappear beneath the table and go through an Edison Bell record. This was very popular for a time, but also ended in disgrace, for one day I added some rather rude noises through the lamp-glass.

Despite the fact that my kindly but Victorian parents were against it, my resolve to go on the stage remained unshaken. This was an era when the stage itself was looked upon as a very doubtful career, and in addition, because of the reverses in the family fortunes, my parents were somewhat dependent on and influenced by relatives who were better off, and who were even more hostile to a theatrical career.

For instance, my well-to-do uncle and godfather, who paid for the greater part of my education, was determined that I should enter his own profession, the law.

Uncle Howard Deighton was a big cheerful-looking man, rather like Mr. Pickwick. Although at first he showed exceptional hostility towards my theatrical aspirations, later on, when he became an under-sheriff of the City of London, he was instrumental in my getting an introduction to Beerbohm Tree.

Other aunts and uncles all had their say. And it was decided that this "ridiculous idea of the boy's" must be squashed.

Ostensibly the family were the victors, but only on the surface. Privately I utilised every spare moment and every spare copper in getting to know more about the theatre and the music-hall.

The Dudley of my boyhood was a cross between a country town and an industrial one. Class distinctions were much in evidence. We were bounded socially on one side by the people whom one *did* know—on the other, by the people one was supposed *not* to know, and who were, according to some of the more dogmatic members of the family, people who never *should* be known.

Rebellious against much in my boyhood, in later life I have more appreciation of the tremendous qualities of the Victorians. Hypocrisy there was—suppression and side-stepping of facts. But there was also a tremendous sense of duty and a great observance of respectability.

I was an 'advanced' child for my years. Both my governess and the family nurse were given special instructions to correct my precocity. Poor Miss Clarke, the governess—poor Agnes, the nurse—what a time they had with me. And how ineffective their efforts to curb me.

Dudley, at the time of which I am writing, had a wooden theatre called the Coliseum, in Trindle Road— and a music-hall, built mainly of corrugated iron and wood, known as the Empire.

Excellent managers ran these respective places. At the Coliseum was Mr. J. Maurice Clement, whom I recall as a quiet, dignified gentleman with a florid complexion, white hair, and a waxed moustache tinged with yellow at the edges. He was a very dapper man, always wore a large flower in his button-hole, and his top-hat was immaculate.

Tom Pritchard at the Empire was an entirely different type, a far more flamboyant showman. I can picture him now, driving through Dudley Market Place with his four-in-hand, accompanied by his wife.

In her stage name of Violet Friend she had been a well-known variety artiste in her day, and particularly popular locally. Mr. Pritchard always sported a grey bowler, rather loud checks and a Newmarket coat, and, like Mr. Winston Churchill, was generally seen smoking a very large cigar.

I was a cheeky young cub, and forced my way into places where I wanted to go. I bearded both these managers in their respective theatres.

When I confided my hopes and aspirations to Mr. Clement he was very affable and, I think, rather amused. "There's plenty of time, dear boy, plenty of time," he said. "Come and see me when you are older."

Tom Pritchard said the same thing, albeit in a rather rougher manner. Both of them turned a blind eye to the fact that I often found my way on to their respective stages on Monday mornings when I should have been at school, and into their galleries at night when I should have been at home in bed.

So far as my parents and nurse knew, I went to bed.

But after waiting until everything was quiet, I would dress and slip out through the bedroom window, jump on to a convenient garden shed, and thence to the ground down a rain-water pipe. These clandestine visits to the two Dudley theatres were the basis of all that I have ever learnt about the stage.

It was in those days, too, that I first saw theatrical newspapers—copies of *The Era*, *The Stage*, *The Encore*, and *The Entr'acte*. When my pocket money would run to it, these publications took the place of *The Boy's Own Paper* and *Chums*.

I read them from cover to cover, and I am quite sure that I learnt some of them by heart. I would record here an incident from my later life which shows how indelibly the contents of the theatrical Press that I read in boyhood were recorded on the tablets of my mind.

Some thirty years later I was on a variety bill at the Chatham Empire with the "Veterans of Variety", Arthur Roberts, "the Prince of Comedians", was talking about the casts of shows in which he had appeared in past years. He could not remember some of the casts who had supported him, and I surprised him considerably by going through them all, name for name.

It was at the Coliseum, Dudley—and later, when Mr. Clement built the Opera House, that I saw some of the finest plays and acting of this period. I do not think that Dudley considered itself particularly well off theatrically. Yet, when I recall the annual visits of Osmond Tearle and his fine Shakespearean company—Edmund Tearle, with a similar but not quite so good a company—the Edward Compton Comedy Company—the D'Oyly Carte Light Opera Company—the Carl Rosa Grand Opera Company—Wilson Barrett in melodrama—then I do not think that Dudley had much to complain about.

Osmond Tearle was one of the finest actors that I have ever seen. He was, of course, the father of Godfrey Tearle, and a fine-looking man. It was generally known that he had many times refused West End engagements because of his preference for, and tremendous drawing powers in, the Provinces.

The story is told that Beerbohm Tree once wrote Osmond Tearle, "I offer you one hundred pounds a week to play Bassanio to my Shylock at His Majesty's." Tearle is supposed to have written back, "Will accept one hundred pounds a week on condition that you play Bassanio to my Shylock."

I used to get to know some of the actors. Many times I was sent out of the theatres and told to go home. But I learnt a lot, and often managed to appear in odd bits of "supering".

It was at the Coliseum that I saw my first pantomime, "Sinbad the Sailor". Vividly I remember the very large principal boy, who sang:

"Down by the ferry
Lives Rosy Lee,
She is very
Fond of me,
We're going to marry,
She'll be my wife,
And away we'll float in our dear little boat,
Down the stream of life."

In the course of time Tom Pritchard's old "tin" Empire was scrapped and a new, and what was then very modern, music-hall built on another site in Hall Street. I saw some very great music-hall artistes there—Cliff Ryland, Pat Rafferty, Marie Loftus, and the one and only Dan Leno, who made a special appearance at the opening in 1904. I think that I am right in saying that a present-day star of the music-halls, another son of the Midlands, Billy Russell, sold programmes on that occasion.

Billy Russell "on behalf of the working classes" is surely to-day one of the funniest acts, with perhaps more universal comedy appeal than any other.

The Opera House, Dudley, had the usual run of dramas and melodramas, and very good they were too.

Melodrama has often been ridiculed—but it was a grand school for getting a broad method. There was nothing clipped or stilted about it, and if one can acquire breadth in technique, gesture and voice—then one has a solid foundation on which to work. It can always be modified. In my submission it is better for an actor or actress to learn the basis of their craft in that way than in the modern colloquial school.

Melodramas such as "The Grip of Iron", "The Face at the Window", or "The Ugliest Woman on Earth" may have been crude. But they were full-blooded, and the student could learn the art of dramatising a situation from them.

It was at the Opera House that I saw my first musical comedies. "The Geisha", "The Greek Slave", "The Runaway Girl", and that delightful operetta, "La Poupée", were some of the musical shows that I saw.

I think that I can still sing every number from "The Runaway Girl". In my boyhood there was danger from this memory of mine. Once, in the bathroom, I was overheard singing:

"Follow the man from Cook's,
    The wonderful man from Cook's,
    Whether his stay be short or long,
    He'll show you the sights that can't go wrong."

"Where on earth did you hear that?" queried my father, as he came in to shave.

"Oh, I picked it up from somewhere," I answered vaguely.

"H'mm," said Dad, "it sounds very good."

Later that same week, when he and Mother had been taken to see "The Runaway Girl", and I had been over-heard singing *The Sly Cigarette* song, the truth came out. This, coupled with the fact that my carefully hidden copies of the stage papers were found by my nurse, caused a lot of trouble for me, and I had to lie low for some time.

There were, of course, no cinemas in those days. But

we had occasional visits from shows like West's "Our Navy" and Poole's "Myriorama". These were magic lantern affairs, with an announcer and a few other artistes to make up the programme.

I applied to West's for a job, and was used by a conjurer as his assistant.

Then there was the visit of the famous Barnum and Bailey Circus. What a wonderful show this was! I recall the man with the elastic skin—the cadaverous-looking sword swallower—the man who drank tea and wrote letters with his feet—and the bearded lady.

Approaching a kindly-looking man outside a caravan, I tried to get a job with the Barnum and Bailey Circus. "I'll do anything," I said. He was a swarthy chap, and his dark eyes twinkled as he said to me, "No, my boy. You run away. This isn't the life for you."

Our greatest annual entertainment was, possibly, the Dudley Castle Fêtes, held every Whitsuntide, for three days in the Castle grounds.

Wonderful acrobats—tight-rope walkers (with the tight-rope stretched from one battlement of the Castle to another, and no safety-net underneath)—trapeze artistes —clowns—famous bands such as the Band of the Coldstream Guards and the Besses o' th' Barn, which massed together at night to play stirring music for the fireworks.

In the fireworks, wonderful set pieces, such as "The Relief of Ladysmith" and huge portraits of Kitchener and Joe Chamberlain. Earlier there would be the excitement of Lt. Lemprière ascending in his balloon, whilst the band played, and we all sang, *Up in a Balloon, Boys*."

Around ten o'clock at night, when the fête was over, there was the breaking away from the parents and the snatched moments with May or Nellie, or whoever it happened to be at the time.

The stage, however, was my main interest. Later, when I had become articled to a solicitor, I was exultant when I discovered that he had a branch office at Birmingham.

This solicitor was my second cousin, Sidney Hooper.

I think that he and his head clerk, Harold Round, had a secret sympathy for me. At any rate, one day a week I was the clerk chosen to take various documents to the Birmingham office.

"Such long hours I have to work at Birmingham, Mother," I used to say, when I arrived home after ten o'clock at night. This subterfuge masked visits to all the Birmingham theatres and music-halls for a long time.

Sometimes the business in the Birmingham office was so 'heavy' that it was finished, so far as I was concerned, by lunch-time. Then I was able to do both a matinée and an evening show, and both the postage account and my tea money suffered on those days.

Eventually Sidney Hooper told me frankly that he did not think my mind was on the law—and I got "the sack". Poor Mother was most upset. There had been many lawyers in our family, and my parents had set their minds on my becoming one also.

In a fit of exasperation one day I said, "Haven't we ever had anything else but lawyers in the family? Haven't we had any actors or criminals?" My query caused consternation, for amidst the family's respectability there had been one alleged "black sheep".

He was an uncle with a craving for the stage. Forced to become a lawyer, he proved a "bad lad" and was promptly exiled to the United States for the rest of his life. He was a great character, a fine cricketer, a grand mixer, and altogether a very lovable type. But he liked a lot of things that the Victorians thought that he should not like—so he had to be hidden.

However, I had lost my job, and that was a most serious thing. It was duly impressed upon me that I was a burden on the family—that I was not "bringing anything into the home."

At this stage in my career the family religious outlook had undergone a change. Mother—and that meant everyone else in the family also—was a Low Churchwoman, and her church, St. Luke's, Dudley, was very low church.

The vicar, Rev. W. Downs, was a big, silver-haired man, with a booming voice. He intoned everything that he said in church and most things in ordinary conversation.

This intoning carried the sound of one word into another until they were almost indistinguishable. I greatly surprised my parents one Sunday when, after church, I asked them what the "tinomies" were.

After a deal of unravelling and questioning, they discovered that Mr. Downs's intoning of the words, "And the seas, and all that in them is . . ." had been so slurred that I had taken the last few words of the sentence as being the name of some fish or other!

In the meanwhile, my elder brother, Claud, who later became a priest, had come under the spell of a High Churchman, and, much to the family's disgust, had transferred his worship to St. Michael's, Tividale, a near-by suburb.

As St. Luke's was very low, so St. Michael's was very high. "Such bowing and scraping and Popery," my mother would say. "I've never heard of such a thing."

But shortly afterwards she herself—and, of course, everyone else in the family—succumbed to ritualism, although dear mother herself to the end jibbed at a real genuflexion, and compromised with a sort of quick bob. But she became a regular worshipper at St. Michael's.

The vicar of St. Michael's, Father Geoffrey Wynn-Griffith, was one of the most outstanding characters that I have ever met. After a few more clashes at home, he told my parents that he would have me at the vicarage to live with him. Picture my joy when I found that he was Chaplain of the Actors' Church Union!

He spoilt me terribly, but he did encourage me in my theatrical ambitions. He allowed me to get up concerts, and he actually introduced me to several theatrical managers, with a view to work. He even took me to Mr. Will Catlin, who was doing a winter season at the Masonic Hall, Birmingham. Mr. Catlin gave me an audition, but turned me down. Father Geoffrey, however, refused to permit me to be discouraged.

"I feel dreadful being out of work," I used to say to him. "Nonsense, my dear boy, you can't help it," he would answer, and he would take me everywhere with him to keep my spirits up.

We went to cricket matches at Edgbaston, Birmingham, where I had my first glimpse of an England–Australia match. For the first time I saw the poise and polish of C. B. Fry's batting—the grace and fluency of Reggie Spooner—the non-stop speed of Walter Brearley's bowling —the dour stolidity of Tom Hayward—a slim young man named Jack Hobbs making his first appearance in big cricket—the "googlies" of B. J. T. Bosanquet—the wily action of Colin Blythe—the tyke-ish George Hirst—the regal Ranjitsinhji—the smiting Gilbert Jessop.

And among Australians, Clem Hill—Joe Darling—the gazelle-like Victor Trumper—Cotter, that amazing fast bowler—and the then very youthful Warwick Armstrong.

I tried to show my gratitude to Father Geoffrey by helping at the church. I served at the altar daily, and also helped with weddings and funerals. Indeed, I was almost annoyed that my assistance was not required for churchings.

One of the curates, Cecil Mason, also lived at the vicarage. He was a fine footballer and cricketer, and had a great sense of humour. He also did all that he could to stop me feeling depressed, and was emphatic in his assurances to me that one day I would be a star.

He took his sense of humour into church with him. One day, when I was helping him into his dalmatic and chasuble, he noticed that I had put out the green vestments for the Trinity period instead of the red for the Whitsuntide. We were already late in starting Mass, so with a humorous twinkle in his eye he said, "No time to change, and the few who are there probably won't notice that we've decided to skip Whitsuntide and get summer over early."

Eventually I inserted an advertisement in the *Birmingham Daily Post*. The following month, much to my surprise, I got a job as a junior clerk at the Norwich Union Fire Office in Birmingham.

This to me was ideal. I spent all my dinner-hours in the public library, munching a sandwich, and going through the files of every stage publication that I could find, and assimilating the contents.

My lunch money was generally spent on visiting theatres and music-halls. Naturally my office work suffered, but being a quick worker and, I suppose, an opportunist, I covered up a lot of my delinquences.

Then "The Swiss Express" came to Dudley, a panto-mimic musical show run by a pair of Continental clowns, Charles and Frederick Renad. These two were wonderful mimes, not using the spoken word throughout the show, and I cannot recall ever seeing more artistic work in this sphere.

I determined that I would be either a Charles or a Frederick Renad, and accordingly went round to see them. On the Friday night one of the small part actors was ill, and I got myself on in his place.

That appearance was the deciding factor. From then on it was obvious that I should never settle to anything but the stage.

On a previous holiday at Rhyl I had won a singing competition organised by Tom Wood's "Merry Men". In this I had sung *She is a sensible girl, Never forgets she's a lady*—but I had also a considerable repertoire of numbers.

One night Mr. Hughes, of the Norwich Union Fire Office, who had heard some of my efforts, asked me if I would go along to a smoker and sing. Naturally I accepted with alacrity.

Much to my joy the promoter gave me a series of six engagements in the Birmingham district. For four of these concerts my fee was to be five shillings per concert, with an increase to seven shillings and sixpence per concert for two special ones.

c

One of these was in the Market Inn of my own home town, Dudley. I do not think that I have ever experienced more joy at seeing my name on bills or in lights than I did when I saw my name scrawled in coloured soap on the mirror of this hostelry!

There it was, and no mistaking it—A. C. ROSE, Comedian.

I kept walking up and down past the window and looking at it, and wondering why other passers-by were not doing likewise.

Of course I was not the star. The "top of the bill" was a very well-known and excellent Staffordshire comedian, Ernie Garner. He used the Black Country dialect, and I have seen him deputise for the first George Formby, Little Tich, and many others with outstanding success.

Moss's Empires gave him a tour and tried to make a star of Ernie Garner. But unlike Lancashire, Yorkshire or Scots dialect, the Black Country has never been successful outside its own area, and Ernie did not make the grade.

Ernie Garner was a natural comedian. He had a big heavy-jowled face, rather sad eyes and a plaintive voice.

On the night of the Dudley concert I was very nervous. In the kitchen, where we dressed, the landlord sent beer through to us. One of the artistes told me that it would buck me up if I had a glass, and I did so. But it rather fuddled me and I started very badly, and was not well received. There was quite a lot of noise, when suddenly Ernie Garner came forward, and with his Staffordshire accent said, "Oosh oop, and give the lad a chance." Then turning to me he said, "Go on, ower kid, yo'll be orlright." I sang three songs—*She is a sensible girl*, *That's how I diddle 'em*, and a parody of *Come into the garden, Maud* —and ended up with a return engagement.

After the concert I hurried home flushed with triumph. But this was short-lived.

The coachman of a neighbour was 'walking out' with Sarah, our housemaid, and he had been at the concert. He told Sarah about my appearance, she confided this to

Lizzie, the cook, and Lizzie thought that it was 'her duty' to tell the mistress.

My mother was a real martinet. She was fully capable of dealing with things herself, but when she wanted to be particularly effective, brought father into the battle.

My father was one of the most gentle men that I have ever met, and he hated fuss and trouble of any description. "Anything for peace and quietness" was his motto—but when mother forced him into the firing-line he had, of course, to shoot.

I was sent for to the dining-room. Father looked very uncomfortable in his armchair. Mother was seated upright at the table. There was a pregnant silence as I entered and shut the door.

With tight lips down curved at the corners Mother said, "Your father wants to speak to you." She was quite wrong. Father would have run a mile rather than deal with the situation.

"Well, my lad, what's this I hear about your singing at the Market Inn?" queried Father, very uneasily.

"I don't know what you've heard, Dad," I replied.

"Don't answer back," said Mother. "And speak the truth."

"If Father asks a question, Mother," I said, "I presume that he expects an answer."

"Don't argue," said Mother. "You are a rude, naughty boy."

"I wasn't rude at all," I protested. "It is you who are being rude, interrupting a conversation between Dad and myself."

"Now, now, now," said Father helplessly, with beads of perspiration breaking out on his dear, wide forehead. "This doesn't settle anything. Come, my boy, tell me all about it."

"You are too lenient with him," broke in Mother. "He should be punished."

The 'dreadful story' was soon told. It was pointed out to me how I had disgraced the family. There were many interjections about, "What do you think Mr. Oakley would think of you?"—"What would Dr. Messiter say?" from Mother. She, dear lady, was fond of quoting the alleged opinions of various people.

Dr. Messiter was a big, fat, jolly man, facially exactly like Lord Kitchener. He was our family doctor, the most sought-after medical man in the district, and most respected. He brought me into the world, occupied the same place in my mother's thoughts as any of the great Biblical characters, and his pronouncements, so far as my mother was concerned, were of equal value to the Ten Commandments.

Mother was quite wrong about Dr. Messiter's supposed or possible reaction. He loved the theatre, and eventually my playmate, his son Eric, went on the stage.

My punishment for appearing at the concert was to be put 'in disgrace'. We were all of us, at various times, put 'in disgrace'. It meant frigid looks from Mother, not being spoken to by anybody, being served last at meals, and, in short, thoroughly ignored for two or three days.

My brothers, no matter how much they might secretly commiserate, would never have dared to ignore the family injunction, and my chief consolation at times like this was the servants, or companions from what mother called "the street urchins". I sought out Sarah and gave her a piece of my mind. But faced with her tearful denials and her assurances that I was the one member of the household that she really liked, I was helpless, and ended up by hugging and kissing her.

Sarah was a very pretty girl. With her in mind I much preferred girls from what were then called "the lower classes" to those in my own station. In reality I suppose this was a sex urge. But sex was never discussed in our home.

We were left to find out things for ourselves. And I got the impression that it was something horrid and awful.

Once, at a big family party, about twenty of us children, whilst the elders retired to their bedrooms, or had a nap in the drawing-room with handkerchiefs over their faces, were told that we could do whatever we liked. I at once sought out a beautiful and roguish little girl called May.

She had long straw-coloured hair down to her waist, with a perfectly-trimmed Alice-in-Wonderland fringe, large blue eyes, and a pink-and-white complexion. In spite of the cold, we repaired to the garden tool-shed, there undressed each other, and with an eiderdown and pillow from one of the bedrooms, made ourselves comfortable.

Some two hours later we were found by a horrified uncle and aunt. The disgrace was terrible. But at the time we couldn't understand it. We had done nothing wrong. Only explored each other's anatomy, from curiosity and without shame. But from the opinions of our respective parents and others, it seemed that we were the most wicked children ever known, and condemned to eternal damnation.

I did not see May again until she was married. And then how we laughed about our escapade.

CHAPTER TWO

LOOKING back, I realise now what a tremendous trial I must have been to my parents. Also at the time they were going through a Victorian 'hell' because of the serious financial setback from which they never recovered.

Yet they always maintained appearances. Rightly, I think, in some instances, wrongly in others.

The final showdown between my parents and myself came about through a parochial party held in the Mechanics' Institute, Dudley, in aid of church funds. A Mr. Hartley, a great friend of the family, who afterwards went on the stage when he was over fifty, told my parents not to curb me too much.

"Let the boy sing a song occasionally. Encourage him openly and he won't do it in secret. He'll soon get tired of it, I expect." That was Mr. Hartley's well-meant advice, and he arranged with the vicar that I should appear at the church concert.

With a battered top-hat, an old coat, a dilapidated umbrella and much red grease-paint on my nose, I walked on the platform in the middle of a concert that, up until then, had been quite sedate. From that great entertainer of the period, Mel B. Spurr, who had made several appearances at Dudley as a "Society Entertainer", and who will be remembered as one of the greatest in his particular line, I had learnt a song called "Oh! be careful; Oh! my young friends, be careful." This was my first song at the concert, and it went off quite successfully. But my second song was received in stony silence except for appreciation from a few choir-boys and the rougher element in the audience seated at the back. The first verse and chorus went:

"I remember when a tiny kid,
    Our 'ouse caught fire one night.

I was in such a dreadful plight,
My face turned deathly white.
I was bundled down the fire escape,
Without the slightest fuss,
When the firemen came and threw our happy
   home,
On top of us.

Chorus: Right in the middle of the road,
Right in the middle of the road,
I saw Pa, half undressed,
Lying in the gutter with a mangle on his chest.
Oh, those flames,
What a loved picture showed,
There was my mother in the wash-hand basin,
Right in the middle of the road."

There were two more verses of a similar nature. But slightly broader!

Afterwards I was shunned by everybody except Mr. Hartley. He had been the other comedian on the programme and had sung Corney Grain's *Four Horse Char-a-banc.* He chuckled a bit, reprimanded me mildly—and from that moment a coolness sprang up between him and my family that was never quite eradicated.

At home another council of war was held. Even my grandmother took part in this one. She was a fine-looking, imperious old woman, who copied Queen Victoria's mode of dress very faithfully, particularly the bonnets. She always smelt of old biscuits and peppermints.

I was supposed to be a favourite of hers. Promptly every Sunday I went to her house, at four o'clock, and read her the fifty-third chapter of Isaiah—"Who hath believed our report, and to whom is the arm of the Lord revealed"—and so on.

This performance became very mechanical with me, but Granny gave me sixpence every other Sunday, and that made me keep it up. Another reason for the regularity of my visits was my Aunt Hettie.

She was the youngest of my mother's sisters, and, like myself, something of a rebel. Many were the packets of sweets that she gave me, and the romps that I had with her.

Sometimes she would wait outside the door while I plodded through Isaiah, and when I had received my sixpence would wait for me in the hall and, taking me into the garden, would ask me to sing one of my "rude comic songs".

Granny had been at the concert and her word was law with all her daughters and in-laws. Something had to be done about the boy, and it was decided that my uncle and godfather, Howard Deighton, should intervene. After some correspondence I was sent to his home in London.

He lived at "Dudley Lodge", Wickham Road, Brockley. He was affluent, and we kids had a good time when we went to stay with him. Howard Deighton was far too good a lawyer and tactitian to say much to me on my arrival at his house, but after I had played his pianola nearly all day for several days, even his patience gave out, and he had the instrument locked.

He was churchwarden of his parish, St. Peter's, Brockley, the vicar of which was the Rev. Charles Grundy, a jolly, perky little man, in great demand as a preacher throughout the country, a really popular parson, in whose house I met, for the first time, Douglas Byng.

Douglas Byng and I were about the same age. One day, when I had been invited round to the Byngs' house for tea, Douglas and I, his brother Noel, and my cousins Muriel, Phyllis and Kathleen, formed ourselves into a concert-party which we called "The Eccentrics".

Douglas and I quarrelled a little as to which of us should do the female impersonations. But his flair for this sort of thing was ahead of mine, he had all the props. ready, and duly sang, *I am the Catch of the Season*.

This concert-party was greatly encouraged by Parson Grundy. "The Eccentrics" made their first appearance at St. Peter's Hall, Brockley—and, after that, proved a great success at various local functions.

My sojourn in London had been one long round of pleasure. Visits to the Crystal Palace with its fireworks, trips to Greenwich Observatory, and a hundred and one excitements that I never had at home. Yet all the time my uncle had been thinking over what was to happen to me, and one day informed me that he was taking me to Lucton School, Herefordshire.

Lucton was a grand school, one of the old Pierrepont foundations. Happy years there passed all too quickly.

I did well at cricket, football, and swimming; passed several examinations, and, above all, was given the chance to develop my dramatic abilities by appearing in school plays.

"Paddy" Ireland, M.A., the headmaster, a fat, lovable man who grunted when he spoke, definitely encouraged me. He was far ahead in his methods of current educational trends, but caused me to be removed from the school by writing and telling my parents that I was cut out for the stage.

"He gave a magnificent performance in 'Whitebait at Greenwich'," he wrote of me to my parents, "and he has faithfully copied all the songs that have been sung here by our entertainers on Speech Days." These entertainers included Harrison Hill, Oldbury Brough and Barclay Gammon. "To my mind, on the stage he will go a long way," "Paddy" Ireland concluded his letter.

I was removed from the school. But on several occasions afterwards I returned to it on Speech Days, both as an old boy and as a paid professional entertainer.

Yet another council of war was held. The upshot of this was, that I was sent to the National Provincial Bank at Shrewsbury as a junior clerk.

Before I went, my parents pointed out to me that they were doing everything with my best interests at heart— that I was very lucky to have got into the National Provincial Bank, and that if I worked hard and steadily, I should eventually become a manager. "As you know, my boy, managers have a house over the bank, they are provided with coal, and their rates are paid. That means security. We have forgiven all the past, and you are going to start with a clean sheet."

Shrewsbury was a lovely country town, and I was very happy there. Work in the bank proved easy, when I did it. And my abilities as a comic singer soon became known.

Smoking concerts were the fashion, and at these functions, together with soirées and garden-parties, I was soon in great demand and, indeed, one of the most popular local entertainers. I had brochures printed— "A. C. Rose—Comedian: Entertainer. Available for all functions. Moderate Fees." I augmented my somewhat meagre income from the bank, considerably, through my efforts as a semi-professional, and finally I launched into management, forming a local concert-party, which I named after a club of which I was a member, "The Pengwern Pierrots".

This troupe commanded a fee of six or seven guineas. I used to pay the seven artistes what I thought they deserved individually—to some, seven-and-six, to others, half a guinea, and some even fifteen shillings. Travelling expenses were paid in addition to the fee, so sometimes I made a couple of guineas for myself from an engagement. But it must be admitted that my work at the bank was suffering.

One June day I was down in the strong-room of the bank sorting out some old cheques and trilling the refrain of Ernest Shand's *La Diddley, Diddley Um*:

"Maud de Vere behind the bar,
Thought she'd like to be a star,
Got a turn somewhere in France,
But the first time that she tried to dance—

Chorus: La diddley diddley um,
La diddley diddley um,
La diddley diddley um,
She fell and broke her contract."

I had just finished this ditty when the voice of the chief cashier, Mr. Pennington, whom we used to call "Old Nappy" because he was rather like Napoleon, reached me down the spiral staircase. "Rose, Mr. Gillett wants to see you in the manager's office." Mr. Gillett was the visiting Bank Inspector, there in Shrewsbury for the June balance.

Up the spiral staircase I went, to be greeted by "Old Nappy" at the top with "Never mind about she fell and broke her contract. What about your bloody contract? Gillett heard you in the strong-room, and he's heard one or two more things as well. Not only that, he's seen your books, and I think you're for it, my lad. Go in there, you're on the carpet."

"Old Nappy" was seldom really angry, though he often pretended to be. Doubtless I had been something of a handful to him, and he was somewhat relieved that I was to be called to account.

Mr. Gillett was a big, courteous man. "Sit down, Rose," he said. "May I congratulate you on the way that you sing comic songs. I have, during the past two or three days, heard several of them. I was also interested in this," he continued, producing one of my brochures.

"I don't think that banking is really your forte, and I do feel that you would be more of an adornment to the stage than you are to the Shrewsbury branch of the National Provincial Bank. Your ledgers are very much behind. It is true that you have been working late quite a lot, as I see by the amount of tea money that you have drawn." (We were allowed eighteen pence for tea in those days if worked after a certain time. In my case, this sum generally went on the purchase of a new song or album.) "I am sorry, Rose, but we shall have to dispense with your services."

Mr. Gillett said all this so calmly and suavely. But I had sufficient common sense to know that there was no appeal. I murmured a polite form of regret—and was given a month's notice.

So I was in disgrace again. Although, personally, I did not think that my time in Shrewsbury had been wasted. I had done a lot of concert work and instinctively knew that I was maturing. Also I had been a member of the Shrewsbury Dramatic Society, and had played with them at the old County Theatre, Shrewsbury, in H. V. Esmond's "When We Were Twenty-one."

I fell in love with the leading lady of this amateur company, Nellie Cross. This was great audacity on my part, for she was a most popular girl locally, daughter of the oldest pharmaceutical chemist in the town, and much sought after by the young men of the district.

My income from the bank was one pound per week. Nellie Cross refused me gently, and when, thirty years later, she came to see me in a Lyceum pantomime, referred to the whole thing with much gracious amusement. "I might have done worse," she said.

"You'd have had a hell of a struggle for a long time," I commented.

Out of work again I went back to my uncle and godfather in London. He received me in his City office.

"If I could only have some help to go on the stage, Uncle, I know I should make good," I said.

"You'd better go to 'Dudley Lodge'," was the reply, "and I'll talk to you in the morning."

On my way to Brockley I called in at a public library and there saw an advertisement in *The Times* which announced that a Mr. Glenville, at some offices in High Holborn, had a vacancy in his "Dramatic Company" for a premium pupil with talent. The premium was ten guineas. I copied it out, and when my uncle came home to Brockley at night I told him about it.

"Well, since you seem set on it I will pay this premium," he said. "But this is the last I shall do."

The following day I called on Mr. Glenville with the ten guineas. His place of business was a two-roomed office on the fourth floor. He was an oily individual, and introduced me to an elderly female who, he said, was his leading lady.

After I had paid the premium he gave me the juvenile part to read in a drama called "The Master Passion". Four or five days after that I called at the office, word-perfect in the part, which I ran through. In fact I ran through the part every day for several days.

Whether I was good or bad I cannot say. But Mr. Glenville was suavely pleasant to me until I started making enquiries as to when I commenced work. He evaded this point for a day or two until my uncle insisted on my having some definite information. Then he said that I should open at Cardiff on the following Monday week, and added that, if I could find another pupil who would pay a similar premium, he might find a vacancy.

When I told my uncle this at night, he ejaculated a very gruff "Bah—rubbish—he sounds like a crook to me. You've got yourself tangled up with some bogus firm."

Alas, Uncle was right. Next morning he sent his chief clerk along to interview Mr. Glenville, but Mr. Glenville had departed, and the caretaker of the offices was as anxious to interview him as we were. My uncle communicated with the police—but Mr. Glenville was never found.

I was too depressed to worry whether he was traced or not. He had put paid to my hopes.

By this time my family had moved to Liverpool and Uncle packed me off there. Not wishing to be a burden to them, in a quixotic moment I signed-on as a steward on the Harrison liner *Gladiator*, and went to South America.

In Pernambuco I contacted a travelling booth show run by an Irishman called Rafferty. It was a conglomeration of circus acts, melodrama and variety, and I was engaged at twenty milreis per week. (A milreis was equivalent to about one and fourpence in English money.)

We played one-night stands in very strange places. It was hard work, for, in addition to appearing in melodramas and singing comic songs, I had to help with the tenting and striking and general packing up.

One night, just outside Buenos Aires, Rafferty had a row with a dago in the company. Soon everybody was fighting, and to this day I carry the mark of a dago's knife on my big toe. After the fight Rafferty absconded, owing money all over the place and to every member of the company.

Stranded, for some time I worked at odd jobs in hotels and clubs. Eventually, much to my joy, I caught up with the *Gladiator* again on its next voyage, and worked my passage back to England as second cook. The *Gladiator* did a long trip. We went up as far as New Orleans and Galveston, and came back to Pernambuco, Rio, Maceo, and then to Las Palmas, Tenerife, Antwerp, and finally to Millwall.

By the time we got to Millwall I was down with a bad dose of malaria, and my toe, where the dago's knife had landed, was septic. The port doctor sent me straight into Poplar Hospital, where the first thing that happened to me was that I was bathed by two very attractive nurses.

I made that bath last a very long time, and whenever either or both of those two nurses came to my bed to enquire how I was, and whether I wanted anything, I always replied, "Yes, another bath, please."

The day that I was discharged from Poplar Hospital I was handed a letter, which informed me that a dear old friend of the family, a Mrs. Waring, had died, leaving me ten pounds. This sum, less legal charges, was enclosed.

Surreptitiously I took the cheque to my uncle's head clerk, who cashed it for me. Then I set out to make merry in no uncertain way.

First I went to Frascati's, where I had an excellent meal. Then I went to the Empire in Leicester Square.

I had heard various stories of the wicked ladies of the Empire promenade, and soon found myself in conversation with one. She was a very beautiful woman, slightly over-dressed, her features were almost classical, and the lazy lids of her violet eyes, with long lashes, lowered and raised invitingly.

I was very nervous, and half turned away. Plucking up courage I looked again, and she too had half turned away, giving me a vision of a wonderful mass of auburn hair, coiled into a large knot which clung to a perfectly shaped, creamy neck.

She looked at me again, and taking my courage in both hands I went up to her.

"Will you come and have a drink?" I asked.

And a rich, low voice answered, "Yes, I will, I'm as dry as a bone." That I was very green must have been quite apparent to her, and she took me by the arm and we went and drank draught champagne.

Suddenly she said, "Well, dark eyes, you look very lonely, and I am very lonely, so you had better come home with me." We got into a cab and went to her flat at Bayswater.

This flat was large and sumptuous, and when we got into the sitting-room there was an excellent cold supper laid out, with a bottle of Chambertin. "Excuse me for a moment, darling," she said. "Help yourself to a drink." Then she departed through some double doors to her bedroom.

Presently she returned wearing a wonderful diaphanous négligé. Physically she was one of the most beautiful women I have ever seen. With a roguish laugh she said, "It's horrible to talk about money, but there you are, it's important, isn't it?"

I had just under six pounds left. I stammered and stuttered, and said, "Do tell me what you want. I don't know much about this sort of thing."

"What I want and what you can give me are two different matters, darling," she trilled. "How much have you got?"

With that I took my money out of my pocket and showed it to her. She separated the gold from the silver and copper and took four pounds. Then she added,

"You won't mind giving me ten shillings for my maid, will you? You understand."

I did not understand. But I gave her the ten shillings.

Then she got up, opened the Chambertin, and we sat down and ate lobster and cold chicken. Then, with a happy sigh of contentment, she lit a cigarette and beckoned me to follow her into the bedroom. "Hurry up, dark eyes," she said. "You're very slow. Don't I appeal to you?"

But by this time remorse had set in. Victorian inhibitions and repressions were at work. I felt a horrible sense of shame and confusion, and when she had disappeared into the bedroom I crept quietly but quickly from the flat.

Once outside I made my way to my Uncle Howard's house with my little legacy almost gone.

"You have learnt your lesson now, I should think, my lad," he said to me, the following morning.

"Well, Uncle," I replied, "I haven't had much chance to learn the lesson that I chiefly want to learn." Then to my surprise and joy he suddenly became kindly, told me that he sympathised with my desire to go on to the stage, although he added that he did not think that I had any talent.

"I have been doing some business," he said, "with Mr. J. D. Langton, of Langton and Passmore, who are Beerbohm Tree's solicitors. I will try once more and see if you have anything in you." With that he gave me a letter to Mr. Langton, and Mr. Langton in turn sent me to Beerbohm Tree.

I could not believe my good luck when I was ushered into Tree's room at His Majesty's Theatre. "Why do you want to be an actor?" he asked me, in his slightly guttural voice.

"Because I feel that I am cut out for it, sir," I replied.

"We will see," he said. "You will walk on in 'Julius Cæsar'." With that, he passed me over to Mr. King, and Mr. King called me for rehearsal the next day.

I do not think that it is possible for anyone to have been

J. H. ROBERTS

DOUGLAS BYNG

SIR BARRY JACKSON

FELIX AYLMER

MY FAVOURITE PHOTOGRAPH OF OLIVE

with Tree in any capacity without benefiting. He paid close attention to the minutest detail and was uncannily observant.

To me he was particularly fair. After some weeks he sent for me and told me that he did not think that I should progress far with the only work that he could offer me. He thought that I needed more varied experience. At this interview he must have given me over an hour of his valuable time and much invaluable advice. Finally he told me that he was communicating with the then newly formed Liverpool Repertory Theatre.

Armed with a letter from the great Beerbohm Tree himself I felt particularly confident when I came to interview Mr. Basil Dean and Miss Darragh. I sensed that Mr. Dean did not want to engage me, and, rightly or wrongly, all the time that I was at Liverpool I felt that he thought nothing of my work. But in 1911 I was engaged at a salary of two pounds per week to play small parts and be assistant stage-manager at the Liverpool Repertory Theatre.

Once engaged I worked like the very devil. We did one play a week. My first appearance was in Galsworthy's "Strife", in which I walked on in the crowd scene and was understudy to Lawrence Hanray.

What a marvellous company the Liverpool Repertory was! It included C. M. Hallard, Wilfred Shine, Lawrence Hanray, Joseph Dodd, Estelle Winwood, Eileen Thorndyke, Aida Jenoure, Doris Lloyd, J. H. Roberts, Norman McKeown, to name but a few. George Harris was the brilliant scenic artist, and Arthur K. Phillips the stage-manager.

Arthur Phillips was a good fellow in his way, but very full of the importance of his job, and he used to use me rather as a butt. In spite of many rebuffs I progressed at this theatre, and appeared in all sorts of plays, from Shakespeare to Shaw.

It was grand experience for a youngster. In those days there were many like myself who never left the theatre.

D

I certainly never wanted to leave it, and because I was always on hand, and made a practice of learning the whole play, I caught the eye of that fine and mellow actor, Wilfred Shine, and received the studious attention of Lawrence Hanray.

Both these men of the theatre took me under their wing. Gratefully I record a tremendous debt of gratitude to them for all that they taught me and for all that I learnt from them.

The Liverpool Repertory season came to an end in the spring, and to fill in the summer vacation I joined Estelle Stead's Shakespearean Company. T. W. Stead had left his daughter Estelle well off, and she launched into management.

I joined this company at the Opera House and Winter Garden, Blackpool, rehearsing on the Monday morning and playing Vincentio in "The Taming of the Shrew" that same night.

We were indeed a motley crowd. Old actors and young actors, good actors and bad actors; but old or young, good or bad, they all knew their business, and since we changed the plays daily there was plenty to do and much to learn. "Hamlet", "Richard the Third", "The Merchant of Venice", "Romeo and Juliet", were all taken in their stride.

In this company were actors like Farmer Skein, Douglas Vigors, Charles Stirling and A. E. Beamish. I formed a friendship with the men who played the comedy parts— Richard Henry Lace and Bernard Marsh (now a successful pantomime dame known to-day as Charles Cardiff)—and we three lived together.

And how well we lived! If we had to pay more than twelve or fifteen shillings a week 'all in' we were most upset. And that 'all in' meant four substantial meals a day!

Farmer Skein, who had been leading man in Lyceum melodramas, was a fine and vigorous all-round actor, albeit a very temperamental one. I have seen him play

Shylock almost perfectly—and I have also seen him tear it to rags and tatters.

Douglas Vigors, who played the second leads, was a fine figure of a man. His Bassanio was one of the best that I have ever seen.

I do not think that Estelle Stead was a very good actress. But she was scholarly and a delightful woman to work for.

Our tour was a strange mixture of number one, number two and, indeed, number zero dates. We went from the beautiful Opera House at Blackpool to the Opera House, Workington, and from thence to the old Royal at Sheffield where, in the height of the summer, the business was dreadful.

One night Farmer Skein, playing Richard, stopped in the middle of a scene and told the audience that he did not think that they understood the play or that they were paying it proper attention. I recall also that at Sheffield, Lace, Marsh and myself lived at some very famous 'digs', Mrs. Cavey, 97 Club Gardens Road. They have gone long ago, but many famous people from the legitimate stage and the music-halls enjoyed the hospitality of Mrs. Cavey's excellent theatrical lodgings.

George Formby, father of the present-day music-hall star, and possibly the greatest natural Lancashire comedian that the stage has ever had, was also staying there. He was top of the bill at Sheffield Empire, but he liked to live quietly and unostentatiously, and could be as quaint and gormless off stage as he was on.

Young George, a little whipper-snapper at the time, was staying with his father, and he used to take a long time in the bathroom, which contained also the W.C. One morning, after making several attempts to get in, I complained to Mr. Formby.

"Ee," he said, "is our George still in there?"

I replied with some heat that he was. With that, George Formby, in his famous croaky voice, shouted upstairs, "Our George, 'urry up and come off closet. Mr. Rose wants to coom."

During that week I had the temerity to submit to Mr. Formby two extra verses that I had written for his song, *John Willie, Come On*. Whether he ever sang them or not I don't know, but he told me that he liked them and, what is more, gave me ten shillings for them, and ten shillings in those days was a godsend!

From Sheffield we went to the Opera House, Burton-on-Trent. The majority of the male members of the company were against the management on some question of fares being paid back to London at the end of the tour. The women were not, apparently, affected, and Lace, Marsh and myself were not prepared to join in with the others in their demands.

On the Friday night at Burton-on-Trent, just before the Trial Scene in "The Merchant of Venice", they decided to strike and not go on. I was playing Salarino, but I knew every part, and so did Lace and Marsh.

Farmer Skein sent for us hurriedly, and we played the scene with the three of us speaking the lines of all the characters. I acted Bassanio and a bit of Gratiano. Cuts were made, and a lot of the Duke's lines were lost. But we got through the scene and the rest of the play.

After the show Skein sent for me and told me that I had to play Lucentio in "The Taming of the Shrew" the following afternoon. Some of the strikers returned, but not the full cast. But once again we got through the play, and Estelle Stead and Farmer Skein repaid us by paying our fares back to London.

Then came another season at Liverpool. Lawrence Hanray was now the producer. I got bigger parts, my salary was increased to two pounds ten shillings—and I was as happy as a sandboy.

CHAPTER THREE

BY 1914 I was married.

This marriage was not successful, and later it came unstuck, and I do not intend to write about it. But it did serve to tie me down, and, when a baby came, I just could not afford to be 'resting'.

So, in the spring of that year, to fill in the summer vacation from the Liverpool Repertory Theatre I joined L. M. Musgrove's concert-party, the "Moonbeams", at Seaford.

In spite of real attention to my work, in all my early engagements I found time to fall in love. At Liverpool I worshipped—very much from afar—at the shrine of Eileen Thorndyke. When my baby was born, although her first name had to be the family one of Ruth, her second had to be Eileen, after Eileen Thorndyke.

I like to think that this second name, coupled with some aptitude inherited from me, was responsible for my daughter, at a very early age, showing that she would have done well in the theatre.

When she was twelve I took her to Italia Conti. She, after hearing Ruth 'do her stuff', said, "Well, Mr. Rose, I think so much of her potentialities that I will train her for nothing."

However, this was not to be. My daughter embraced a commercial career in which she found her theatrical propensities very useful.

In Estelle Stead's company I formed a great attachment for Dorothy Drury, a delightful girl with a tremendous sense of humour, and a very capable actress. She kept me well and truly in my place, and we were great pals.

At Seaford I fell in love with Frances Walkley. She was the soubrette, and much of our work was done together. She, however, although fond of me, was engaged to some-one else, and that affair did not develop very far.

53

The "Moonbeams" was a little five-handed show and a very good one. At my interview with Mr. Musgrove I had so impressed him that he made me principal comedian and producer, although I was not fitted for these important roles.

Norman Griffin and myself had supplied much of the material for this show, and in the fateful summer of 1914 we opened at the quaintly named Spot Pavilion. The show was very successful and the cast Paul Freeman, Horace Bernard, Frances Walkley, Gladys Glover and myself, occasionally augmented by a visit from Mr. Musgrove's partner, that excellent entertainer Brett Hayden.

The Seaford of those days was an exclusive resort where well-to-do families rented a house for two or three months. One of these was the well-known stage family, the Reeves-Smiths. The vivacious Alma Reeves-Smith was a tremendous 'fan' of our show, and my own work.

Paul Freeman and I became great pals. Our mutual respect was not lessened when, right through a night of vicious gale, together with Brett Hayden, we hung on to our tent to prevent it being blown away.

The outbreak of the 1914 war terminated our season. With others who had been re-engaged for Liverpool, I received notification that the directors did not feel like taking the responsibility of opening the theatre.

Then it was that the famous Liverpool Commonwealth Company was formed. Granville Barker once described this company as the finest all-round acting combination that he had ever seen.

The well-known actress, Madge McIntosh, had been engaged as our new producer, and she was assisted from time to time by Lawrence Hanray and Wilfred Shine. The whole of the company were on minimum salaries, and a huge banner was put outside the theatre with this quotation from "The Merchant of Venice" on it—"You take my life when you do take the means by which I live."

A departure was made from the accepted repertory standards of the time, and many popular plays were presented. The fact that we were dependent upon ourselves had a definite appeal to the good people of Liverpool; there were never any empty seats, and this company was probably the most successful theatrical enterprise in the country.

Madge McIntosh and Estelle Winwood were the prime movers in achieving the initial successes. And in addition to Hanray and Shine, the cast included Pennington Gush, Phillip Lesley, Cecil Rose, Dorothy Thomas, Harvey Adams, Lawrence Anderson, Frederick Cooper, George Dewhurst, Percy Marmont, Lois Hatherley, Nina Henderson, Maire O'Neil and her sister Sara Allgood, Shiel Barry, Algernon Grieg, Olive Wilmott-Davies, and many others. What a powerful band of players was this! And in the background, watching over our interests, Alec Rea, Professor Riley and Ronald Jeans.

The autumn season went from success to success, and then, at Christmas, it was decided to put on "Twelfth Night", twice daily. This particular production of "Twelfth Night" is entitled to rank as high as any in the history of Shakespearean presentations.

It was played as a pantomime and at pantomime time. Wilfred Shine as Sir Toby, Lawrence Hanray as Malvolio, Pennington Gush as Aguecheek, and Patrick Curwen as "Feste", kept it going at tremendous pace. But when the curtain went up on Boxing Day I did not dream of the great chance that was coming to me.

Curwen lost his voice during the matinée and the understudy was not ready. Hearing this, I dashed to Lawrence Hanray and said, "I know it. Don't worry."

Some were against me playing the part, and shook their heads. There was no time for rehearsals between shows, however. Hanray stood firm, and said, "I have every confidence in him"—and I played.

The part of Feste carries three songs. It was something of an ordeal, but the arrogance and confidence of youth took no account of these things, and on I went, confidently and fearlessly.

What a fine feeling it was, at the fall of the curtain, to receive the congratulations of my fellow-players, and such men as Hanray and Shine! Moreover, Patrick Curwen's misfortune was my good luck—he did not return to the cast, and I played the part for the whole of the run. So far as the Liverpool Repertory Company was concerned I had established myself as definitely 'belonging'.

I was fortunate enough to have an excellent Press. And, perhaps to me the most important of all, I received an increase in salary of ten shillings a week.

It was the custom of many of us to slip over to the 'Ormskirk', a public-house which stood opposite our stage door and which now no longer exists. Here you could get an excellent cut off the joint for sixpence, vegetables for a penny a portion, and a huge piece of bread from a perfectly baked cottage loaf cost another penny.

If you did not want to spend as much as that, a substantial slice of Welsh rarebit and various other snacks could be obtained for twopence. Since, up to 1914, a glass of Guinness cost twopence-halfpenny, or at the most threepence, it will be evident that a gargantuan repast could be had for a shilling. Cheese was free, and a sweet cost only twopence or threepence.

There was no stopping the Liverpool Commonwealth Company. Madge McIntosh and Estelle Winwood had a definite West End complex; they were determined that the company should go there, and eventually a short season was fixed at the Kingsway Theatre, London.

The play chosen for the famous Liverpool Commonwealth Company to startle the West End of London with was Pineros "Trelawney of the Wells". In Liverpool it had been one of our most successful productions, but, unhappily for us, it had recently been revived in London for charity performances with an all-star cast.

I played the small but effective part of Captain de Phœnix, and enjoyed every minute of it.

When we did eventually put on a new play—John Galsworthy's "Full Moon", the title of which was afterwards changed to "A Bit of Love"—it was too late to save the season at the Kingsway, which was, in the phrase of the theatre, "a disaster", and we returned to Liverpool with wiser and possibly smaller heads.

What a kind and understanding and gentle man was John Galsworthy. He took immense pains and trouble with me in creating my minor, but nevertheless important, role in the new play.

After the Liverpool season I was out of work, and disconsolate in 'digs', which I shared with Oscar Waddington, in Guilford Street, Russell Square, London. "Waddy" was a real character, happy-go-lucky and always optimistic.

He was the assistant-manager of the Liverpool Repertory Company, but I don't think he took it very seriously. Luckily we each had a watch which would fetch five shillings when necessary, but even so, we had to be content with one frugal meal a day, eaten at Chick's in Long Acre.

Sometimes a windfall would come our way. "Waddy" would say, "Let's go and call on Arthur Chesney: he's in work and we can borrow a bit." So down we'd go to Ebury Street and dig out Arthur.

Arthur Chesney was a superb actor, especially in unctuous and kindly parts. I have always thought that if Chesney's brother had not been Edmund Gwenn, Arthur would have achieved just as prominent a position in the theatre as Gwenn.

He was a generous man, and once lent "Waddy" and I three quid, whereon we lived like fighting cocks for three days. You could get a seven-course meal at the Café d'Italie in Soho for one and sixpence—and for another ninepence a half-bottle of Chianti.

When we were extra 'flush' we used to go to the Chanticleer, which was the height of our gourmet ideas in those days. We always started a meal at the Chanticleer with bisque d'homard, which was the speciality of the house. It was the first time that I had ever tasted lobster soup, and I thought that it was wonderful.

Since then I have had it in world-famous hotels and restaurants, but I don't think it has ever tasted so wonderful, so luscious, as at the Chanticleer. Perhaps the special tang, given by the knowledge that it was a special and extravagant luxury, has been absent.

One day, at Guilford Street, I received a letter from Philip Howley who, at the time, was running an excellent show called "The Vagrants" at, of all places, the Undercliffe Pavilion, Bradford, Yorks.

Howley had seen me in "Twelfth Night" at Liverpool and thought, quite wrongly, that I would add tone to his Northern show. He had engaged me to take the place of a most popular Northern comedian, Mickie O'Brien.

I went to Bradford to rehearse and found a grand company—Philip Howley, Eileen Desmond, Winnie Victoria (almost the perfect soubrette), Darroll Richards (the tenor), Tom Braham-Fox (Will Catlin's brother), and others equally good.

They were all expert dancers, and when I watched the show at night I saw that the man whose place I was to take was a local idol. Everything that he said and did registered, and I knew that Philip Howley, in booking me, had made a mistake.

I had borrowed two pounds in advance from the management. But early one morning I went silently from my 'digs' and took the train to Liverpool. It was the first—and the only time—that I have run away from a job.

From Liverpool I wrote to Philip Howley and explained, and said that I hadn't got the pluck to face them. Later on I returned his loan.

Philip Howley, who afterwards became an eminent Wylie-Tate producer, was very understanding about it. Years afterwards he engaged me for cabaret at the Grafton Galleries with Beatrice Lillie.

Financially things were serious with me. So I decided

to "have a go" at the music-halls. I persuaded Harris Fineberg, the Liverpool agent, to get me a date at the Lyric Music Hall, Everton Street, Liverpool.

I had written myself two light comedy songs, and somehow had acquired a morning-suit complete with lavender waistcoat and top-hat. I was first turn at the Lyric, and quite definitely not a success.

Whatever should we do without the ladies? was the title of my first song, and as I sang it I walked up and down in the approved light comedy style, and kept raising my hat. I got 'the bird' nightly, and in addition quite a number of coins and at least one piece of fish!

"Why don't you pack it up?" said Chesney Allen, who was sharing a dressing-room with me. "It must be agony."

"I can't afford to," I replied.

"In a way I don't blame you," said Ches., "since you're earning such a big salary."

Chesney Allen was, at that time, playing a light comedy part in Johnny McElroy's sketch, "Helping a Pal". He was, so he told me, getting two pounds ten shillings a week. I was getting seven pounds.

On that bill also was Billy Bennett's father, who, with Bill's sister, appeared in an act called "Howard and Bennett". He encouraged me in many ways through a terrifying experience.

When I went for my salary to the offices in Seymour Street, Mr. Carnell, the manager, when he paid me, said:

"Well, you haven't done very well, Rose, have you?"

"No," I replied, "but I'll get some different songs." Then I promptly asked him for some more work.

"Well, I don't know," he said, "but I'll tell you what— I can fix you three nights at the Empire, Skelmersdale." This was a little picture-house near Ormskirk. My salary was three pounds ten shillings, and to save fares I bicycled out to Skelmersdale from Garston, Liverpool, where I was living, some fourteen miles every day.

My act was to follow one of Charlie Chaplin's old Essanay pictures. The audience was already in an uproar when I started, and remained in an uproar throughout my performance.

The proprietor came round and said very bluntly, "Mai God, Carnell's sent me some b—s in his time, but I think thee takes the cake! Tha can't go on next house!"

"They don't understand my songs," I said.

"Aye," he replied, "and I don't rightly know why they should."

I begged and implored to be kept on. Finally he relented a little, and said, "Well, the only thing about thee is tha voice. Go and see ma daughter at the grocer's shop opposite. She's got some sentimental songs, and if tha likes to have a smack at 'em I'll let thee go on second house and see what tha's like then."

With the paramount thought in my mind that my three pounds ten shillings must not vanish, I rushed and found the lady. She was a lovely girl, with a mass of raven hair and pale-blue eyes. Her appearance somehow did not seem to fit in with her very broad accent.

She got out the songs and tried them over, and I think that she fell for me. Anyway, at the second performance, A. C. Rose, Light Comedian and Raconteur, went on and sang *The Sunshine of Your Smile* and *Somewhere a Voice is Calling*, and was retained, not only for the three days, but for the entire week.

The following week Mr. Carnell sent for me. "I want you to go to Dublin next week, Rose," he said. "To the Tivoli. And I want you to sing the same songs as you sang at the Lyric."

"But I thought that you didn't think much of those songs, Mr. Carnell?" I said.

"No," he replied, "I didn't. But to tell you the truth, they don't bother much with the first two turns at the Tivoli, Dublin, and they like to have a serio or a light comedian that they can chi-ike. It isn't very comfortable, and some don't like it. But if you can take what you took at the Lyric, you can take it in Dublin. And you'll get an extra thirty shillings, as it's a long journey to Ireland."

Poverty prevents one being 'choosey'. So off to Dublin I went and duly endured what I had been promised!

Following these first experiences of the music-halls it was the start of a new season at the Liverpool Repertory Theatre. To my joy I found that I was cast for the lead in James Sexton's play "The Riot Act".

This play was based on the Liverpool strike riots of a year or two previously. Jimmy Sexton was a cheerful little chap who scattered good humour and aitches around him everywhere, and was one of the first of the Labour M.P.'s.

It was a bad play. Jimmy Sexton was no playwright. But so far as we were concerned it had definite local appeal. Later we took it on tour to such places as Wigan and Warrington, but after that nothing more was heard of it.

Playing opposite me was Sara Allgood. She was a typical Irishwoman, lovable, tempestuous, sensible and non-sensible—all within the space of five minutes.

At the end of the spring season Ronald Jeans had a brilliant idea—that we should do a revue. He wrote this, his first revue, and called it "Hullo, Repertory".

It was a magnificently constructed entertainment, and was 'revue' in the real sense of that much-abused word— "a current cartoon of matters of the moment."

For a highbrow dramatic company, one of the pioneers of experimental repertory in the country, it was, of course, an unheard-of thing to do. But in deciding to do it Jeans showed real genius. He wrote it for the Repertory Theatre audience, and for the Repertory Company players. He realised that our vast public—and it was a vast public in Liverpool—would delight in seeing their favourites in what was, for them, a completely different form of entertainment.

Lawrence Hanray, a fine musician who had, in past years, composed some excellent songs, wrote the music.

So tuneful was it that even now, forty years later, I could hum every tune.

I was given some excellent parts, amongst them an appearance as Miss Horniman of the Gaiety Theatre, Manchester, and an impression of George Lashwood. I am glad to record here a sincere "Thank you" to Ronald Jeans for these parts.

Miss Horniman lent me her own clothes and some of her personal belongings. And when I had a word with him at the Liverpool Empire, Lashwood helped me to reproduce some of his mannerisms.

Jeans had combined my impression of Lashwood with a skit on the recent innovation of a "Beauty Chorus", and I had a backing of 'girls' in gorgeous gowns. The 'girls' included such clever actors and men of the theatre as William Armstrong, Harvey Adams, Frederick Cooper, Lawrence Anderson, J. H. Roberts, and I often think that no other artiste can have had a "beauty chorus" of so many people who were later to achieve distinction in the theatre.

"The Passing Show" revue was running at the Palace Theatre, in London, at the time, and Jeans cleverly travestied some of this show in our production. Percy Marmont, wearing a brown suit and grey top-hat, in the style of Basil Hallam, sang a burlesque of *Gilbert the Filbert* as *Basil from Balham*. The chorus went:

> "I'm Basil from Balham,
>   The bolt from the blue,
>   The absolute essential of every revue,
>   No suiting from Tooting
>   Can imitate the cut,
>   Of Basil from Balham,
>   The pride of Alfred Butt."

Wilfred Shine, amongst other parts, gave a wonderful impression of the Liverpool theatre proprietor, W. W. Kelly.

Success is almost an inadequate word to describe the

reception of this revue. We ran on with it, to capacity houses, for many weeks.

Sir Oswald Stoll, with Harris Fineberg, saw it, with the result that it was booked for a tour of his music-halls, including the London Coliseum. This booking was to show that even an astute theatrical manager like Sir Oswald Stoll could make mistakes.

We opened on the Stoll tour at the old Manchester Hippodrome. So quietly was the show received by the audience at the Monday matinée that at the first house on Monday night various music-hall turns from Sir Oswald's Ardwick Green Empire were brought in to bolster-up the entertainment, and "Hullo, Repertory", was cut down to some forty minutes.

Knowing that we were a failure some of us wanted to contact Sir Oswald Stoll and terminate the engagement. But Madge McIntosh, in many ways a dominating and autocratic woman, said, "Nonsense. Never mind about what Manchester thinks to-day. The show is obviously right for London."

In between Manchester and our London début we were booked for the world-famous music-hall the Argyle, Birkenhead, by its renowned proprietor, D. J. Clarke. His judgment was usually very sound but, like Sir Oswald Stoll, he made a mistake in booking "Hullo, Repertory", for the show was a definite failure at Birkenhead.

How the big company all got on at the tiny Argyle puzzled me. But that we all got off again safe and sound was an even bigger mystery.

The failure on tour benefited me personally. Because I had had some experience in concert-party, and so was used to handling audiences in this type of entertainment, I was given a lot more songs and a lot more to do.

Billy Armstrong, at Liverpool, had made a great success in a clever burlesque of an Ohio American song. After his first performance at Birkenhead he came along to my dressing-room between the shows and said, "Arthur" (he always called me Arthur), "here is the suit, here is the hat—it gives me the greatest pleasure to relinquish the song and ask you to do it. I would much rather that the audience hated you than me."

Madge McIntosh was still optimistic. So off we went to London.

When the London Coliseum was a twice-a-day variety theatre the programmes always contained a great number of stars. The bill on which "Hullo, Repertory" was booked was no exception. Wilkie Bard was there; Owen Nares in a sketch; and the Irish Players from the famous Abbey Theatre, Dublin.

At the opening matinée on Monday we occupied the whole of the second part of the programme. Our concluding item was a burlesque march of the nations in which we all came down carrying flags. So ghastly was our flop at this first performance, that when we were all lined up carrying our flags, and waiting for the applause that did not come, Hanray very quietly lowered his flag to half-mast!

At night we found that we had been moved to first turn and cut to twenty minutes. It was a sad experience, but Madge McIntosh refused to be daunted, and sailed through the whole engagement with an imperious manner and her head held high.

Because it showed me off to greater advantage than the others, the engagement benefited me personally, and I had offers from various managements.

"What shall I do?" I asked Percy Marmont one day, "I've been offered eight pounds a week, and I'm under contract to return to Liverpool."

"Good heavens," said Percy, "you must tell them, and of course they'll release you. Eight pounds a week! Do you realise that that is four hundred a year? It is more than I get."

Shortly after that Percy Marmont was making a big success in silent films, and at salaries that made four hundred a year look minute.

The summer of that year I spent with the Millar Ander-

THE MOONBEAMS, SEAFORD, 1914. WITH FRANCES WALKLEY, CLARKSON ROSE,
GLADYS GLOVER, PAUL FREEMAN, AND HORACE AINSLIE

Left: THE AUTHOR AS FESTE IN "TWELFTH NIGHT" AT LIVERPOOL REPERTORY
THEATRE, 1914. Right: THE LATE SIR HARRY LAUDER

GILLIE POTTER

THE AUTHOR IN 1922

ADA REEVE AS ALADDIN

WILKIE BARD

son and Mabel Mannering Repertoire Company. Millar Anderson was a well-known touring manager, who had in his repertoire such plays as "Mrs. Dane's Defence", "The Liars", "Joseph Entangled", and "Cousin Kate". Mabel Mannering was his wife, an excellent emotional heavy lead. But unfortunately she brought heavy emotion into every part that she played, even those requiring more delicate treatment.

I behaved very badly with this management, talking a lot of 'flaf' about having been with the famous Liverpool Repertory Company, and treating the whole thing as though I were doing Mr. Anderson a favour. Naturally he did not appreciate this. But his wife liked me, and I stayed with the company playing the juveniles in every play.

The company included many capable all-round players, such as Robert Dalzell, old Charlie Stone (an excellent comedy character actor), Vernon Crabtree, Gladys Lloyd, and Gordon Fleming. We were expected to put the plays on quickly—and we did.

If not too much attention was paid to detail, well— three nights at Clacton followed by three nights at Cromer, and dreadful journeys such as from the Marina Theatre, Lowestoft to the Pier Theatre, Lytham, Lancashire, did not leave much time for the finer points.

Again I lived as one of a trio, with Robert Dalzell, Gordon Fleming and myself always 'digging' together.

When we played at Clacton the three of us stayed at a farmhouse a little way out. We all occupied one bedroom, and had ample excellent country food. The cost was seven shillings and sixpence each for the four nights!

The farmer had a most attractive daughter who brought us in early morning tea and waited on us. Each of us tried to get friendly with her—and I won.

Swift work was done in four days. On the third day the sweet girl was ordered out of my dressing-room by Mr. Anderson, and I was ordered out of the farmhouse by her father that same night.

E

But the farmer had reckoned without making due allowance for his daughter's spirit. She promptly told him that if I went she went, and he, knowing that he would soon be rid of us, used his discretion.

By this time the war was absorbing man-power and the Derby Scheme was in full force. It was an unenviable time for men like myself who looked fit but were not, for busybodies of the female sex went about presenting them with white feathers.

I was a victim on several occasions. But in point of fact, as a volunteer, twice I had been totally rejected by medical boards for a suspected spot on one lung, which was later to prove serious.

CHAPTER FOUR

IN the autumn I returned again to Liverpool.

Even if I did not fully appreciate it then, looking back now I realise how fortunate I was there to come into contact with such great people of the theatre as Granville Barker, Bernard Shaw, John Galsworthy, John Masefield, Harold Brighouse, Stanley Houghton, Lascelles Abercrombie, Eden Philpotts, Ronald Jeans and Miss Horniman. These apart from and in addition to the splendid actors and actresses from whom a young actor like myself could learn so much.

I was privileged to have the companionship and friendship of people like William Armstrong, J. H. Roberts, Lawrence Hanray and Wilfred Shine. What professors for a youngster in the university of the drama.

"Billy" Armstrong came to Liverpool to open in the "Music Cure". I do not think that he was ever fond of acting, but his Dubedate in "The Doctor's Dilemma" was a magnificent performance. Subsequently he found his right métier as a producer and director. His artistry was tempered with sound Scots philosophy and a great sense of humour.

J. H. ("Jack") Roberts was a favourite with everybody. A gentleman in every sense, as he rose in stature he still had time for the smaller fry. He gave a wonderful performance as Gaffer Pearce in Masefield's "Tragedy of Nan".

Hauptmann's dream play, "Hannele", was a typically German heavy myth to which Basil Dean gave an ambitious production. Shiel Barry, son of the famous old tragedian, came to our company to play the part of Mattern, the cruel, drunken father of Hannele, who in the course of the play killed his daughter, who was duly transported to heaven.

That fine actor Baliol Holloway played The Christ

beautifully and reverently; Maire O'Neil played The Angel of Light; Norman McKeown, The Angel of Death; and I was his understudy. Among the 'angels' engaged from Italia Conti's school were Noël Coward, Gertrude Lawrence, Roy Royston and Harold French.

Since I was assistant stage-manager this redoubtable quartette were put partly in my charge. They never did anything that I told them to do, and cheeked me unmercifully.

Noël Coward's tongue gave early promise of his later success with the pen.

"Please don't forget that I'm the assistant stage-manager," I said to him one day.

"Of course I shan't," was his reply, "but what a pity that *you* can't forget it sometimes."

These four 'angels' had to carry the dead body of Hannele in a crystal coffin into heaven, and then cavort about swinging incense.

Basil Dean had arranged to make the entrance of The Angel of Death more impressive and terrifying by having him enter right from the back of the theatre auditorium, down the centre gangway, over a huge rostrum and up to heaven brandishing his sword. One night I had to go on for Norman McKeown.

I went to the back of the pit and found that I had some ten minutes, as I thought, to spare before my cue. So I went into the bar to chat to the beautiful barmaid, Peggy, and have a Guinness. I kept opening the door an inch or two to watch for my cue, but I had miscalculated the time, and suddenly it was upon me.

Hurriedly I picked up my sword, wangled my wings through the door and stalked down the pit gangway. Half way down to the stage I realised that I still held the glass of Guinness in the hand that was not brandishing the sword, so I pushed it quickly into the hand of a patron in the stalls.

This incident had not escaped the watchful eye of 'angel' Roy Royston, who in his angelic garb looked

the picture of innocence. As I clambered up over the
rostrum on to the stage he whispered through his teeth,
"You might have brought us one."

I was not wanted for the Christmas season. So I went
to London to look for work. I had an interview with the
famous Mr. Blackmore at his agency in Garrick Street,
and with the cool cheek of youth turned down several
excellent opportunities.

Then I went to see Charles St. John Denton in Whit-
combe Street. I had a great affection for Mr. Denton,
and I think that he liked me. I told him that I did not
want to remain in straight work, but wanted a pantomime
engagement.

"It's very difficult, my boy," he said, "and you have
not been in pantomime. However, I will see what I can
do. Come back this afternoon."

When I got back, Mr. Milton Bode, a very influential
theatre manager, was in Denton's office. I can picture
Bode now, in his tightly fitting Chesterfield overcoat and
jaunty bowler hat, wearing lavender gloves and with a
large carnation in his button-hole. He had a narrow
outlook, a wide vocabulary and a high-pitched voice.
"Sing us a song," he said, "I want somebody to play
Prince Abdullah in 'Sinbad the Sailor' at Brighton."

I had no song with me and offered to go home and get
one, but Mr. Bode would not wait. Could I give him some
idea of what my voice was like?

"Yes," I said, "I could sing a hymn."

"That should do," said Bode, quite unconcerned.

In came Miss Lind, a beautiful girl who was Mr.
Denton's secretary, to play the piano. I whispered to her,
and she played the *Old Hundredth*, and in the approved
light comedy style I walked up and down Denton's office,
raising my hat at intervals, and singing *Praise God from
whom all blessings flow*.

Charles Denton, afterwards when I had signed the
contract, told me that it was the most extraordinary
audition he had ever seen, unique in his experience. But

Bode said, "I don't know whether you're any good or not, but your appearance is all right, the clothes will fit you, so you're booked. Six quid a week for all performances."

When I presented myself on the stage of the Theatre Royal, Brighton, for the 1915 pantomime "Sinbad the Sailor," Bode said, "Who are you?"

"Arthur C. Rose, Liverpool Repertory Theatre," I replied promptly and proudly.

"My God, Gus," Bode said to his producer, Gus Hammond, "we've booked a bloody actor." Then turning to me he said, "We don't want any actors in this pantomime, you'll have to be a bloody comic."

At the Theatre Royal, Brighton, pantomimes Milton Bode would have all the comedians, irrespective of status, dress together in the big room at the end of the corridor on the ground floor, so in I went with the others.

These included the Brothers Bass, one of whom is now Billy Danvers, the "cheery, chubby" comedian; Barry Mills; and Tom E. Sinclair, the dame; also Bert Maddison. Since Phil Ray, the original abbreviating comedian, whose wife, Nellie Wrigley, was our Principal Boy, spent most of every evening in our dressing-room, it will be readily apparent that we were all somewhat cramped.

This was my first appearance in pantomime, and the other comedians rather left me out of things, getting together in corners and arranging gags and business amongst themselves. But this turned out to be a blessing in disguise. Mine was a light comedy part: Renee Reel was playing Principal Girl for the first time, and she and I had three excellent scenes and two duets together, which were amongst the hits of the pantomime.

Renee Reel was a lovely girl, with masses of long auburn hair, and I fell in love with her. But she had another suitor and a watchful mother, and I didn't get very far.

Since I was young, and when made-up looked fit for military service, one night, from the stalls, some young subalterns who had had several 'over the eight' started chi-iking me and made some uncomplimentary remarks. Phil Ray insisted on them coming round and seeing my rejection certificate, whereon they apologised, bought champagne all round, and ended up tremendous pals of the pantomime, and myself in particular.

But tired of such ignominious happenings I destroyed my medical certificate and once more presented myself to a Medical Board. Again I was turned down the moment that the doctor sounded my chest.

Billy Danvers was, in those days, a thin fair-haired boy with a quizzical look and a burning ambition. He and I became great friends. We used to play dominoes in the 'digs' for pennies. When our means would permit, we used to have a whole tin of salmon for our supper. Billy was engaged, and used to watch every post for letters from his Guila.

When the Brighton pantomime ended I went to London to look for work, and started rehearsals at the Savoy Theatre, with H. B. Irving, in "The Angel in the House". The Birmingham Repertory Theatre wanted someone to take Ion Swinley's place: I was interviewed, offered the engagement, and Mr. Irving very graciously released me from my contract with him for what he said "was obviously a more permanent job".

So to the Birmingham Repertory Theatre I went, and immediately started rehearsing the lead in Charles McEvoy's "When the Devil was Ill". This was a colossal part for which I was not nearly experienced enough. Crompton Rhodes, the dramatic critic of the *Birmingham Post*, whilst giving me some credit, disparaged my performance by saying, "Mr. Rose made his hero somewhat like a picture palace cowboy". This upset me very much at the time, although afterwards I was to have many excellent notices from Crompton Rhodes.

There was tremendous enthusiasm at the Birmingham Rep., and one could forgive the 'arti-craftiness' because of the great underlying sincerity. After my first essay in a leading part I was given minor roles for a time.

It was a wonderful company, including John Drinkwater, Felix Aylmer, Scott Sunderland, Paul Smythe, Ivor Barnard, Stuart Vinden, Mary Merrall, Miele Maunde, William Rea, Margaret Chatwin, Maud Gill, Phyllis Relph, Vera Bassano, Dorothy Taylor, Cathleen Orford, Isabel Thornton, Noel Shannon, Mary Raby, Frank Moore, Harcourt Williams, and Betty Pinchard. Bache Matthews was the manager.

John Drinkwater, Barry Jackson and Stuart Vinden all did production. It was another grand experience, but it took me a long time to fit in.

John Drinkwater was a dear, sweet and very gentle man, who lived a greater part of his days in the clouds. I think that he looked upon me as being 'music-hally'. But when he found that I had written several parodies of some of his beautiful poems and plays, including a full-length burlesque of "The Storm", with many sly digs at his dreaminess, he laughed like a schoolboy and insisted on the company and other guests being invited to a reading of it at a party one Sunday night.

After that, whenever he saw me with a piece of paper in my hand, he would say, "Read me what you have written, Rose. I know that it will be ribald and probably scurrilous, but I want something to laugh at."

Barry Jackson cast a devoted and æsthetic eye over everything. For a time I think that I was suspect to him. But I do remember him watching me singing comic songs at a concert he had arranged for soldiers, after which he gave me the part of "Feste" in "Twelfth Night".

Scott Sunderland, whilst he regarded his work seriously, loved the rough-and-tumble part of stage work. He was always playing practical jokes on me.

Felix Aylmer, at that time, was just starting in the profession. At first I thought him cold, frigid and austere. But when I got to know him I found that behind this apparent façade was a tremendous sense of humour. Since he was a musician he took a great interest in my song-writing efforts.

He approached every part that he played from an academic and scholarly viewpoint. When he matured he became a great asset to the stage, and the studios' gain is the theatres' loss when he is occupied with his present-day successful work in films.

One of the greatest characters back stage was Father Arnold Pinchard. With his daughter Betty in the company, he took a great interest in the theatre, and his house was always open to any of us who cared to go up.

He was a great personality. People came from miles away to hear him preach at the near-by St. Jude's.

Ivor Barnard was a grand comedy actor who, since Birmingham Rep. days, has done some notable work. He was the perfect example of the helpless little man who always looks as though he needs 'mothering'.

Margaret Chatwin—known to us all as "Margot"—was the "Queen Mother" of the theatre. She was more prone to laughter at the slightest thing than any woman I have ever known. Once when she was playing Lady Macbeth I nearly got into terrible trouble by making her laugh heartily just before she went on for the sleep-walking scene. "Margot," with her usual generosity, got me out of it, of course.

Another girl at the theatre with a great sense of humour was Vera Bassano. One of the most vivacious persons that I have ever met, she looked like Lee White, and laughter danced behind her eyes all the time. She had tremendous character and her attraction was magnetic.

She had leanings towards the musical stage. After experience in concert-parties she made a name for herself with Anglo-French songs and monologues. On the air she was known as Yvette.

I shall never forget the fun we all had when we produced Ben Jonson's "The Alchemist". The lurid language was played uncensored.

The value of the Birmingham Repertory Theatre as a nursery can readily be gauged when one ponders the names in the theatre to-day who started their careers there.

But my own training apart, I was delighted to be back in my beloved Birmingham.

I have heard Birmingham described as an ugly industrial town, and I suppose in many ways this is correct. But despite the fact that my early associations were ones of struggle and extreme poverty, I have great affection for the city, and to me, born in Dudley, it has always seemed a wonderful place.

I can picture now Corporation Street with its shops and stores, and, above all, Pattison's Restaurant, where, as a kid, I was taken by indulgent aunts and given wonderful chocolate éclairs and, on occasions, cold salmon with Pattison's own special salad cream, which really was made from thick rich cream, and then was given a bag of farthing buns to munch on the way home: Barnby's toy shop, from whose outside display I had, one Christmas, stolen a wooden engine.

Narrow and busy New Street, with the Theatre Royal so tucked away that you were right on top of it before you knew that it was there; Broad Street, with the Prince of Wales Theatre; Coleshill Street, with the old Gaiety; John Bright Street, where, at the old Alexandra, I used to try to persuade Lester Collingwood to take me on in some capacity or other; the 'pros' digs' in Bath Row, Belgrave Road and Bristol Road; the Bull Ring, with its Market Hall where at one time you could get a dozen oysters for sixpence; Mountford's cook shop with huge, luscious joints sizzling on large pans in the window, and where you could get a 'good blow-out' for a 'tanner'; the smoke and grime from the factories.

When, as an office-boy, I used to gaze at the Tivoli with its tall tower like a lighthouse, little did I think that, when it had been rebuilt by Charles Gulliver and opened as Birmingham Hippodrome, "the Palladium of the Provinces", I should be co-starred there with Shirley Kellogg.

Whilst I was at the Birmingham Repertory I had yet another medical. Someone thought fit to write to the authorities and say that I was avoiding military service.

A civilian and a sergeant came down to the theatre, and I
was hiked off very unceremoniously. Again I was rejected,
and this time a doctor told me that my lung was very bad.
I could never understand this, because I felt very well
myself.

The Birmingham Repertory Theatre at that time had
a kind and pleasant custom of paying artistes during the
vacation on condition that they did not do any other work.
I did not take advantage of this, and on my first summer
vacation from the theatre, joined Hickman Smith's
"Royal Entertainers", and had a happy if somewhat
ramshackle tour to places like Burnham-on-Sea, Pwllheli,
Bohemia, Finchley, and other odd spots.

I had much varied work to do in this show. Hickman
Smith was a grand old trouper who knew his job, and he
gave me considerable help. But I think that he was
getting rather tired of it all at the time, for he even
allowed me to take over some of his compèring.

The main thing about this job was that Hickman Smith
was willing to book Vera Bassano with me. That, at the
time, meant everything.

Despite parental disapproval—and opposition from both
our families—Vera and I, both young and hot-headed,
were determined to go our own way, and that way was to
be, and to work, together.

Vera Bassano had a wonderful home at Old Hill in
Staffordshire, and all I could offer her was a joint engagement in a small concert-party and hand-to-mouth living
in cheap rooms. But for a long time our romance was
impervious to mundane considerations.

We worked very hard arranging duets and double-
acts, and these were a great asset to the show. During the
autumn and winter of that year, instead of wisely returning
to the Birmingham Repertory Theatre, we both joined
Fred Spencer's resident company at Seaford.

Seaford, although a tiny place, at that time had a
tremendously swollen temporary population from the
adjacent army camps. The concert-party season ran

right through the winter, with a change of programme every week.

Fred Spencer was a big name, in those days, as a summer show proprietor and as a pantomime dame. He was a fussy, nervous man. His partner, Harry Rogerson, was one of the most brilliant tumbling comedians that I have ever seen.

But in every programme Fred Spencer would do a dame scene, and Harry Rogerson would tumble. Vera and I, with our youth, our vitality and much new material, were more than welcome.

By this time I was doing a considerable amount of writing. Daily I could be found with Loie Milne, a magnificent pianist, working out new melodies, and week by week the new songs went on.

Fred Spencer realised full well the value of our success, but for some obtuse reason he resented it. So, taking advantage of an enquiry I had received from Edgar Allan Brown at the Devonshire Park Winter Garden at Eastbourne, I went over to see him.

Edgar Allan Brown was a strange man—and Mrs. Brown stranger still. They were both enthusiasts and pioneers in making concert-parties something more than just haphazard shows.

Their show "Charivari", a superb and most original presentation, was playing at the old Vaudeville Pavilion in the Park. Douglas Furber, playing Punch, was the leading spirit, and the cast included such grand artistes as Noel Leyland, Elsie Ingle, Lilian Byrne and George Ellis.

Vera and I did a public audition in the middle of the "Charivari" show. Listening to the roars of laughter and applause that greeted the well-established favourites, as I waited in the dressing-room I felt very humble and nervous. But "Douggie" Furber gave us a magnificent 'build-up', we were most successful, and were engaged to open in a few weeks' time in Edgar Allan Brown's "Moonshine".

When we went to rehearse this show, at the Shaftesbury Hotel in London, we found that our fellow artistes were Agnes Croxton, Phœbe Hodgson, Felgate King, Elsie Mayfair, Phyllis Rose, Richard Crawford, Blake Adams and Norah Roylánce. The producer was Philip Howley. I was appointed manager and principal comedian.

Agnes Croxton was, I think, the best all-round soprano I have ever seen in concert-party. Her singing was effortless, and her appearance that of the traditional Dresden china shepherdess, with natural platinum hair.

Blake Adams was an excellent little comedian of the Billy Merson type, but inclined to be worried if anyone else got laughs.

Phœbe Hodgson was a natural comedy actress, a sheer joy to work with. She has since proved her worth in many West End shows.

Felgate King was a brilliant if somewhat temperamental musician. His wife, Elsie Mayfair, was an extremely versatile artiste. She had a marvellous mezzo-soprano voice, and could and did sing ballads, which she followed with as happy a routine of clog-walloping as one could find, and then, still not breathless, she would join Felgate King in an excellent double-piano turn.

My own work, with Phœbe Hodgson, with Vera Bassano, and on my own was, with the possible exception of Elsie Mayfair and Felgate King's piano double, the hit of the programme. But Mrs. Brown did not like it. It was probably not artistic enough for the Brown pattern.

I also had rigid ideas about managing a show. One night, at the old New Theatre at Oxford, I stopped one of the girls in a ballet doing something to attract the attention of young cadets in the stalls. When I went, for support in my action, to the management, I found the same lady in an intriguing position on the knees of an official in the office. Knowing that I was powerless locally, I telephoned Eastbourne, and was told to overlook the matter.

The next night the same thing happened again. So I telephoned Eastbourne and said that either my authority as the manager was established and respected, or I resigned. The upshot was that I gave in my notice, and two weeks later, when I brought the show into Eastbourne, I handed in my books and cash and said good-bye.

I was particularly glad to hand in the cash to Edgar Mockett, then chief cashier at the Winter Gardens, because, for some reason best known to Mr. Brown, I had been instructed not to bank any moneys in the various towns for several weeks, and I was carrying a considerable amount of cash around in a linen bag, and terrified of losing it. Edgar Mockett and I became great pals, and I often pop in to the Park Saloon at Eastbourne, where he is now the landlord. We talk over old times, and he generally has a new story for me.

Since I hadn't a penny in the world, to resign was probably a foolish thing to do. But in a couple of days the man who had taken my place was found to be unsuitable, and I was sent for. After that, law and order prevailed in "Moonshine", and we had a most successful tour.

Edgar Allan Brown's shows, "Moonshine", "Vogue", and "Charivari", certainly blazed a trail, and made other managements look to their dressing and decor.

After "Moonshine" I had an unpleasant period out of work. I filled-in with some 'after dinner' entertaining in London, a type of work which I never really liked. I did a trial turn at the old Surrey Music Hall without success, but quite undaunted tried the same thing at the Foresters, and did secure a week's engagement.

From squalid 'digs' it eventually became a question of earning, somehow, enough for board and lodging at Rowton House. There were many worse places than Rowton House in those days.

There, very cheaply, one could have a good bed, plenty of facilities for washing, slabs of bread and margarine, mugs of cocoa and hard-boiled eggs. In addition to eating hard-boiled eggs, in Rowton House one met them.

Here was a community of men drawn from all ranks of life but with one basic underlying factor—their common poverty. I found it very interesting to meet humanity in the raw, to explore London with the lid off.

I even tried entertaining the theatre queues. But I found that this branch of show business was the special preserve of certain people, and in finding myself pitches I had not a few fights.

One night, after entertaining the Lyceum queue and collecting three 'bob', I was strolling down the Strand feeling almost affluent when, just as I passed the Hotel Cecil, three magnificent Daimler cars drew up. Quick as lightning, before the commissionaire could get to them, I opened one of the car doors and handed out a lady.

"Dearest, give this nice man a half-crown, he looks so cold," she said in a shrill voice. The lady was Mrs. Asquith—and the gentleman who handed me the coin was Mr. Asquith.

When they had disappeared inside, the commissionaire, who had been attending to the other cars, gave me to understand, in no uncertain manner, that he disapproved of my interference. In fact, he planted a well-aimed kick on my behind. But I'd have taken—and indeed did take —many kicks for a half-crown in those days.

CHAPTER FIVE

WHEN Phil Ray gave me a letter of introduction to Wallis Arthur, Dame Fortune smiled on me again.

Wallis Arthur was a remarkable man. He had been, in his day, a very successful entertainer in London concert circles, particularly in the more Bohemian type of concerts. He had a reputation for being risqué in his own work, but he never allowed anything of this nature in his own shows.

With his partner, Paul Mill, he had established a summer entertainment syndicate with shows at Lowestoft, Bognor, Westcliff-on-Sea, Eastbourne, Hastings and Weston-super-Mare. Outside these Pierrot pitches one saw neat boards, "Wallis Arthur's Season, nightly at eight o'clock". Then would follow the names of the cast, and finally the line, so redolent of graceful and leisurely days, "Carriages at 10.15".

Under the Wallis Arthur banner were gathered some of the best artistes in this class of work, including Milton Hayes, Gillie Potter, Alice Lilley, Doris Lee, Olive Fox, Ambrose Thorne, Winnie Melville, Stuart Debnam, Fred Wildon, George Blackmore, Fred Rome, Rupert Hazell, Ernest Sewell, Carrie Herwin, and Frederic Gregory. He had been astute enough to engage these people long before they became well known, and most were paid salaries which did not reach double figures.

It was two shows a day with Wallis Arthur, and an artiste had to have at least thirty items in his repertoire. He was looked upon as a hard man—but admitted to be just.

In his time he had been something of a writer. He had an uncanny knack of putting his finger on the very spot in a song or sketch where some slight alteration would vastly improve it.

His London office was at 156 Strand, but at Westcliff-on-Sea he lived at the Welcome Club. He wore large glasses, which helped to hide the cute expression in his eyes, and had a disarming effect on everyone at whom he looked. He always made his own cigarettes, taking out a tobacco pouch and a cigarette paper. In an emergency he always rolled a cigarette, and the more critical the situation the longer time was taken in the rolling, whilst one stood by and waited patiently for an answer. He was always placid, calm and unruffled.

It was his custom to have the first few rehearsals with all the various shows together. By that method he achieved a cheerful rivalry among them.

Wallis Arthur, shrewd man that he was, saw that the day of the rather staid six-handed concert-party was passing. I had new ideas and he approved of them, but left me personally to pass them on to the heads of the various companies.

Very naturally, people like Franklyn Vernon of the Eastbourne company, Fred Rome of the Bognor company, and George Blackmore of the Hastings company, were somewhat resentful of the newcomer. Blackmore, however, gave me every co-operation. He had been at Hastings for sixteen or seventeen consecutive seasons, and was something of a god there. But he had a marvellous sense of humour and a philosophic acceptance of changing circumstances.

"It had to come sometime, my lad," he said to me. "I don't mind. It will keep the shows going a bit longer. But go easy with the old 'uns. They're in a comfortable groove, and won't like being shaken out of it."

At Westcliff-on-Sea I had a new company which was taking the place of one that had been very popular the previous year. My cast included Kenneth Blain, Alan Stainer the ventriloquist, Maud Davidson the soprano, Jimmie Saker the baritone, Melanie Castel a child impersonator, Hilda Bertram the pianist, and myself.

The previous year's cast had included Fred Wildon,

F

Fred Gibson, and Ambrose Thorne. After our first performance the report was that we were not so good as the year before, and for a week or two all I could hear about the town was praise of Fred Gibson. I was very crestfallen, and asked Wallis Arthur what was wrong.

"There's nothing wrong," he said. "You'll eventually be more popular than any Pierrot who has been here."

For a number of seasons the intervals at the matinée performances had always been long enough for someone to be sent to a near-by café for a huge pot of tea and a selection of cakes, which, after taking off their pierrot ruffles, the company leisurely enjoyed whilst the audience sank into a coma. There was almost a revolution when I cut the interval down to five minutes.

When, at the end of three weeks, I still went in for intensive rehearsals and proposed putting on a further three programmes, the cast threatened to strike. Wallis Arthur, however, stood firm with me, and the season proceeded to a normal close, although the word went round London concert circles that I was "an impossible man and a slave-driver."

On the last night Alan Stainer said to me, "You're bound to get on. You've an absolute disregard for anybody's feelings. People like that always get on."

A prolonged interview with Wallis Arthur and myself, after tea one afternoon, on the lawn at Shorefields, started Milton Hayes doing his famous "Meanderings of Monty" act.

Milton Hayes was a fine writer, particularly of monologues like *The Green Eye of the Little Yellow God*, but he decided that he wanted a song of mine that he had heard that afternoon, called *If You Belonged to Me*.

When the deal had been negotiated, reminiscences among three Pierrots obliterated time. Suddenly Hayes realised that he was late for his turn at Southend Hippodrome.

He ran all the way to the theatre and just managed to get on the stage one turn later than he should have done.

He had no time to get into his immaculate evening-dress clothes, and went on in his lounge suit, carrying a newspaper. He was too breathless to go into his usual entertainer's routine, and with this and nervousness he jabbered inconsequently.

Members of the Head Office booking department were in the audience, and from that night Milton Hayes never went back to his evening-dress suit, but just strolled on in a well-cut but negligent lounge suit, and chattered. That accident took him from £25 or £30 a week to £250 or £300!

When the Westcliff season ended I went to spend a few days with Wallis Arthur at Bognor. Since the Zeppelins were making London uncomfortable, he decided to keep the Bognor Pavilion open through October, with a composite company that included George Blackmore, Harold Humphries and Marion Ruth from Hastings, Muriel McGregor from the Bognor season company, and myself from Westcliff.

During that month I got to know George Blackmore very well, and had much encouragement from his sense of humour and philosophical outlook. I was seen also by a representative of George Grossmith and Edward Laurillard, the musical-comedy management, and received a letter from St. John Denton arranging for me to give Mr. Grossmith and Mr. Laurillard an audition some weeks ahead.

I had no money saved and no work to go to, and wondered how I was going to get through these weeks. Wallis Arthur lent me ten pounds, and I went up to London and stayed with Mrs. Dyer at 123 Kennington Road.

Calling on Charles Denton I pressed for an earlier audition. He recognised my plight and, seeing that I was very shabby, he took me out to a hosier's shop, bought me a shirt, collar and tie, made me put them on in his office, and then walked me round to Grossmith and Laurillard's headquarters in Golden Square, and took me in to see Felix Edwards, their production manager.

The firm had "Theodore & Co." running successfully at the Gaiety Theatre, and an understudy was wanted for Davy Burnaby and Fred Leslie. It was arranged for me to do an audition on the Gaiety stage the following morning.

Amongst others at this audition were Kenneth Blain and Arthur Margetson. When it came to my turn I could dimly discern the naval uniform of George Grossmith out in the auditorium, and felt rather than saw the cold, pale-blue eyes of Edward Laurillard. I rendered my pet item, Clifford Grey's *The Art of Song Writing*, but did not achieve any reaction.

"Have you anything else?" asked the slightly lisping voice of Grossmith.

"Yes. I've got some more songs," I replied.

"Should like to hear something more," said Grossmith. And Laurillard added a guttural murmur.

I took out another song called *In These Hard Times*, and handed it to the pianist. Before starting on this I advanced down to the footlights and said, "Excuse me, gentlemen, but would you mind, even if you don't laugh, making some sort of noise where it is obvious that the laughs would come from an audience? It will at any rate let me know that you are listening."

Grossmith was most amused at this, and I started to sing. When I had done the first comedy couplet in the chorus and there was still no reaction I said, "That's where you should laugh. Or stop me from going any further." Charles Maynard, the stage-manager, rushed on from the side and told me to get on with it, but the upshot of this audition was that Kenneth Blain, Arthur Margetson and myself were engaged for the first provincial tour of "Theodore & Co." starting out in some weeks' time, and I was given an immediate job at four pounds a week understudying Burnaby and Leslie at the Gaiety Theatre.

Four pounds a week would not enable me to meet my commitments and keep clear of debt. I shall not forget the sweet, gracious kindliness of dear Mrs. Dyer, at 123 Kennington Road.

Amongst those living with her and sharing her table were Little Zola, who would have been a star except that there could not be a Little Tich and a Little Zola, and his large-sized wife; Harry Marvello the illusionist, and his wife; a couple of German acrobats; a real "actor laddie" named Gregory; and two chorus-boys. They were all permanent residents, and seemed permanently out of work, but they were all grand people.

A huge, underground, cellar-like room was our dining-room, sitting-room, common-room. Mrs. Dyer, attended by a maid-of-all-work, cooked for us and waited upon us. We had ample portions of meat and vegetables, and could always have more when our plates were empty. After the meat and vegetables, Mrs. Dyer walked round the table with a huge dish of rice, or some similar pudding, and ladled out large portions upon the same plates.

We used to sit far into the night after supper, playing cards for matches, the value of the matches being six to a penny. We borrowed small sums from each other, lent each other clothes, and if a letter came for any of us giving promise of a job, we were all as pleased as Punch, and gave any further help needed.

There was great consternation and not a little laughter one night when I enquired where the bathroom was.

"Bathroom, indeed," said one of the ladies; "this ain't the 'Otel Cecil, you know."

But Mrs. Dyer said, "You leave 'im alone. 'E probably likes a bath."

Then turning to me she said, "Well, ducks, I 'ave got a bathroom, but at the present moment it's got a bed in it and is let to a composer, so you can't go in it. But after you've 'ad your supper, you get undressed and come along to the kitchen and I'll 'ave a big 'ip bath full of boiling water for you."

During the six weeks that I stayed with Mrs. Dyer I never knew her to go to bed or even take off her clothes.

She sat in an old rocking-chair in her kitchen, and at the slightest pretext, at any hour of the day or night, she would make tea for herself and her clients.

Understudying at the Gaiety Theatre was a pleasant experience, and I got to know Leslie Henson very well. It was in this show, "Theodore & Co.", that he and Davy Burnaby were singing that grand topical song *Three Hundred and Sixty-five Days*.

After I had reported and seen that my principals were in the theatre, and exchanged a few words with that great character, Mr. Jupp, the Gaiety Theatre stage door-keeper, I would go over to the "Wellington" or the "Bell" and write topical couplets for this song. Some of my efforts were good and some were bad, but when I had done them I would go back to the theatre and take them in to Leslie Henson and Davy Burnaby. Leslie would often give me half a crown or five 'bob' for them, and occasionally he would use them.

I alternated between a silent admiration and passion for Julia James, and an equally unspoken devotion to Madge Saunders. I was emotionally very unsettled at this time.

What a diplomat was Mr. Jupp! He was a monument of tact, a mine of information, and a master at dealing with awkward situations. He was no snob and had just as much time for the minor artistes as the big stars, and was ready to help in anything. I suppose that he and one or two other stage door-keepers in the West End of London knew more about famous people than anybody.

Well, the time came for the number one touring company of "Theodore & Co." to embark at St. Pancras for Edinburgh. On that Sunday morning, at the door of 123 Kennington Road, Mrs. Dyer said, "'Ow are you fixed, ducks?"

"Oh, I'm all right, I shall manage," I said.

"Give us a kiss, love, and come back and see us again."

She pressed her gnarled, rather dirty but lovely face against mine, and pushed a pound-note into my hand.

"Send it back when you've been in work a week or two. And be a good boy."

Mrs. Dyer was a grand, loving soul. Her whole life was spent serving others.

Again I was one of a trio in 'digs', for Kenneth Blain, Arthur Margetson and myself had decided to live together. At Edinburgh we fixed at Mrs. Cowell's, 16 Grindlay Street, just opposite the Lyceum Theatre.

Margetson was playing a footman and understudying the part created in London by George Grossmith and taken over by Austin Melford when Grossmith returned to the Admiralty for the remainder of the war; Kenneth Blain was understudying Billy Pringle, who was playing the Leslie Henson role; and I had Fred Leslie's part, and was delighted to find myself working again with Agnes Croxton, who was in the Julia James role.

It was an unlucky month for the principals, but a lucky time for the understudies. Billy Pringle was taken ill, and Kenneth Blain went on for him and gave a grand show. Willoughby was taken ill and on went Margetson in the Grossmith role, and showed early promise of what he was eventually to become, an exceptionally fine musical-comedy leading man.

The Grossmith and Laurillard management were very strict and did not approve of their men living in the same 'digs' as their ladies, and a careful check was kept. But we managed to have some carefree love affairs.

Agnes Croxton, Arthur Margetson, Kenneth Blain, Amy Verity, Wilson James and myself were all from the concert-party school. We were unknown in the big provincial cities, where the George Edwardes's musical-comedy favourites, such as W. H. Rawlins, Horace Mills, Lionel Victor, Frank Hector, George Gregory and Louis Bradfield, were established stars. The grand business done by "Theodore & Co." with this cast must have been a revelation to Grossmith and Laurillard, on whose shoulders, by this time, the mantle of George Edwardes had fallen.

Wilson James had been a well-known London concert entertainer and proprietor of an excellent concert-party, "The Gaieties". This was his first incursion into musical-comedy, and his tall, dignified appearance was eminently suited to the part of the Duke. He was a 'dandy', and belonged to the age when the dandies flourished, an age that the 1914 war had ended.

He was of far greater standing in the concert-party world than any of us were at the time. He had been a proprietor—whereas Margetson, Blain and myself were employees—and he was not slow to register the difference in our status. Later on he worked for me as manager at Shanklin, where his vast experience and competence were invaluable.

Kenneth Blain and I spent a lot of time writing material. Since we were both to rejoin Wallis Arthur again the following summer, we were able to turn this ability to good account. I began to learn that I must treat my writing seriously and learn to market my efforts.

The tour of "Theodore & Co." came to an end at Cardiff. Just before that date I received a letter from Wallis Arthur giving me the personnel of the company I was to control at Westcliff.

In the final paragraph he said, ". . . and Olive Fox, who, as you know, is a noted piano entertainer and comedienne. She is a grand artiste, but somebody you will find very difficult. You will have to mind your P's and Q's, my lad."

Little did I think as I read the letter that, in that 1918 season at Westcliff, I was to meet the woman who was to play such a tremendous part in my life, who was to cement me to foundations, and give me a better sense of the fitness, not of some things—but of all things.

CHAPTER SIX

ON a day before the commencement of the 1918 season at Westcliff, in Wallis Arthur's office at 156 Strand, I first met the dynamic Olive Fox. There were other women in the room, but Olive was outstanding.

She was wearing a perfectly tailored blue coat and skirt, a blouse of paler blue, a large and immaculate white fox fur, a closely fitting little hat edged with shaded flowers around the brim, gossamer stockings, and shoes artfully made to conceal the fact that her feet were rather large. She was a great friend of the famous woman entertainer at the piano, Margaret Cooper, who passed on to Olive a lot of the work that she herself could not undertake. In addition, Olive Fox herself had a large and lucrative connection in the concert world.

Knowing that she was used to the good things of life and the best places, I hesitated about asking her out to dinner, but eventually plucked up courage and took her to that very nice temperance hotel, the Bonington. Since she was familiar with the Ritz, the Savoy, the Cecil, the Monico and the Carlton, Olive Fox must have thought it very funny. But she has since assured me that it was the nicest meal she has ever had.

I seem to recall that it cost me nine shillings, and left me nearly 'broke'!

At rehearsals she worked like the proverbial 'nigger', and since Olive Fox was a notable and respected artiste, her example had its due effect on the others. Consequently we opened at Westcliff to a flying start, and put on a series of programmes that are talked about there to this day.

This supposedly 'difficult' woman turned out to be just the opposite. But then she liked to be with me, and so the longer the rehearsal the more she enjoyed it.

Almost at once I fell in love with her, and she with me.

She was, as I have said, a well-known artiste. I was completely unknown.

Both of us were tied, and neither could voice to the other their inmost thoughts.

Wallis Arthur knew that I was in love with Olive, and that it was the real thing in my life at last. Whether he thought that Olive might take me away from his organisation, or whether he really believed in the creed of "playing the game and doing the right thing" I do not know—for his was a complex nature.

But he used to stress to me the disadvantages that would face me if I kept on "chasing Olive", and then he would tell Olive the same things about me. It made no difference—such advice never has under similar circumstances. The surest way of drawing two people together is to try to force them apart.

Yet with that weapon of "doing the right thing" on his side Wallis Arthur nearly won. At the end of that wonderful season Olive Fox and I agreed to part. She went back to her London concert world—but it nearly broke her up. I went off to try to find a job—with the bottom fallen out of my life.

Then something happened that seemed almost too good to be true. My domestic affairs straightened themselves out, and the way was made clear for me to go to Olive. Very soon afterwards Olive, too, got her divorce.

That was in 1918, and we have been at each other's side ever since.

It was bitterly cold the day that I went to Olive to tell her my news. Dressed in nurse's uniform, she was standing outside Clarendon Court, Maida Vale, where she lived, selling flags for a hospital. I, thin and emaciated, met her on the corner.

"Where is your overcoat?" she asked. "You will be frozen."

As nonchalantly as I could I said that I never wore an overcoat if I possibly could avoid doing so, and in any case

I had left it at home. Then we made an appointment to meet that night, and went our separate ways.

As soon as I was out of sight Olive took a taxi to my 'digs' at Kilburn and found out from my landlady, not only that I did not possess an overcoat, but that I was short of other necessities also. When I got to Clarendon Court that night, and was shown to her room, she had some half-dozen overcoats from Whiteley's, and she would do nothing and discuss nothing until I had selected one.

This incident was typical of Olive Fox. To anyone in need she would give the clothes off her own back.

Olive and I then formed a double-act that was known as 'Fox and Rose'. As I have said, her concert connection was extensive, and from that moment she would not accept a booking unless I also was engaged.

Many of her clients were annoyed. But Olive was adamant. She would fulfil faithfully contracts already made, although even with these engagements she would try to get me in wherever possible. But she turned down everything else unless her new partner could be included.

We made steady progress, and soon the National Sunday League sent us double bookings. At one National Sunday League concert we were seen by a small agent named Cooke Frankish.

He was an unusual type of man with many good points, but to me he always seemed to have a grudge against life. To him no artistes were any good unless he had booked them.

He took a great interest in us and booked us our first week on the music-halls, at Rotherhithe Hippodrome, at a salary of eighteen pounds. Although our act was somewhat 'concert-y', I had seen its faults, and by Tuesday had corrected them, and Cooke Frankish had many offers for us, including the Syndicate theatres and the much-coveted by artistes because it gave them a cachet, Stoll tour.

Frankish became dictatorial, and this led to my leaving

him, amicably as I thought at the time. But he sued me, the case being a question of 'sole agency'.

It was heard by Mr. Justice Tobin, at the Westminster County Court, and I had to come all the way from the Isle of Wight to appear.

Charles Doughty, an eminent legal light, was my counsel, Mr. Lever appearing for the other side. When the break came for lunch I felt sure that I was on the losing side, so did Mr. Doughty, and in the interval we made an offer to settle, which Cooke Frankish refused.

In the afternoon the fact was elicited that I had come from the Isle of Wight to appear. Mr. Justice Tobin stopped the proceedings and said, "Why was it necessary to bring Mr. Rose from the Isle of Wight on this case, when there's a perfectly good County Court at Newport? It seems vindictive to me."

A few more questions from both sides, a few more statements from me—and I had won. I caught my train at Waterloo, and got back to Ryde just in time to walk on in the opening chorus in my lounge suit.

Our next agent was Bernard Sherek. Old man Sherek was a German, a grand character and a great agent, with a particular pull on the music-halls controlled by Charles Gulliver.

In his black alpaca jacket he would sit all day in his little office in Lisle Street. His uncompromising exterior and brusque guttural tones were frightening to many artistes. But once you got behind that exterior you found a nice, homely soul.

At my first interview he said sharply, "Haf you effer played for Mr. Collifer?" When I replied that we had not, he said, "Zen I book you and you play vit him."

He picked up his telephone, barked a series of orders, and when he had finished said, "You go to Villesden Hippodrome next week, and also you go to Kilburn Empire as deputy for Shak and Efelyn" (Jack and Evelyn).

I felt very proud to deputise for Jack O'Connor and his sister, but sorry for the reasons that made it necessary.

Jack, with whom I had worked in my early days at Liverpool, was, to my mind, one of the finest natural comedians that we have ever had.

Old man Sherek continued to take a great interest in us, and we were never out of work. He took a personal liking to us, and would often take us round to his favourite place in Soho for coffee, and would sit and talk about music, books or any other subject except variety.

Young Henry Sherek was finding his feet in the office, and we became excellent friends. I did not visualise then that he would one day become one of the biggest (in every sense of the word) impresarios.

That Christmas Olive had a lot of previously booked concerts to fulfil. So I fixed pantomime with Joe Graham and Milton Bode at the old Kennington Theatre.

This pantomime, "Cinderella", had been produced originally by Robert Courtneidge at Manchester and at the Adelphi Theatre, London, and was known as the "White Cinderella" because of its white ballet and transformation scenes. It had made pantomime history, and most of the noted pantomime names had played in it.

My part was Dandini. It had been played by George Lashwood, Eric Thorne and Fred Allandale, and was, in my opinion, one of the best male parts in the show.

The cast was a notable one for a suburban pantomime. Charles Garry, a West End actor, played the Baroness on very cultured lines; Robb Gilmore was the Baron, the part originally played by Dan Rolyat; "Cinders" was Elsie Gregory, and one of the best I have seen in the part; the page, "Buttons", was, in this production, known as "Choddles", and played by Eddie Walker, a comedian with a very funny face, a good voice, and when on, a peculiarly hurt sense of humour.

The Ugly Sisters were that grand little comedy actress Nellie Sheffield and a more austere actress of the eccentric type, Rita Rae Vivienne. The Principal Boy was a really lovely girl named Ernestine Cesnere, who was booked as an experiment. When she was in the mood, Ernestine was excellent. But she treated the whole thing as a joke, often laughed in the part, which is bad in any show, but particularly terrible in pantomime, when the children are looking for dignity and chivalry from Prince Charming.

Bluff, hearty Wentworth Croke was the manager at the Kennington Theatre. Olive came down in her spare moments to see that I was taking my cod-liver oil and malt and other medicines, and altogether it was a particularly happy season.

A link of strong friendship was forged between old Joe Graham and myself. In many ways he was a hard nut to crack, and in conversation he had a curious intake of the breath, making a sort of hissing sound that was always a warning that he was not going to agree with you. But first and foremost he was a lover of the theatre and of tradition, a great pantomime man and a great man of the theatre, and it was illuminating to work with him. He was a very lovable eccentric, and we could do with more of his kidney in our profession to-day.

He could go on for any male part in the pantomime at a moment's notice. Once at Kennington he was fetched in from the pit door, where he was taking the tickets in lieu of someone absent from the staff, and in place of Eddie Walker, who was ill, appeared as "Choddles", wearing Eddie's clothes, and even singing his song.

After the Kennington pantomime Olive and I resumed concert engagements. For one of these I was taken down to Maidenhead, and there introduced to Frank Trevoe, who lived at a house called "Carrig Cleana".

An American by birth he was possibly the most famous Bohemian of that time in theatrical circles, and noted for the lavishness of his parties, particularly on American Thanksgiving Day, when the peak of the festivities was the turkey and cranberry sauce, and his house full of famous names, with others accommodated in Skindle's and other hotels in the district.

An illness had caused him to lose both his eyes. But he was always cheerful, humorous, and a perfect host.

Frank Trevoe was very fond of Olive and her mother—
Florence Venning, a noted contralto in her day—but he
was jealous of his friendships and resented newcomers.
I was taken to his chair to be introduced.

"This is 'Clarkie', my new partner," Olive said.

Frank grunted something, and then said, "Come
closer."

He felt with his hands all over my face, then my
shoulders, and finally took hold of my hand and said, "I
think I'm going to like you."

It was at "Carrig Cleana" that I first met Pauline
Chase. She was the lovely American actress brought to
this country by the impresario, Frohman, for whom
Barrie wrote "Peter Pan". I still think her the best of all
Peter Pans.

It was Thanksgiving Day, and around the table were
the Two Bobs, Odette Myrtle, Bobby Mitten, Stewart
Gardner, Norah Blaney, Gwen Farrar, one of the Du Cros,
Marie Dressler, Lew Hearn, Lee White, Clay Smith,
Hope Jackson and others. After the meal we all had to
sit around Frank, and he, with the uncanny instinct of the
blind, could tell almost the exact spot where any given
person sat. He would point suddenly with his finger and
say, "Odette, darling, play something on your violin and
sing me a song."

On that particular day Odette tried out for the first
time a song that was to become the rage, *Maryland*.
Stewart Gardner and Bobby Mitten, with wonderful
voices and, what is rarer still in these days, perfect
phrasing, sang ballad after ballad. Then Frank's finger
suddenly pointed at me.

"Come along, Olive's 'Clarkie'. Let's hear what you
can do."

I got up and sang *Don't get the wind up, Walter*. It was
different from anything that had been done in that
assembly, and from that day I was taken right into
Frank Trevoe's circle, and whenever I went to the house
always had to sing that particular song.

Until the start of the summer season Olive and I played music-hall engagements. Then we returned to Westcliff-on-Sea and a wonderful welcome.

Wallis Arthur rather wondered whether the publicity in the more sensational papers of the divorce case would adversely affect us with the more respectable resident supporters of the show. But in our first season they had, in their own minds, formed a romance between Olive and myself, and there was the culmination of that romance for them all to see, and they loved us.

Wallis was, by this time, a great influence in my life. He used to say of me to other people that I always came up under the punch—and he could certainly punch pretty hard. But if any young artiste under his banner was ready to listen, and could suffer bluntly spoken home truths about their work, and, if necessary, their private lives, they could learn much.

After the Westcliff season Olive and I played more music-hall dates, and then I managed to bring to successful fruition a scheme I had evolved for getting Olive booked into pantomime with me. Although her professional experience had been that of an entertainer at the piano and a comedienne, I felt instinctively that she had all the necessary flair for Principal Boy. Anyway, I managed to get Joe Graham to give her an audition at the Duke of York's Theatre.

Olive could 'put over songs' as well as anybody that I knew. But she was not a top-ranking vocalist when it came to the ballad or straight song that Joe Graham always expected from his Principal Boys.

Her first song at the audition was a rollicking affair that was just right. Then she started the ballad, and I heard the quick intake of Joe's breath, but I walked him to the back of the pit, and by conversation managed to keep him from too intent concentration on Olive's vocal deficiencies. Another vivid swinging song from her, and Joe called us both into the office.

"You did say that she had played Boy before, Rose?"

"Of course," I replied.

"I'd like to see some photographs of her in tights."

I saw Olive's face fall and, what is more, I felt that she was about to blurt out the truth, but it was arranged that we were to go to the office in a week's time. Olive has perfect Principal Boy's legs, so I took her to Raynes's, hired a Boy's costume, had the photographs taken, and these, together with my persistence, did the trick.

For her first pantomime engagement Olive was booked to play Principal Boy in "Cinderella"—the "white Cinderella"—at the Opera House, Leicester, where she achieved immediate success. Big, burly Nat Lewis played the Baroness and little Roddy Hughes the Baron, otherwise the cast was as at the Kennington Theatre.

Leicester is an interesting place, a mixture of industry, agriculture and Quorn aristocracy. The audience is pleasant, but seems to have neither the warmth of the south nor the discrimination of the north.

Working Men's Clubs abound there, and in this sphere many professionals earn a living. Some of the stars of the music-halls graduated from the clubs, many music-hall artistes return to the clubs in their declining years, a few remain club artistes all their lives.

In the days of which I am writing few artistes stayed in hotels, and in every town there were excellent professional 'digs'. The landladies were staunch supporters of the theatre, and followed the careers of their clients with interest.

Olive and I stayed with Mrs. Woodford of Pelham Place, Leicester. Round her room were photographs of many stars who stayed in her house regularly, but her favourite was Hetty King.

In her old age dear Mrs. Woodford went blind. But despite her infirmity she went on 'letting', and many of her clients went on going back.

"Cinderella" had a phenomenal run but, as was the custom of Joe Graham and Milton Bode, it was taken off whilst still playing to capacity. "I don't take chances,

G

my boy," said Milton Bode when I tried to persuade him to run longer.

Sitting on the fence of middle-age and looking back I cannot help feeling how happy and carefree "the profession" was in the past. Certainly, at that time, I used to worry a lot about the future—I was scraping and saving to get a home together, writing incessantly to sell summer rights of songs for odd guineas, but I still found time to play cards every night after the show until the small hours of the morning, and had any amount of fun off-stage in the theatre.

After the run of the Leicester pantomime we had several weeks out of work. 'Weeks out' meant a hand-to-mouth existence with, sometimes, the hand not going as often to the mouth as one could have wished.

Olive and I had a furnished flat in a rather notorious block not far from Russell Square. The gentleman in the flat next door, who always appeared to me to be an affable and harmless type, decided one night to murder his wife, which he did with great thoroughness before putting his own head in the gas oven.

In the flat on the other side of us lived a couple who were always quarrelling. Their quarrels were not merely verbal ones, and we heard many exciting conflicts.

In the flat above us lived a lady of easy virtue who appeared to have no reluctance to work overtime, and had never heard of the five-day week. Since she was at her busiest between the hours of eleven at night and two in the morning, sleep in our flat was an elusive thing.

One night I could stand it no longer and, throwing an overcoat over my pyjamas, I went up and knocked at her door. She opened the door herself, wearing a faded négligé and with a cigarette in her mouth.

"Madame," I said, "please do not think that I wish to interfere, nor that I am a prude, but we find it difficult to sleep, your bed is so noisy."

With a merry laugh she said, "Ze bed he very old.

Next week I get a new one, but now I oil 'eem and stop 'eem squeak."

There was no more noise that night. The following day this amazing woman sent us down an excellent French confection that she had prepared herself, and invited us to tea.

The time came for the commencement of our Stoll tour, and the first date was Manchester Hippodrome. We travelled from London on the midnight train, and it was bitterly cold. I managed to get a pillow for Olive, but could not waste another 'bob' on one for myself.

All through that cheerless journey I buoyed Olive up with verbal pictures of the wonderful Manchester Hippodrome. "Not only that," I told her, "but George Reynolds, the manager there, is an old concert-party performer, and he'll look after us."

Manchester is a city whose grim surface I have been fortunate enough to dig beneath, and have found much to love in the place and its inhabitants. But I must admit that Manchester, at six o'clock in the morning, with sleet, rain, and a dense atmosphere almost like a London fog through which an occasional amber light winked mockingly, did not present itself winningly to Olive, who for some reason 'funked' going there in any case.

We were staying with Mrs. Wood, 92 Lloyd Street, Greenheys. I had stayed there in my musical-comedy days and was one of her favourite boarders. In fact my photographs, with some of Henry Lytton of the D'Oyly Carte Opera Company, were the only ones that adorned her mantelpiece. But I was to find that, whilst Mrs. Wood took a possessive pride in looking after her men boarders when they stayed on their own, when they arrived with wives, mothers, or other female appendages, fits of jealousy attacked her, and she looked Olive up and down with a real Lancashire sniff.

But Mrs. Wood's table, always beautifully laid with spotless white linen and shining crockery, sizzling bacon and eggs, and a good bright fire, all had a thawing and comforting effect on Olive, who went to bed exhausted, whilst I, after a short rest, went to the theatre for the Monday morning band rehearsal.

When I got off the tram in the Oxford Road I saw the Manchester Hippodrome posters. But I had to look very closely before I could find the names "Fox and Rose", which were little bigger than the printer's imprint.

In the theatre Joe Williams, the stage-manager, told me that we were first turn, nine minutes. George Reynolds, who was managing Manchester Hippodrome at this time, told me that he could do nothing about our bad spot because the programme order was made out by the head office.

Olive, when she arrived at the theatre, thought that we should go back to London. I had to remind her gently that we were in desperate need of the money.

At the matinée we went on first turn and did well, running sixteen minutes instead of our nine. George Reynolds, when he came round, was very pleased.

"So you will put us later in the programme, George, won't you?" I asked eagerly.

With a disarming twinkle in his eye he said, "Can't possibly do that, old man; the way that you opened the programme was magnificent. There's not another act on the bill that could have done it the way that you two did."

At night, however, fate intervened on our behalf. It was Manchester University Rag Night, and Olive and I were the only ones who stoically withstood the fusillade of banter and the unholy noise.

Noni, the clown, who was doing an act in the Grock tradition, and Yvonne Granville, the diseuse, were both giving performances that made it difficult for them to deal with the rather frightening barrage from the students in the audience, their acts were curtailed, and the programme was running short. George Reynolds, knowing that Olive and myself would have something up our sleeves from our concert-party repertoires, came round and asked us to make a second appearance, which we did, in the coveted last-act-but-one position.

We had an excellent reception. Olive received a large box of chocolates and I a box of Punch Coronas from the students, and George Reynolds must have sent in an excellent report, for we were never again first turn on a Stoll programme. Although we played Manchester many times afterwards, Olive never got over her dread of the place.

"Fox and Rose" had a wonderful run. Although not of star value we were known as a 'safe act', one that would always hold its position, and we were lucky enough to have made our vehicle a universal one—that is, of equal appeal to rough or high-class audiences.

On our first appearance at Warrington, where we made a great hit, the top of the bill was that excellent comedy actor, Charles Windermere, in a sketch. Charles was supported by a lovable, carefree juvenile named Archie Arbuthnot, and a nervous little comedian named Robertson Hare.

It did not seem long after that week in Warrington when "Bunny" Hare achieved great success in London. He has continued this since with his inimitable studies of the harassed, bullied, or henpecked but always prim and 'indubitably correct' little man.

CHAPTER SEVEN

FROM steady work on the music-halls we returned, at Whitsuntide, to Westcliff for another season. Everything was now left to me, for by this time Wallis Arthur was a sick man and spent much of the year at Harrogate.

When he was at Westcliff he liked me to massage him. This, I think, was more to ensure having my company than for any specific benefits obtained from the treatment.

He had a strange outlook on life peculiarly his own. In many ways he was very wise and in others very warped. He would talk to me by the hour expressing his emphatic opinions on life in general and people in particular, and for a long time I was indeed a "Trilby" to his Svengali.

Possibly I was too impressionable. But I freely admit that much of the great success of my own show "Twinkle" in this and other countries came from ideas germinated in my association with Wallis Arthur.

Many people advised me to leave him. Sometimes I made the attempt.

"May I have a word with you, Wallis?" I would ask, with a tense and serious expression on my face.

"Half a dozen, if you like, my boy," he would reply. "You're not sending a telegram, and there's no charge per word."

Then I would start. When I had finished he would roll a cigarette slowly, and then systematically demolish my arguments. Often he would say, "Olive has been putting in a lot of work in the munition factory lately making bullets for you to fire."

This, in the main, was quite wrong. Certainly Olive thought that I should be making better financial progress. But, on the other hand, she was quite content to be working in the same show as myself, and at Westcliff we both had big followings.

Wallis, cleverly and quite rightly, played on the matter of my health. "You came to Westcliff almost a dying man," he would say. "Don't you think that you're better off here in this wonderful air, earning what you call a small wage, but building up your health, than playing the music-halls in the industrial north?"

Westcliff did indeed benefit my health. Quite apart from and in addition to this, it also helped me to build up a south coast connection which has been extremely valuable.

Wallis Arthur was a great man. Like most great men he had his weaknesses, one of which was his intense dislike of anybody differing from him. It was almost a phobia, and covered every field, social, domestic and political.

His philosophical and unruffled acceptance of catastrophe was one of his better characteristics. In 1919 a tremendous gale swept the south coast, and the Shorefields tent was blown into the sea.

Old Arthur, a grizzly old man with a stubbly beard, who took the tickets, sold the programmes and was Wallis's general factotum, came up to my room that particular morning, peremptorily knocked on the door, put his head inside and said, "The pavilion's in the sea."

Nothing appeared to be left but a part of the stage and the piano. Seats were all over the place, in chaos; tattered and torn tarpaulin was intertwined with pieces of broken wood—in short, Shorefields was a picture of complete destruction.

Presently Wallis, in his immaculate white suit, was picking his way through the debris. He stood by my side and surveyed the scene.

A telegraph boy wended his way through the wreckage and handed Wallis a telegram. It was reply paid and from George Blackmore, at Hastings, and read, "Marquee demolished. What shall I do? George."

Wallis took the reply-paid form and carefully found a piece of wood to press it on. Then he wrote this reply: "So is mine. Do what you can. Wallis."

Old Arthur had caught some of the philosophy and calm of his employer. Once in 1918, just as our matinée was about to start, German 'planes sailed up the estuary, our fighters from Hornchurch went up to tackle them, and soon bombs were being dropped.

"Do you think that we should start this matinée? The tent is vulnerable and there's a lot of kids inside," I said.

"One and sixpence first four rows, programmes a penny," Arthur continued to chant.

Just then the crump of a bomb sounded very near. Almost immediately another bomb came down even closer. Arthur looked up, and remarked laconically, "I think they're 'ostile."

At that moment some of our fighters zoomed across from Rochford and the Taubes turned tail and fled. Arthur smiled triumphantly, showing his chrome-coloured teeth through his beard, and said, "Well, they've b—d off now, so you can start the matinée."

For all the alarums and excursions of those years Westcliff was a very pleasant place. The Welcome Club in particular was a cheery spot, and since it was attached to our pitch at Shorefields, it was handy and convenient.

Harry Davis, its proprietor, was a curious mixture of good humour and bad temper. But he had a weak spot for our profession.

During my time at Westcliff, amongst the members of the Welcome Club I can recall Nelson Keys, who at that time lived in the town, Ambrose Thorne, Eugene Corri, and several prominent journalists.

I can remember Nelson Keys arriving one night, after a heavy raid in London, and giving most astounding vocal and facial imitations of the people who had been sheltering with him in a Tube station. It was one of the spontaneous flashes of genius for which "Bunch" was noted.

His sons, Paddy, Roderick and Tony, received their introductions to show business with our Pierrots. "Bunch" asked me to keep an eye on them, and I used to let them come to our rehearsals. Best-seller Paddy Carstairs refers to these happy days in several of his books.

Ambrose Thorne was a remarkable mimic, although, strangely enough, he never used this gift in his professional work. When he lived at the Welcome Club it was quite a usual thing to hear the voices of George Robey, Violet Loraine, Harry Tate, Shirley Kellogg, and other leading artistes of the time, coming from "Brosie's" bedroom. Harry Davis, Wallis and I would creep up outside his bedroom door and listen, and not until we collapsed with laughter did he know of our proximity.

"Do Vi Loraine again for us," Wallis would ask. And "Brosie" would do it, albeit reluctantly, and with only half the faithfulness and genius he had shown when he thought that nobody was about or listening.

Winnie Melville was a graduate from Shorefields. When she left Wallis Arthur's management she went almost straight into "Bubbly" at the Comedy Theatre.

She had been a tremendous favourite at Shorefields, and the following year we persuaded her to come down and appear on Olive Fox's Benefit Night programme. West End success evidently had affected her sense of values, and she was not her natural self, which was a pity, for she had been a real personality.

Winnie Melville went on to make several notable successes, particularly with Derek Oldham. But in my opinion she never allowed the urchin that was in her, and which was such a great part of her personal charm, to come out.

Olive and I returned to the music-halls at the end of the summer season. When we were appearing at Chelsea Palace, Fred Warden, the Irish pantomime producer, called round to see us.

Fred Warden was a big, bulky, fleshy type of man, and recognised as a great pantomime producer. For many years he ruled theatrically in Dublin and Belfast.

When the Chelsea Palace hall-keeper brought him to

the dressing-room he said, "Good evening, Miss Fox. I want to book you for my Belfast pantomime."

I intervened and said, "Please sit down, Mr. Warden. I do all the business."

"I'm not concerned with you," snapped Warden, "and I don't want to book you, either. But I do want to book Miss Fox."

When I made it quite plain that Olive Fox could not be booked without me, and that I should transact the business details, a long and acrimonious discussion and argument ensued. But eventually Olive was booked to play "Aladdin", and I " Pekoe ", at Belfast.

Doubtless it was because we got the fight over early, but Fred Warden and I became firm friends. The following year, at Dublin, he insisted that Olive and I shared the same house with him because he liked us around.

We arrived for the Belfast pantomime right in the midst of the religious trouble. At the first rehearsal Warden said that the artiste who was to play Abanazar had 'ratted'—as he described it—because of the shooting that was going on in the city. He added, "I don't know what I am going to do."

With an audacity that I would not have to-day I stepped forward and said, "You have nothing to worry about, Mr. Warden. I can play Abanazar, and I shall be excellent in the part."

His huge moustache bristled, eyes nearly bulged out of his massive head, he turned a fluent vocabulary on to express his opinion of my inability to play Abanazar, and the rehearsal proceeded with my playing Pekoe and the stage-manager reading the part of the missing artiste. The next day even his friend and booker, Karl Hooper, had been unable to find a suitable substitute.

I went to Karl Hooper and said, "I don't know what Fred's worrying about. I could play the part standing on my head."

"Sure, I think so too," said Karl, with the soft burr of the Western States still in his voice.

"Then for heaven's sake tell Fred so, and let's get on with the pantomime."

Fred Warden would not hear of it for a long time, but eventually gave in. I played the part, and was lucky enough to be the hit of the pantomime.

Immediately after the first night Fred Warden served his option on us for the following year. I pointed out that I had been engaged to play Pekoe and had only helped him out of a hole.

"Never heard such sauce in my life," he blustered. I was adamant.

"All right," said Fred, "I can still serve my option and make you play Pekoe. How will you like that?"

"I shall have no choice in the matter, Guv'nor," I replied. "But how will you like having a first-class Abanazar in your pantomime thrown away on Pekoe, and another Abanazar who, for all you know, may not be so good, but to whom you will have to pay a salary for playing the part?"

For the next three or four days there was not the usual pleasant atmosphere in the Opera House bar. Old Jimmy McCann, Fred's manager, who suffered very badly from asthma but had a great sense of humour about it, came to me and said, "For God's sake, 'Clarkie', get hold of the Guv'nor and come to some arrangement. The bar's like a morgue at nights now, it's worse than the 'throuble'."

I made no further move. But some days later Fred called me to the office, and we fixed up an agreement satisfactory to both parties.

Benefit Nights were still in existence in those days, and Olive and I had a benefit. The beneficiary had a third of the receipts, but since he or she had to pay for a buffet, boxes of chocolates for the lady artistes and cigarettes for the men, they didn't benefit much personally out of it. They were jolly evenings, however, for all that, and I was sorry to see them pass.

The following year the pantomime was played at the Gaiety Theatre, Dublin, with the Belfast cast, and was again an outstanding success. After the Dublin run Fred Warden booked us for two more years, and for the first of these, Olive Fox and I returned to Belfast with "Dick Whittington". I was cast for Idle Jack—and was probably the worst Idle Jack ever known.

There was a curfew on in Belfast, and everybody had to be indoors by nine o'clock. Nine o'clock was very early for pros. to retire to bed, so, when we did meet after the show, it meant staying in the 'digs' where we had forgathered, until daylight.

One Saturday night a gang were gathered at my 'digs' for supper and cards, and included in the party was the American comedy team, Cornalla and Eddie. Eddie was a great practical joker. After supper we found that the cards had been left in his 'digs' three doors away.

Despite the fact that, just opposite, was the Police Barracks, Eddie said, "Listen, folks—I'm going to get those 'broads'. Keep a look-out."

We raised the window—everything appeared to be all clear. Eddie crept out and, keeping in the shadow of the wall, got to his 'digs' and secured the cards.

Just as he was entering our gate three reverberating shots rang out. Eddie fell to the ground, and packs of cards went all over the place.

In point of fact the firing was nowhere near. As he admitted later, he had fallen to the ground from sheer fright. Just as I rushed out to help him, a policeman came round the corner.

At first he was intensely official, and I feared that we were for it. But eventually he melted, came in "for a quick one", and after that he was our friend for the run of the pantomime. Despite the curfew, whenever we had forgotten anything, he was nearly always on hand to escort us to and from the different 'digs'.

Olive was a grand "Dick Whittington". I was not happy in the Idle Jack part, but although I implored Fred Warden to get someone else to play it, he would not budge.

Shortly after the pantomime we were playing Bristol Hippodrome with the "Fox and Rose" double act. On the Monday, as we were going to the theatre, Olive jumped off the tram at the Centre, and in doing so ricked her neck and set up acute fibrositis. She could not even turn her head and was in intense pain. I rushed her back to the 'digs', sent for a doctor, and then went to the theatre to tell Fortescue Harrison, the manager, that we could not appear.

Mr. Fortescue Harrison was one of the dignified school of managers. Sir Oswald Stoll had a high opinion of him. He listened sympathetically, and then said, "I'm sorry, Rose—but we never ask for deputies from other local theatres. It is too late for us to get one from London. You will have to appear and do something."

"I can't, Mr. Harrison," I said. "You know our act—without Miss Fox there just isn't an act."

"Then, Mr. Rose, you had better go on and sing some of those songs that I heard you sing with the Pierrots at Bognor last summer. If you sing that song, *Rule, Britannia*, I am sure that it will be all right."

I protested in vain that I had no orchestrations of the songs, and the outcome was that, instead of "Fox and Rose", the curtain went up on Mr. Galpin, the musical-director of Bristol Hippodrome, seated somewhat uneasily at a piano; on I came, made an announcement about the absence of Miss Olive Fox, and then went into an improvised entertainment.

To my amazement my songs were, to use Mr. Harrison's own words, "an outstanding success". "Let Miss Fox have the rest of the week off," he said. "Your double-turn is very good, but such turns are far more common than outstanding single acts. When you have assembled your songs properly and had them orchestrated, you will be a head-liner, Mr. Clarkson Rose. I am 'phoning Sir Oswald Stoll to tell him so."

That, in short, was the end of the act "Fox and Rose". Although we had several years booked ahead, managements took me over as a single act, and Olive appeared as a single act on the same programmes.

When I played Wood Green Empire, I found, to my amazement, that I was one of the head-liners with George Carney and T. E. Dunville. Personally I never thought much of my act. But I was young and virile and had original songs.

Every agent in London got wind of the newcomer, and after the first performance on the Monday night most of them came round and wanted to represent me. In point of fact, Karl Hooper took me over. He was a very good agent, and there is no doubt that his handling of Victoria Monks, then his wife, was a considerable factor in her success.

In 1922 I played the Alhambra for the first time. I was in very small print on the posters, and second turn on the programme. But to my amazement I stopped the show.

In two weeks' time I returned to the Alhambra as one of the head-liners. A number of the leading newspaper critics were in front, and the following day five of them gave most of their space to praise of my performance. "Buckie" Taylor, then writing in the popular *Town Topics*, gave me a full page.

Whatever one's abilities may be, success on the stage is often a matter of luck. In my case I happened to hit the music-halls as a single act at a time when many of the established head-liners were getting stale. And I was particularly fortunate in having original songs that fitted exactly the public taste and mood of the moment.

Contracts at salaries I had never dreamed of earning came pouring in—but I still had another year to do with Wallis Arthur. Complex and difficult decisions had to be made. On the one hand, I did not want to give up my seaside work, because I knew how my health benefited from it. On the other hand, agents and bookers kept saying, "Now you've hit the head-lines, don't drop out of the market. You can always go back to your seaside shows later."

Wallis Arthur had said, "One day you'll go on the music-halls, and since I never knew a man with a big voice, clear diction and good songs who wasn't a music-hall success, you'll do likewise. You'll be inundated with offers—but don't let them get you away from your seaside season."

Eventually I went along with Olive to 156 Strand, and asked Wallis Arthur if he would release me. I should have known better. It was a long and acrimonious interview. Finally he agreed to my release, rather in the manner of an irate father in melodrama saying to an erring son, "Go—and never darken my doors again."

Olive and I walked out into the Strand and for a long time I was upset and depressed. However, with the resilience of youth and the excitement of the music-hall offers, I cheered up.

It was not until the question came up of signing the music-hall contracts that I realised that I had nothing in writing from Wallis Arthur giving me my release. So I wrote him. He took his time in replying—Wallis enjoyed doing a "cat and mouse" act sometimes—and then imposed conditions that I was unable to accept.

"There's nothing for it," I said to Olive, "except that I should play out my contract with Wallis Arthur." So I went back to him and told him that I did not want release.

Wallis Arthur was livid. This did not suit his plan at all, for in point of fact he no longer had the branch to which he intended to send me for the season. Had I known that, my methods would have been different. He was artful in business, and probably rightly so, but he was faced with the fact that I was willing to play my contract and he had nowhere to send me.

There was another unpleasant interview, and eventually I was definitely released. But all this took some time, and when it was finally settled, a further variety slump had set in, and bookers were not nearly so ready to book up artistes ahead. Faced with the alternative of taking a cut in salary or being without work to go to, much to Karl Hooper's horror I refused the cut.

It was sad that my association with Wallis Arthur should end as it did. I owed him much but, on the other hand, he was in many ways indebted to me, and the curtain should have come down on our relationship in a much warmer atmosphere.

MADE UP AND READY TO AMUSE

THE AUTHOR AS OLD KING COLE AT
BIRMINGHAM IN 1928

Above: CLARKSON ROSE AS THE
BARONESS IN "CINDERELLA". Right:
AS MOTHER HUBBARD IN "GOODY
TWO SHOES"

GEORGE ROBEY, FRED CONQUEST AND THE AUTHOR AT FREE TRADE HALL
MANCHESTER

A T Chiswick Empire, one night in 1921, Powis Pinder came round to see me. "Papa" Pinder, as everyone affectionately called him, was for long the chief *entrepeneur* of summer entertainments on the Isle of Wight.

After congratulating me on my act, he blinked his butterfly-like eyelids and said, rather tentatively, "I've got Ryde Pier on my hands. Quite frankly, it hasn't been very successful, and I was not going to put on a show of my own this year. Would you like to tackle it?"

He was very open about everything, and the prospects did not seem bright. But I was always impulsive in certain matters, and I said "Yes" immediately.

Thus was my own show, "Twinkle", formed and born.

Olive and I scraped together what bits and pieces we had, ordered a set of Pierrot costumes, booked four other artistes, and the six of us went off to Ryde Pier to open at Whitsun, which was early that year. Ryde Pier is a long one, and about a mile from the inhabited part of the town.

On our "Grand Opening Night," which was Whit Saturday, we took sixteen pounds. But there in that Pavilion, with its incandescent gas footlights and its poor equipment, and with nothing much but a couple of baskets of props, and a ton of enthusiasm, we plodded along.

Olive and I were very depressed. Our former seasons at Westcliff had made us used to large and enthusiastic audiences, and for our first six weeks at Ryde very few people came to the show.

I cannot pay too high a tribute to Powis Pinder's generosity and understanding. He refused to take any of the percentage of the takings due to him during that first six weeks. He allowed the contra account that I owed him for tickets and other things to remain unsettled until such times as things improved.

Olive and I had got down to our last pound, and were

contemplating selling-up our bits and pieces of furniture back in London to meet our commitments, and closing down, when the tide turned! On that memorable Friday night, from their yachts in the Solent, Sir Walter Runciman, Sir James Redhead and Lord Inchcape came to our show. With them they brought a large party, and they were all tremendously enthusiastic.

The following day I was relieving in the box-office myself, because I could afford to pay only one box-office clerk, when Sir Walter Runciman came to the window. He asked how we were doing, and I told him the truth.

"Damn shame," he said. "Anyway, I shall be bringing my party from the *Sunbeam* every week, and I'll send a lot of others." Whereupon he made a block reservation of seats for every Friday night for a number of weeks, and gave me a cheque in advance! Naturally, being a leader of his own particular set on the island, many of his friends followed suit, and in a matter of a few days "Twinkle" became the success of the Isle of Wight season.

The company were invited to the various yachts and houses, and business increased by leaps and bounds. Every Tuesday we used to interchange with Powis Pinder's Ventnor show, and on another night with his Shanklin show. To use Powis Pinder's own words, "Much to my amazement, Rose, your little six-handed Pierrot show has swept the island. My own far more elaborate shows are not nearly so popular."

Powis Pinder's "Sunshine" was always the top show of the island. But that year we packed them in at Shanklin and Ventnor, and the shows from those places fell below our business at Ryde.

Wilby Lunn was that year the principal comedian in "Sunshine". Physically he had many assets for comedy —a compact little figure, a bald head, and an expressive voice. Had he continued in comedy I think he would have gone far in this sphere, but he decided to become a concert-party proprietor.

First he entered into partnership with Murray Ashford, a clever and experienced concert-party proprietor who had a long record of success at Margate. And after Murray's unfortunate passing, Wilby Lunn joined forces with that lovable trouper Will Seymour, and these two have provided many seaside resorts with grand summer entertainment.

Will Seymour is a fine, homely comedian who oozes kindliness. His show, "Bubbles", has brought many artistes to the front, notably Nan Kenway and Douglas Young.

The news of "Twinkle's" success soon spread in the world of the theatre, and managers like Bannister Howard, Murray King, Julian Wylie and Sir Oswald Stoll all came to see the little show. Our farewell night of the season was indeed a contrast to our opening night.

The doors of that old Pavilion had to be taken off the hinges, and people sat on beer barrels and other improvised seats, right out into the tramway station. This little company, which had opened to sixteen pounds on its first night, played, on its farewell night, in the same Pavilion, to just over one hundred and thirty pounds!

Unknown to me, during the last fortnight of the season, Olive had slipped up to London and paid the deposit on a house at Golders Green of which she saw only the foundations. It took us fifteen years to buy this house, with the aid of a building society. At the time, as I told her, I thought that Olive had been very extravagant and too optimistic. But in this matter, as so often in others, Olive was proved right.

The good people of the Isle of Wight had got to hear of our home-planning, and on the last night the presents handed up to us almost furnished the house. Glass, silver, antique furniture, pictures, carpets, linen, fire-irons, coal scuttles, china—all came up to us over the footlights; and from Sir Walter Runciman a huge case containing a varied assortment of wines and spirits, to which was attached a message, "May 'Twinkle' have as many successful voyages as the *Sunbeam*. Here is something for the cellar of the new home."

Olive and I returned to London, she to rest, and I to go back on the music-halls. I had written a song called *Back I went to the Ministry of Labour*.

When I first wrote it, having sat up until the small hours of the morning, I thought it so tedious that I tore it up and threw it into the waste-paper basket. Olive, down before me the next morning, salvaged it and put it away.

One day she heard me grumbling, when making out a new programme at Ryde, that I hadn't a good enough song. "Oh yes, you have," she said, and produced the torn manuscript. I argued about it, but Olive was emphatic, so on it went.

Because I needed a new song I put it into my music-hall act. It was sensationally successful. I was at the Alhambra a month, doing three shows a day, and at every show it held up the performance. It was just "one of those things", and it 'made' me as a comic singer.

My early days as a single-turn were interesting because many of the great names of the music-halls were still about. From great artistes like Malcolm Scott, Arthur Roberts, Harry Randall, Whit Cunliffe, George Carney, Wilkie Bard, George Mozart, Eugene Stratton, Bransby Williams, Alec Hurley, Robb Wilton, Harry Tate, Charles Austin, Cecilia Loftus, Arthur Prince, Tom Coram, and Marie Lloyd, I had much help and encouragement. There was nothing 'high hat' or superior about them, and they all found time to listen to my hopes and aspirations and to give me their advice. There were others, of course, who were different. But I had so great an admiration for them that I accepted their rebuffs and still learnt what I could.

T. E. Dunville was a strange man. The physical disability of a withered arm had made him something of a recluse, and he had a sharp tongue. That he felt his style was getting out of date undoubtedly led to the tragedy of his death.

Many stories were told of the meanness of that great international star, Sir Harry Lauder, but he proved, so far as I was concerned, completely the reverse. When Olive and I were still "Fox and Rose" we had our first date for Moss's Empires, at the old Liverpool Empire.

There were only five acts on the programme, because Lauder himself was doing about an hour of the show. For this, our trial week on the circuit, we found ourselves second turn and down for nine minutes.

"We'll never get the tour on this," I said. "We can't possibly show our value in nine minutes."

Big, bluff, military-looking George Manners, the manager, hadn't much time to worry about us. Whilst programme running orders are made out by head office, in Sir Harry Lauder's case it was provisional because, at band rehearsal, Manners asked him where he liked to go on. "Well, if you put me on first they'll go out when I've been on, and if you put me on last they'll wait until I come on," Sir Harry replied.

When it was settled where Sir Harry was to appear— last act but one—I summoned-up the courage to explain to him the private predicament of "Fox and Rose". "You see, Sir Harry," I said, "I've got everything newly orchestrated, new dresses for Miss Fox, and the act absolutely right. But it takes eighteen minutes and they've only given me nine."

He took me to his room. We had a long talk, and he listened very patiently. Then he said, "Leave it to me. I'll see you to-night before the show."

What he said to George Manners I don't know. But I do know that at night Mr. Manners came and told us that we could do our full time, and that Sir Harry Lauder shortened his own act to enable us to do it.

Not only that, he came down to the side of the stage every night and watched us. We were doing an old-fashioned medley that included impressions of some of the

old-time stars, such as Charles Coburn, George Beau-
champ, Tom Costello, Harriet Vernon, Victoria Monks,
and others. Most were evolved from youthful memories,
and Olive had never seen Harriet Vernon at all, and had to
rely on my description.

Every night Sir Harry Lauder, who had known and had
worked with them all, took us on one side and gave us odd
little bits of business and mannerisms appertaining to
these artistes, and also gave us one or two suggestions that
helped to pull rounds of applause in certain spots in our
act. He was as pleased as we were when, before the end
of the week, Moss's Empires booked us for the coveted tour.

He made us a very attractive offer to tour South Africa
with him on his own variety combination. I have always
regretted that other commitments made it impossible for
us to accept.

Whit Cunliffe was another artiste who delighted in
seeing newcomers coming along. He retired long before
he need have done, but strangely enough, in the years
immediately before his retirement, he became extremely
nervous, and it was really agony to watch him put on a
new song.

Once at the Palace, Leicester, I recall him being so
nervous with a new song, that he trembled and shook
in the corner when the introduction was played. Talking
to him about it, I who have always been a quick study,
said that I could not understand what caused such nervous
tension. "You can't understand now," he replied,
"because you are young and because you are climbing.
But you will later on. You won't always have song
winners in your repertoire, and you'll be snatching at
anything in the hope of trying to find one, knowing that
you must maintain the position and reputation that you
have achieved."

An interesting point not generally known is that Whit
Cunliffe was the writer and original singer of Sir Harry
Lauder's world-famous song success, *Just a wee deoch and
doris*.

Charles Austin was one of the biggest-hearted men in the profession. At the height of his success in variety and revue he always had time for lesser artistes.

Arthur Roberts, in spite of a caustic wit, was a kindly man. He was a friend of Wallis Arthur and Sydney Josiffe, and used to come down to Westcliff when I was a pierrot there.

Josiffe was a well-to-do wine merchant who loved being with pros. One day when we were seated at coffee and liqueurs after lunch, Arthur Roberts was dozing with a half-smoked cigar, and Josiffe was rambling on in a long dissertation on the rise of Sir Walter de Frece, the music-hall magnate:

"I knew him when he was plain Walter de Frece, and now he's Sir Walter de Frece. How he's changed. Now he's Sir Walter, how he's changed. Ah, plain Walter de Frece, now he's Sir Walter de Frece, and how he's changed," Josiffe droned on. Arthur Roberts woke up and said, "After that, I think we ought to call him Sir Altered de Frece."

The story of Arthur Roberts arriving at the Gaiety Theatre for a rehearsal and feeling a sudden call of nature, is a gem. He left the stage quickly, and walked into the first lavatory that he saw. This happened to be a "Ladies" with the old type of door which ended about six inches from the floor.

Whilst he was in there a cleaner approached scrubbing the floor, and as she passed the door she noticed a man's boots and trousers. A man in the "Ladies"!

The horrified cleaner shouted, "What are you doing in there?"

Quick as lightning came Roberts's staccato reply, "I'll give you two guesses."

Harry Randall was a dapper little man, always perfectly tailored. He saved his money and retired much earlier than he need have done. He took a keen interest in my work, and gave me much valuable advice.

I used to meet him a lot during the summer seasons at

Bognor, and we would play cards together for very small stakes. Harry would worry like the devil if he lost three-pence.

We went together to Kilburn Empire to see the "Veterans of Variety". They had tried to persuade him to join them, but without success. As we sat and heard the old songs, and saw the old stars—Leo Dryden, Tom Costello, Sable Fern, Florrie Robina, Arthur Roberts and others—tears streamed down his face. For their final number the "Veterans" all lined up and sang *Comrades*—it was too much for Harry Randall, he broke down completely.

For Malcolm Scott I had a great affection. With his satire and culture he was about twenty years ahead of his time, absolutely right for variety bills at the Palace Theatre, London, but not with the same appeal in the provinces or at rougher music-halls.

Malcolm had been an Adeler and Sutton Pierrot and never forgot it. The first time I saw him in pantomime he played Cogia in the "Forty Thieves", at the Court Theatre, Liverpool.

He had had a trying time at rehearsal with the other comedians leaving him out of things. But they had reckoned without Malcolm's brilliant brain, and he was the hit of the pantomime.

Towards the end of the production, with another comedian he had to work the famous duet *We don't want a Girl from* . . . Malcolm had prepared a brilliant series of local verses with the most amusing and ingenious rhymes about places like Wallasey, Hoylake, Aigburth and Birken-head. The other comedian was sunk under this barrage of clever word play.

In between two of the verses Malcolm folded his arms, pursed those mobile lips, and in his austere woman's voice said to the other comedian, "What is the matter? Where are all those funny things that you did at rehearsal? Why don't you do them now?"

Malcolm Scott and I were together on the bill at

Hackney Empire not long before he died. His humour
was somewhat above the Hackney audience. At the end
of his turn he walked forward, and in quiet, sibilant tones
said, "Mr. and Mrs. Hack-er-ney, I am aware that my
songs and chatter are above your heads. Luckily I have
a sweet shop at Brighton, and so I'm not worried. But in
about a quarter of an hour's time a great friend of mine,
Mr. Clarkson Rose, will appear before you. He has a
loud, raucous voice and some excellent comic songs which
he has been wise enough to keep to the level of your
understanding. So although you haven't liked me, please
give Mr. Rose a grand welcome. In the meantime, get
on with whatever food you are eating."

One of my most treasured possessions is the dress that
he wore as Katherine Parr—and his stage jewellery. He
gave them to Ambrose Thorne, and said, "When you don't
want them, give them to Clarkson Rose. He'll be a very
good 'dame' one day."

Once on a Monday matinée I was seen at the Alhambra
by Arthur Burton, who was manager of the Palace, Blackburn. He was one of the old type of managers who really
managed, who could alter their programme to suit their
own or their patrons' needs, and who could advise on
what artistes should be booked for their theatres.

The Palace, Blackburn, was on the Macnaughten tour.
This embraced the smaller industrial towns of Lancashire
and Yorkshire, and the Palace, Southampton, and the
Pavilion, Leicester.

After Burton had seen my act at the Alhambra he came
round with my agent and booked me for the Palace,
Blackburn. I arrived on a cold, dank Sunday night, and
as I left the station I saw workmen fixing the electric
installation outside the theatre and trying it out. The
wording—THIS WEEK A NEW STAR—CLARKSON
ROSE—was flashed into the darkness. I felt very proud,
albeit nervous.

On Monday night I went on, and made no impression
on the Blackburn audience. I tried and tried, came off

wet through with perspiration, but all to no purpose. I was a dreadful flop, and as I left the theatre the sign, flashing my name into the darkness, seemed to mock me.

Although I may not show it I am a very sensitive person, and I shall not readily forget that week. I had the feeling of being "sent to Coventry" even by the stage-hands. They have no respect for an artiste who cannot hold his position. I heard snatches of conversation that I was not meant to hear, and the direct, unequivocal phrasing in the Lancashire dialect left me in no doubt as to what they were thinking. I found myself walking along the streets hoping that I should not be recognised.

During the week a telephone call came through from London asking me to appear at a charity matinée in London on the Sunday. This could only be arranged if I could catch an early train from Blackburn on the Saturday night.

I went to Arthur Burton and explained the position. He left it to me to ask the other artistes if any would change places with me, but the change did not suit any of them except the first turn.

"I'm afraid it's off," I said to Burton. "Only the first turn can change with me, and even though I am not a success, I don't suppose you'll agree to the top of your bill being first turn."

"I don't mind, if you don't," he said.

The change was made. And that week the top of the bill at the Palace, Blackburn, went on directly after a short overture, at the second house on Saturday night. Strangely enough I was received with much more applause as first turn than I had achieved in the star position on the programme.

The following week I was back at the Alhambra, and round to my dressing-room came Ernest Edelsten's henchman, Charlie Ferrier. With a broad grin he said, "So you were a big flop at Blackburn, 'Clarkie'? I've just been on the 'phone to Macnaughten's head office.

They'll give you the rest of the tour if you'll take a cut of ten pounds, and they will not include a return date to Blackburn."

Success at the Alhambra had put me in a happier and cockier frame of mind. I turned to Charles and said, "Give my compliments to Mr. Sydney Arthur, the Macnaughten booker, and say that I am entirely unsuitable for their Palaces, and in any case I should not think of taking a cut. I'll play for them at the same money I got at Blackburn and not a penny less."

"All right," he replied, "but you won't get the tour." To my surprise he came back in a couple of days' time and said, "Mr. Sydney Arthur's compliments, he thinks that you're very tough and uncompromising. But he's given you the tour with the exception that they are not going to give you a return date at Blackburn. You open at the Palace, Southampton."

When the time came for me to open on the Macnaughten tour at Southampton, judge of my consternation when Ferrier 'phoned me to say that my opening week had been transferred to the Palace, Blackburn!

"Have they forgotten what a tremendous flop I was there?" I asked.

"No, they haven't," he replied. "But they can't help themselves. They have got to clear the Palace, Southampton, bill for a revue, and all the other programmes except Blackburn are full."

Here is one of the strange things that happen in show business. I went back to Blackburn in fear and trembling. This time there was no electric installation outside carrying my name, and I shared the head-lining position with another act. My act, with the exception of one number, was exactly the same as on my previous visit, and I was appearing to the same audience.

But this time they reacted in a marvellous manner to everything that I did. So much so that, before the end of the week, I was, with Arthur Burton's permission, trying out new material, and at the Palace, Blackburn, that week

I did for the first time one of my big successes, *The Girls of the Old Brigade*.

No one can explain these things. On this second week my act was the talk of the town—and I have never been back to Blackburn since. Yet, when the act was a flop, I returned in a few months.

CHAPTER NINE

THIS Blackburn incident did me a lot of good. It taught me to have ready alternative items in my music-hall repertoire, so that I could always change if a "one-horse wire" came unstuck. I was to have further examples of this happening in my career, and I was grateful for the Blackburn experience that made me ready for emergencies.

The type of entertainment that audiences like in the British Isles varies considerably according to districts. Artistes who are a big success in the West End are not always a success in the provinces and *vice versa*.

Some West End impresarios think it policy to try out their shows in the provinces. In my submission, all that a manager can glean from a provincial try-out is the reaction of that particular audience.

He can, of course, cut and prune his show. But that can be done anywhere. I don't agree with the saying that what Manchester thinks to-day, London will think to-morrow.

Except in rare cases an artiste—or a show—has to have the London cachet before making news in show business. There are, of course, provincial artistes who have achieved success when they struck London. The late Sid Field and the late Sydney Howard are two outstanding examples of this. Both were successful provincial comedians before they became West End names.

Through the year I continued to work on the music-halls, and then went back to Dublin for the Fred Warden pantomime. This time the engagement was not to be so happy.

Prior to the pantomime Fred Warden had produced a musical show called "Gabrielle", and he wrote and asked for two topical songs I had written, to include in this production. I sent them, together with the assignment and my bill, which I had made very reasonable, charging him only ten guineas.

Fred Warden did not send the cheque. When I got to Dublin I reminded him of it, and found that he objected to being charged at all. "You're working for me, you're in the firm, so to speak. I've given you a fine chance in pantomime. I should have thought that you would give me those songs," he blustered.

I reminded him that originally he did not want to book me, but only wanted Olive, and that it was only by a series of accidents that I had ever played principal comedy for him. "Further," I added, "my performing has nothing to do with my song-writing business. I charge other managers, there is no reason why I should not charge you, but in any case I've charged you less."

"All right, you stubborn so-and-so," he said, "but you'll be sorry." And he wrote out the cheque.

His way of making me feel sorry was by not giving the Principal Boy and myself the customary Benefit Night. The public were not slow to show their resentment of the slight that had been put upon us, and the presents that came up over the footlights, and the ovation that they gave us were almost embarrassing.

As I have said, I loathed the part of Idle Jack, and the song that I had to sing in the last spot of the show was not so good as the number I had had in "Aladdin". Fred Warden made it more difficult for me by putting the Cornalla and Eddie act directly ahead of me. Their china-breaking left the stage covered in debris—and the audience in an uproar at their clever fooling.

"For the good of the pantomime can't you alter that spot?" I asked him.

But he was adamant—he would "teach me to charge him ten guineas for lyrics." "You can't follow Cornalla and Eddie," he continued, with malignant glee.

"I'll bet you a pound that before the end of the pantomime I find a song that will follow them," I said.

"You can have twenty-to-one, you conceited so-and-so,"
he replied, "but you won't do it."

The following Sunday I noticed a leader in the Dublin
Sunday Independent commenting on the dirtiness of Dublin
and its thoroughfares. Inspiration came to me. I wrote
some topical doggerel called *Dear Old Dirty Dublin*, and I
was lucky enough to compose a simple tune with a lilt.
The chorus went:

> "In Dublin, in Dublin,
> That's the place to make you gay,
> And keep your spirits bubblin'.
> In London town six pence is paid
> For a bottle of Guinness's lemonade,
> So why charge ninepence where it's made?
> In dear old dirty Dublin."

I wrote about twelve choruses to it, each with a topical
reference, found Mr. Nabarro, the musical-director, who
sat up all night doing the orchestration, and on Monday
night it went on. I started by singing four choruses and
went off. The audience nearly raised the roof. Then I
used the old trick of coming back, singing another topical
chorus, making a false exit, and coming back and singing
another—and so on, almost *ad infinitum*. The last couplet
I sang was:

> "The town would look so nice and neat,
> And the unemployed would get a treat,
> If they'd rebuild O'Connell Street,
> In dear old dirty Dublin."

With the possible exception of Norah Bayes's first
appearance at the London Palladium, the audience
reaction was the most amazing thing I have ever seen in
a theatre.

After my song there was nothing left but the finale
walk-down of the pantomime. When a Dublin audience
makes up its mind that it wants something, no power on

earth will stop it. They refused to allow the walk-down of the pantomime to continue. They clamoured and roared and stamped, and in the general hold-up I slipped back and sang another topical chorus with a punch.

I did this for five minutes in all, and at the end of the show Fred Warden rushed back-stage, livid with rage, and said, "There's your twenty quid, you so-and-so," and he continued to give his opinion of me to the world at large for nearly as long as I had taken with my topical choruses.

Flushed with triumph, and feeling much more gentle, I said, "Fred, don't be silly. The song is just one of those lucky things, a natural. You can't stop it."

"Can't I?" he shouted, almost purple with rage. "I can always black-out on you, and a black-out will stop any applause."

The musical-director was ordered to play into the finale music, and the electrician to black-out the lights, as soon as I had done four choruses. It made no difference. When I did take my place in the finale walk-down, the audience stood up and cheered and cheered. So I stepped forward from my place in the finale line-up and sang them another chorus, and then stepped back into line again. But the audience would have none of it, so I stepped forward again, and then again, and then again.

After the show that night, in the bar, Fred Warden came up to me and said, "You've won. We'll call it quits now."

There were no more black-outs, and I was allowed to sing my song in my own way. The *Daily Independent*, which was under the same proprietorship as the *Sunday Independent*, every day quoted one of the many verses I wrote during the run of the pantomime.

For the rest of the run there was complete harmony between Fred Warden and myself. We were in Dublin when the news of the Free State Treaty being ratified came through, and Fred rushed to my dressing-room

THE LAST PANTOMIME IN THE OLD ALEXANDRA THEATRE, BIRMINGHAM, BEFORE IT WAS REBUILT. "DICK WHITTINGTON", 1934. Left to right (front row): FRANK VICTOR AS THE RAT, HANNAH WATT AS THE PRINCE, JACK WILLIAMS AS COOK, CLARKSON ROSE AS ALDERMAN FITZWARREN, IRENE NORTH AS ALICE, LILY LAPIDUS AS DICK WHITTINGTON, HAL BRYAN AS IDLE JACK, AND HARRY GILMORE AS THE CAT. IN THE BACKGROUND, THE SAM LINFIELD TROUPE

FLORRIE FORDE, HELEN BREEN, ARTHUR ASKEY, CLARKSON ROSE, CORA GO?
DOROTHY WARD AND "WEE" GEORGIE WOOD AT THE AUTHOR'S PA
QUEEN'S, BIRMINGHAM, 1935

THE AUTHOR AT 5CL STUDIO, SYDNEY, AUSTRALIA, WITH HASTINGS MANN
"UNCLE BERT" WOOLLEY WHEN THEY ENTERTAINED THE AUSTRALIAN BOYS'

and said, "Announce it to the audience on your next entrance."

So, as Abanazar, in front of the Cave Scene, I tried to do it artistically in the dialogue between Olive, who was Aladdin, and myself. The moment that I had done it I realised what a mistake I had made. There were people with all sorts of differing creeds, religious and political, in the theatre. In a few seconds there were boos, cheers, free fights, and even a bit of shooting—and Olive was left to sing *The Tears of an Old Irish Mother* in the midst of this pandemonium.

Very little of the second half of the pantomime was heard the rest of that evening. Feeling ran high and near the surface with all types of people.

Fred Warden had many bad qualities, but I would also pay tribute to his good points. He was a fine producer—I have yet to see any man get a pantomime on with less fuss. On one occasion his pantomime was ready within four days of the first rehearsal. Another of his good points was his honesty in business. His word was his bond. I am grateful to him for the fact that, in four seasons I played under his management in Ireland, I made many wonderful friends.

At Belfast, Isaac and Aimee Stewart practically threw open "Kelvin House" to us, and made it in every sense of the word a home. In Dublin, Dr. Jim Macguinness was another open-handed friend, and how grateful I was to him for his care of Olive when I had to leave her behind there for a nasal operation.

A well-known Dublin character was "Bird" Flanagan, a brother-in-law of the then President Cosgrove. He was a great Bohemian and a very lovable man.

Our introduction to him was a strange one. One matinée he walked right down the centre of the theatre, placed a huge tray of meringues in the conductor's hands, and in his rich Irish brogue shouted, "Give that to Dick Whittington."

Olive took the tray of meringues and went on with

I

the scene. In a short while the "Bird" came back and, evidently encouraged by the fact that Olive had taken the meringues, produced two bottles of Bollinger from his overcoat pocket. This was in the Highgate Hill scene and very embarrassing. But Harry Gilmour, as the cat, rose to the situation, clambered over the foot-lights, took the bottles and placed them very carefully by the milestone.

After that we were to see a lot of the "Bird". He always called Olive "Dick Whittington", and, with a twinkle in his eye, always said that he loved her, but did not mind my being around.

One night he took us out to supper at Mother Mason's rather drab but very popular Oyster Saloon. Seated at a table near by were some young members of the Irish Free State Army in their new green uniforms. The "Bird" was an Irishman through and through, but he was what was known as a "loyal Irishman", and being a *bon viveur* he deplored the passing of the Vice Regal Lodge, and all the splendours attached to it.

"In the name of God, phwat sort of a uniform is that you're afther wearing? Sure and it looks like something from a musical comedy. There's many a foine regiment in the British Army could show you a proper uniform. God Save The King! Up the Dublin Fusiliers!" Thus "Bird", with his piercing eye on the young Free State soldiers.

There was an ominous silence. One of the young soldiers came over and said, "We heard what you said, Flanagan, and we all know you. You've got guests with you. But shut up or else there'll be trouble."

"Bird" would not be silenced. In a few moments there was a scuffle. Canes were brandished, water thrown—and in a few moments revolvers were produced.

This was enough for me. Shootings were taking place in Ireland anywhere and everywhere. Many of our girls were present, and I thought it time to leave.

"Come on, Olive," I said to her, and to the others.

"It's time we got out. The 'Bird's' intent on trouble. There'll be shooting in a minute."

"Bird" was an old man, but as game as they make 'em, and he was soon in the midst of things with obvious joy. One of the young soldiers fired his revolver at some glasses on a shelf.

At this, in spite of my entreaties, Olive walked right into the midst of the scuffle. She talked to the youngsters like a mother and, what is more, they listened. And she got the "Bird" back to his table.

The police, hearing the shots, came inside. It was not long before they insisted on "Bird" Flanagan leaving. As his guests we could only follow: we got taxis, said a good-night to him, and went home.

We had been indoors but an hour when the front-door bell rang. We went down and found that it was the "Bird", his valet and his chauffeur, carrying huge wooden boxes. In our sitting-room, from these boxes they produced cold chickens, tongues, bread, butter, cheese, even a couple of cruets, knives and forks, and several bottles of champagne and other wines.

"Glory be to God," said the "Bird", "it's luck's way I am in, to find you not in bed. Come on, 'Dick Whittington', we had to leave our supper at Mother Mason's, but we'll make up for it now." And make up for it we did!

The "Bird" was always in the midst of some escapade. He once rode his horse into the Shelbourne Hotel and demanded a pint of beer for it.

There was tension in Ireland in those days, but bitter as was the feeling, there was still some chivalry. I was, on one occasion, at a party where Michael Collins and Arthur Griffiths were present. We were about to play cards, when word came through from a high-ranking British officer that they knew where these two Irish patriots, both with a price upon his head, could be found. The British would give them half an hour's grace to get out. The two great men took full advantage of the respite.

What a lovable man was Michael Collins. It seems appalling to me that lives such as his should be given for a cause that could and should be settled by means other than fighting.

From pantomime I went back on the music-halls. And then another summer season with "Twinkle" followed on the Isle of Wight.

This year "Papa" Pinder's "Sunshine" was the finest all-round show of its type that I have ever seen. It had the further advantage of the return of a great Shanklin favourite, Edwin Styles.

"Teddy" Styles was one of the best summer-show personalities I have known. His easy, nonchalant style, his good looks, his tall ambling figure, together with his cultured approach and original touches all combined to make him outstanding.

I had tried to expand "Twinkle", increasing its numbers from six to eight, and going in for more elaborate costuming. Maybe I had allowed my ambition to outrun my sense of proportion, and I had lost some of the sweet simplicity of the first year's production.

"Twinkle" did not lose prestige that year. But "Sunshine" was unquestionably the show of the Isle of Wight that year.

"Momma" Pinder, a very shrewd judge, put her finger on my trouble when she said, after watching the show one night at Shanklin, "The show's as good as ever, 'Clarkie', and I admire the way that you've expanded it. But you yourself, in your work, appear to me to be over-anxious."

That's it, I thought to myself later, "Momma" Pinder has put it in a nut-shell. I was frightened of being a failure—and over-anxiety can spread, from the leader, through a company.

After the season I returned to the Alhambra. Lily Morris, Billy Bennett, and myself were all head-lining there at the time, and, strangely enough, we had all developed from other types of acts.

Lily Morris had for years been a well-known and

excellent principal boy. Then she turned to low comedy. Billy Bennett had been doing a war-time act in khaki when he suddenly hit upon his "almost a gentleman" attire.

I had been very much the second partner of a good but never startling double-act, and had become the most talked-of comic singer of that time.

CHAPTER TEN

ALTHOUGH variety acts were included in the programmes, the London Coliseum could not, by any
stretch of the imagination, be described as a music-hall.
When I first played it, one might see there such items
as the Diaghileff Ballet; Arthur Bourchier, Owen Nares
or Fay Compton in sketches; the great clown Grock;
Margaret Cooper the famous pianist-entertainer, with her
unforgettable songs at the piano; that great character
comedian, Wilkie Bard; the Irish Players. I first saw
Bernhardt there in an abridged version of "La Dame Aux
Camelias".

I could not understand a word that she said, but I could
feel her genius. She had the same effect on me as Mrs.
Patrick Campbell, Eugene Stratton or Marie Lloyd. To
watch and listen to such great artistes tightened my chest,
brought tears to my eyes and made me feel humble about
my own work upon the stage.

Apart from and in addition to their genius I wonder
what quality it was they possessed that made them outstanding? Certainly they had authority. Authority in
work is important. But they also had something else—a
tremendous love of humanity which came right through
their work.

They 'rang true'. There was nothing 'phoney' about
them. Alas, this cannot be said for some present-day
artistes. The stars of the past had time for people, and
not, as so many of our present-day stars have, time only
for useful people.

Throughout the Sir Oswald Stoll regime the London
Coliseum was a difficult house for the average variety act.
All the Stoll theatres were strictly run and no one with
sense will quibble at that, but the London Coliseum was
unique in its austerity. To many it seemed the cathedral
of the Stoll diocese, and the staff, who served Sir Oswald

faithfully for so many years, acolytes reverent in some pontifical ceremony.

Arthur Croxton the manager was a figure of whom one heard, but he was seldom seen by the small fry. Agnew, the assistant-manager, was much more human, and Maurice Harbor in the box-office section always cheery and affable. Many artistes were nervous of Alfred Dove, the conductor. Frankly, I thought him a very bad variety conductor, although, since he was a friend of Olive's father—Professor Albert Fox of the Guildhall School of Music—he and I became very friendly, and he would often come and have tea with me in my dressing-room between the shows. Mr. Crocker the stage-manager was very conscious of his position, and the stage-staff included also the famous Coliseum carpenter "Tizzy".

A strict censorship was kept on artistes' material, any deviation from the approved script being noticed at once. Sometimes an artiste would be tackled on his way back to his dressing-room, so quickly had the news travelled.

Sir Oswald Stoll was once responsible, indirectly, for giving me an excellent and cheeky line in one of my songs. I was singing a comparison song about girls, the lines of which were:

> "Any girl looks all right
> In a bath marble white,
> With beautiful bath salts like peaches
> But the queen of my soul
> Has to stand in a bowl,
> And wash down as far as it reaches."

Mr. Crocker arrived at my dressing-room followed by Llewellyn Johns of the booking-committee, who was a delightful fellow, very understanding and tolerant. "Sir Oswald Stoll doesn't like that line about 'washing down as far as it reaches', and Lady Stoll, who always likes your work, was very surprised and said that it was not like Mr. Rose at all," said Johns.

"All right, Mr. Johns," I said, "I'll alter it."
I altered it to:

> "Any girl looks all right
> In a bath marble white,
> With beautiful bath salts she'll frolic,
> But the queen of my soul
> Has to stand in a bowl,
> And do what she can with carbolic."

If anything, I think the latter version is a trifle more crude. But that night Mr. Johns passed it, and when later in the week Sir Oswald came to take another 'peek' at his programme, he sent round a message to thank me for the 'much nicer' alteration. The revised got a far bigger laugh than the original version.

The first time I appeared at the London Coliseum as a single-act I was second on the programme. I got to the theatre about two hours before I was due to face the audience, a fatal thing to do, because in my beautiful ornate and expensively furnished dressing-room I was gradually reduced by apprehension and imagination to a shaking, nervous wreck.

A waitress knocked on the door to know if I wanted anything from the restaurant. I didn't really want a meal, but I ordered poached eggs on toast and coffee. I ate the poached eggs, which 'jiggered' my make-up, which I had to re-do, and in the middle of this an ear-piercing buzzer went off in the room.

I jumped up, knocking my make-up tray on to the floor, and dashed to the house-phone. A rasping voice said, "Fifteen minutes, Mr. Rose, please," and crashed down the receiver his end.

Beads of perspiration were breaking through my make-up. With a supreme effort I tried to take command of myself. I put on my hat, looked at it in the mirror, decided that it was at the wrong angle, took it off and put it on again. Then my trousers seemed braced the wrong length. Everything seemed wrong.

Then the dreadful buzzer went again. "Five minutes," said the voice the other end, "on the stage, please."

I walked out of my dressing-room and down the long silent corridors, through the swing doors and on to the huge stage. I picked my way nervously to the corner. Mr. Crocker said, "Don't exceed your time, Mr. Rose, please. We have a very long programme."

My mind was in a whirl. Somewhere in the distance I could hear the music of the act that preceded me, finishing. Somehow I got mixed up with some curtains on the side. "Not there!" shouted a voice. Before I knew what was happening, my music was being played. Down came a vast cloth nearly hitting me. I jumped out of the way and found myself on the revolving part of the stage. This immediately started turning—and over I went, base over apex.

"Mr. Rose, you're on," said someone. And Mr. Clarkson Rose, not knowing by this time whether he was at the London Coliseum or Wembley Stadium, picked up his hat and stick, and burst forth into the full glare of many lights, to face the vast Coliseum auditorium.

Alfred Dove was conducting the *ad lib* to my song at about five times the rate that it should have been played. Vainly I tried to bring him back to tempo—and then I started.

I seemed to have been in front of that audience a week before any reaction came. Finally there was a titter, and that so much encouraged me that I had the temerity to lean over to Mr. Dove and say, "Slower, please, take it from me." I finished the song, there was a smattering of applause, and I changed quickly for my next number, *Back I went to the Ministry of Labour*, in which, between every verse, I walked round the stage, lifting my knees almost chin high, in a sort of endless tramp for work.

The song began to get the audience and things were going splendidly until, during one of the *ad libs*, as I was walking round I saw Alfred Dove pointing his baton directly at my middle. He meant well, but it was completely the wrong thing to do, for when I looked down I saw that my flybuttons were undone, and each time I lifted my knees, a gap appeared displaying a large expanse of shirt.

That was "the pay off"—as they say to-day. How I finished the song I do not know. But the audience were quite obviously sympathetic, and the reception of my act at the end, for a second turn, was quite good.

Afterwards an irate Alfred Dove came to my room and asked me what I meant by telling him of all people, and the London Coliseum orchestra, about tempo. "My advice to you, my lad," he concluded, "is to look after your flybuttons and leave the music to me."

In reaction from the tension I had gone through I turned on him like a trapped rat. Having told him what I thought about the way he had conducted my music, I pointed out that he could have little sense of psychology or he would never have drawn my attention to my ill-adjusted attire, since in any case it had to remain for the rest of my performance unless I stopped my act and drew further attention to it by fastening the buttons up. Whether or not my virulence took Alfred Dove by surprise I don't know, but after it the atmosphere became calmer, the conversation moved into smoother channels, and at night my music was played perfectly.

In the summer Olive and I returned to our beloved Shorefields Pavilion, Westcliff-on-Sea, with our own show "Twinkle". A grand Westcliff welcome awaited us, and we opened on the Whit Saturday to a packed house, but somehow I felt, through the evening, that the show was not gripping.

"Twinkle" was still a Pierrot show, albeit a large one. I was confident that the Pierrot type of show was the right one for summer entertainment, but I was wrong.

During our absence for two seasons on the Isle of Wight two indifferent shows had occupied Shorefields, and the astute George Royle had seen the opportunity and had established his "Fol-de-Rols" at the Floral Hall.

The "Fol-de-Rols" were a company of some twenty artistes who played in the old English costumes of the Beau Brummell and crinoline period. They came to West-cliff from Scarborough where they had been immensely popular for years. The "Fol-de-Rols" were a grand show. Moreover, the seating, equipment and general presentation at the Floral Hall were far ahead of ours.

As the season wore on our houses were less and less. It was a terrible blow to my pride, and I was broken-hearted. Our small capital was dwindling, and then we started to sell things; first Olive's small car, and then some jewellery. My humiliation was complete when, one Sunday afternoon, I sat drowsily in a deck-chair by the band-stand with a handkerchief over my face as a protection from the sun, and heard a conversation going on in the chairs behind me.

"Have you seen Clarkson Rose's show?"

"Yes—once and once only."

"I feel terribly sorry for him. He and Olive were such favourites here, but now the whole town seems 'Fol-de-Rols' mad."

"Probably do him a lot of good. Personally I could never see why the town made him and Olive such idols. Anyway, he can't possibly compete with a super show like the 'Fol-de-Rols'. One is a show and the other is a little Pierrot troupe."

"'Twinkle' is doing a new programme to-morrow. Will you come?"

"No," emphatically. "I won't."

Under my handkerchief I was hot with shame and sorrow. I was at my wit's end for money and I could see myself losing Shorefields Pavilion, a place I had always longed to have. But I think the words "cannot compete" did something to me, and I formulated a plan.

First of all I went to Harry Davis, the landlord of Shore-fields, who, to do him justice, had great faith in me, and I persuaded him to agree to my having the pitch for a further year. Although it is going ahead in my story, I would say here that the following year I took back a new pattern for "Twinkle", introduced a quartette of dancers, lavish dresses, and paid higher salaries than hitherto for artistes of first-class ability.

I took the bit between my teeth to make the best of the remaining season. Several of my artistes were unsuitable, and I made changes. Then I decided on a policy of three programme changes a week and, by sheer hard work and slogging, managed to get a few more people in each week.

Back on the music-halls again in the winter, I found myself on the bill at Leicester Palace with Beatrice Lillie. She was appearing on the music-halls for the first time, and was assisted in her act by Joan Fred-Emney and Dennis Cowles. Bea was doing her cabaret character "Snoops" the lawyer, her burlesque of "The Floral Dance", and a sketch from one of the Charlot revues.

Her art was too fragile, sophisticated and delicate for a provincial music-hall audience, and she was not successful. She was distressed, but retained her sense of humour. I made one or two suggestions which improved her act from a music-hall viewpoint and we became firm friends.

From Leicester I went to Bristol, and Bea Lillie to Manchester. Every night she 'phoned me, or I 'phoned her, to see how things were going.

When I got back to the Alhambra some weeks later, Bea was waiting at the stage-door to greet me. She was having tea with me in my dressing-room when Olive arrived, and it was a case of mutual understanding and liking at once. Two days later she came to stay with us in our little house at Golders Green, and remained there until she sailed for America with Jack Buchanan and Gertie Lawrence to appear in the Charlot Revue in New York.

She was an amazing person and a source of joy the whole time that she was in our house. Both she and I were working at the Grafton Galleries Cabaret, and often it was daylight before she came home, but our old housekeeper, "Mother" Veasey, never objected.

When Bea was in America she often cabled us. Then, about a year later, at two o'clock in the morning, Olive and I heard stones being thrown up at our bedroom window. I opened it, asked who was there, and the well-known Bea Lillie voice announced, "Hit his hi, the prodigal daughter. Returned 'ome with American honours thick upon my baack—and what is more, a title."

Beatrice Lillie had become Lady Peel.

I let her in, Mrs. Veasey fussed around, and soon she was back in her old bedroom. In the morning, Mrs. Veasey devastated us by saying, in her grandest manner, "Good-morning, your ladyship. Would your ladyship like one or two heggs this morning?"

I often felt sensitive about Bea and our little suburban home. I knew that she was used to the Savoy, the Ritz and the Carlton, and the general run of London night-life. But, on Sunday nights, she would sit at the table for cold supper, thoroughly happy, completely at home, and perhaps looking on the domestic atmosphere as a welcome change.

The time came for us to return to Westcliff and the new "Twinkle". George Royle had heard of my plans, and, like the wise competitor that he is, he switched his principal company from Scarborough to be my opposition at Westcliff.

Westcliff, however, did not 'take' to the Scarborough company, and the new "Twinkle" was an instantaneous success, remaining for three more seasons at Westcliff in undisputed leadership in summer entertainment. The "Fol-de-Rols" and "Twinkle" were to be rivals again in the future, but an account of that will come in its proper place in this narrative.

Doubtless George Royle, myself, and other managers were making rods for our own backs when we elaborated summer shows. But other forms of entertainment had altered audiences considerably, and the plain Pierrot show was no longer enough.

After the summer I had just commenced a series of

music-hall bookings when Harry Norris put before me a
proposition to go into an Albert de Courville revue. "I
can get your music-hall dates postponed," said Harry;
"this will be a great chance for you. De Courville is
going to co-star you with Shirley Kellogg."

Albert de Courville was a man who had revolutionised
certain branches of the entertainment industry. His
revues at the London Hippodrome—"Hullo Ragtime",
"Hullo Tango", "Business as Usual" and others—were
large and lavish in conception. He brought to this
country transatlantic stars such as Ethel Levey, Lew
Hearne, Jack Norworth, and Shirley Kellogg.

At my first interview with him he explained, in his
excitable manner and marked accent, that the revue was
to be the biggest show that had ever been in the provinces.
"I feel sure that you will be successful, Rose," he
said.

Certainly no expense was spared with "Happy Hours",
as it was called. When I went to the first rehearsal at the
Oxford Music Hall the place seemed alive with executives.
Frank Collins—for so long Cochran's right-hand man—
was the producer. Jack Mason, who had done the dances
for "Hullo Ragtime", was in charge of the ensemble.

The cast, a tremendous one for a touring show, included
Shirley Kellogg, Dewey Gibson fresh from D'Oyly Carte
success; Marjorie Lotinga, now known as Marjorie Sandford and one of the famous Luck family; Fred Hastings;
George Thomas; Gordon Keith; Luke Dawe; several
specialities; a chorus of thirty-two girls; a male chorus;
and a crowd of small part men and women.

Shirley Kellogg was one of the most beautiful women I
have ever seen, but many people thought that her looks were
her only asset. In Hippodrome revues de Courville had
surrounded her with platoons of chorus in vast spectacular
scenes.

Chatting to her at rehearsals I was convinced that her
talents had never been properly exploited. I wrote much
of the book for "Happy Hours"; luckily for me she liked

what I had written, and my scripts fitted perfectly her
personality.

We produced at Leeds at Christmas, and I thought that
the dress rehearsal would never end. De Courville seemed
to have no idea of money, and at one stroke would scrap a
number that had cost thousands of pounds to dress and
stage.

On the opening the show was successful but obviously
unwieldy, and I did not see how they could possibly get
out with the huge overheads. I talked this over with
Shirley Kellogg at the Queen's Hotel after the opening
performance, and we tried to arrive at an economic basis.

The next day, with authority and tremendous enthusiasm, she called a rehearsal. I do not know what
happened between Frank Collins, Jack Mason and Shirley
Kellogg, but they were on their way back to London the
same night, and the show was put in my charge.

So wholeheartedly and untiringly did Shirley Kellogg
throw herself into the work that "Happy Hours" might
have been her first job in the profession. By the end of the
first two weeks at Leeds it was one of the best all-round
musical presentations, if not the best, in which I have ever
appeared.

CHAPTER ELEVEN

THE tour of "Happy Hours" was a phenomenal success. On several occasions mounted police had to be
requisitioned to keep back the crowds.

Shirley Kellogg was a strange mixture of simplicity and
sophistication—of niceness and temper. Fortunately I
understood her and she liked me.

One night she said to me, "What salary are you getting,
'Clarkie'?" I told her. "You should receive another
twenty pounds a week," she said.

At the end of the week another twenty pounds was put
in my envelope. Charlie Seymour, the manager of the
company, told me that he had no authority from de
Courville for this, but Shirley Kellogg had insisted.

She was a great baby in many ways, and most jealous.
When we were at Leeds, Gwladys Stanley, the wife of
Francis Laidler, was then making a huge success as
Principal Boy at the Leeds Theatre Royal. One night she
came into the hotel restaurant, on Francis Laidler's arm,
followed by two waiters carrying an enormous bouquet and
a basket of fruit. All eyes were focussed on Miss Stanley,
and Shirley, tight-lipped, turned to me and said, "To-
morrow I'll show her where she gets off with bouquets."

That night she delayed her entrance into the restaurant.
Then, bidding me accompany her, she swept in wearing
a beautiful gown, and followed by two page-boys, two
waiters, and two small-part men from our show, all
carrying the most ostentatious bouquets and baskets of
flowers that I have ever seen. The procession passed right
round the dance floor, and then she took her seat in
triumph almost hidden by the floral display around her.

Her favourite supper dish was oyster stew. She would
have the ingredients, the utensils and a burner taken to
her on a trolley, and she would make it herself.

A big Press conference took place in Leeds whilst we

THE FIRST TWINKLE COMPANY, 1921. Front row: MURIEL
FARQUHAR, OLIVE FOX, KATHLEEN JAMES. Back row: JAMES
WALTON, THE AUTHOR, AND FRANK WATTS

Left: WALLIS ARTHUR'S PIERROTS. Left to right: FRANK WATTS,
LAMBERT HARVEY, LESLIE WESTON, OLIVE FOX, VIOLET LOCKE, WINIFRED
GAWTHORNE, AND THE AUTHOR. Right: THE AUTHOR AS COLONEL
BLIMP

OLIVE FOX IN 1927

were there. Shirley, an excitable and delightful hostess, and exhibiting a side of her nature that few people knew—delicious and wicked mimicry, out-of-the-ordinary anecdotes, and swift and witty conversation—kept several prominent editors and journalists of national repute spellbound by her personality until the small hours.

"Isn't this woman remarkable? I have never seen anybody lovelier. I have never heard such wit. And I have never been entertained by such a hostess," said Hilton Crowther to me. He was a prominent man in the North of England at that time, and very friendly with many theatrical folk.

Around four o'clock in the morning the people started to leave. "Don't go," said Shirley, "we are all hungry again." And she sent for Paul Vachet, head waiter of the French restaurant. Paul told her that the kitchens were closed and that everything was finished. "Then we'll open them," said Shirley, "and I'll show you how to make a Maryland omelette."

Paul supplied her with eggs and other things, and she was soon turning out the most delicious omelettes that I have ever tasted, cooking with an expert and deft touch, and at the same time keeping up a fascinating running commentary. The newspaper men were her admiring and adoring slaves.

For a time I could do no wrong. Then I began to see her other side.

At Lewisham Hippodrome Charles Gulliver had put streamers outside the theatre with my name exactly the same size as Shirley Kellogg's. After sending for Mr. Vasco the manager, she went outside with her dresser and actually removed my name from the walls.

Technically I think that I was in the wrong. But the affront was there for all to see, I felt that I must make a stand, and I refused to appear until my name was replaced. Streamer letters were found from somewhere, my name was put back, and the curtain rose ten minutes late.

All the week she would not speak to me. But she

K

telephoned Mr. Gulliver, and she telephoned the head office. She threatened this and she threatened that. Finally, in a towering rage she came to my dressing-room and, breaking the silence, said, "Clarkson Rose, I've made you a star. Now I'm going to show you what quarrelling with Shirley Kellogg means. I'm telling Mr. Gulliver that unless you are removed from the show, I am not going on next week."

She told Mr. Gulliver this, and he acted at once. He sent Cissie Williams out to see her. I was in a strong position. My contract provided that all the material I had supplied reverted to me the moment I left the show. All the comedy scenes in the show were my material.

Cissie Williams was one of Gulliver's most brilliant head-office executives. To-day she is the chief booker for Moss Empires. I doubt if there has ever been a better business woman in the variety world.

Cissie Williams's sole idea in life has always struck me as being to get the best possible results for her firm. In business she has set herself a standard from which she has never deviated. Out of business, I doubt if there are half a dozen people who really know Cissie Williams the woman.

My own dealings with her have always been pleasant. You can't 'put anything over' on Cissie Williams. And she would not attempt to do so herself.

This was the woman sent to deal with Shirley Kellogg. After Shirley had tried the high-handed stuff, Cissie came to me and said quietly, "Don't worry, Mr. Rose, just carry on. Miss Kellogg will not be with the show next week."

The following week at Croydon Empire she was not in the cast, and her name was blanked-out on the posters. Marjorie Lotinga gave a brilliant performance in Shirley Kellogg's part. It was a joy to work with her, and the business was excellent throughout the week.

Shirley Kellogg was back in the show the following Monday. The tour continued, with the barometer sometimes "fair" and sometimes "stormy".

On the last night of "Happy Hours", at the Kilburn Empire, she sent for me. It must have been five or six weeks since any word other than the dialogue on the stage had passed between us. With tears in her eyes she held out her hand and said, "I'm sorry, 'Clarkie'. You've won, and you're the only man who has ever beaten Shirley Kellogg. You and I could have been the grandest partnership in the show business, but it just wasn't to be. I can't help my nature."

She left the country shortly after the tour of "Happy Hours" ended. I have never heard of her since.

I learnt much from Albert de Courville. Many people looked upon him merely as a producer of spectacles. But he was far more than that.

In the early days of "Happy Hours" I said to him, "D. C. I'm nervous. I'm not a low comedian in the accepted sense of the word, and I am not a clown. I'm wondering how I shall go over."

Excitedly he answered, "Eet does not matter, Clarkson. Low comedians are good, but eet ees not only low comedians who get laughs. Give me a good actor like yourself who understands timing perfectly, and he will get more laughs throughout the show than the clown. You have a sense of character and situation, and with your artful timing you will be all right."

He came to several rehearsals and I was astonished to find how able he was at suggesting business and gags to comedians.

After "Happy Hours" came another season at Westcliff, where "Twinkle" was the outstanding summer entertainment. I was fortunate with my cast. George Buchanan, one of the most artistic musicians it has been my lot to meet, was in charge of the musical department, and Dennis Brogan helped with the production.

George Buchanan had been with the famous concertparty, R. B. Salisbury's "The Quaints". Facially he resembled almost exactly Sir Gerald du Maurier and, careless in his personal appearance, yet he always looked

like an undergraduate on vacation. His coat collar might
be frayed—but it was a good coat. His flannel 'bags'
might be threadbare, but they were perfectly cut. His
soft hat, with the exception of Frederick Melville's, was the
oldest hat that I have ever seen. Long use in all weathers,
and various stains, gave it an appearance of many colours.
Yet it was always worn at the correct angle. And what a
dreamer he was!

Dennis Brogan had evolved some excellent miniature
ballets for which George provided the music. Quite often
he would extemporise new melodies every night, but he
always gave the girls the correct number of bars, and
when they got over the first shock of the change in music,
they began to know what to expect. He lifted the music
of "Twinkle" to a new high standard.

Dennis Brogan, when he joined me, had rather a bitter
outlook, for life had not treated him well. But the family
influence of our show mellowed him. I had to watch Dennis
and George carefully or the show would have become a
combination of the Russian Ballet and weird music.

On one occasion I had to go away to Bognor to attend
to the number two company of "Twinkle" that was there.
I left George and Dennis in charge, laid out a programme,
and told them to have it ready for my return the following
Monday.

When I returned I arrived in the middle of a rehearsal.
George was in his shirt sleeves at the piano, the girls,
looking very weary, were in their practice frocks, and
Dennis, bathed in perspiration, was shouting, "No, no.
That's ordinary. We Must be different."

I asked what was going on, and partly from Dennis, and
partly from George, had a long description of a new ballet
concerned with the death of Pierette in a wood, and which,
apparently, was to end with my entrance as the Figure of
Death brandishing the Sword of Death over Pierette's
body, as the curtains slowly closed. Worked up to a
fever heat by enthusiasm for their conception, they waited
for my verdict.

"I think that you've forgotten that 'Twinkle' is summer entertainment. Surely the Figure of Death would be incongruous?" I commented.

"But, 'Clarkie'," they said, "you're overlooking the beauty of the situation."

"Maybe," I said. "But there ain't going to be no death in my show."

"You don't understand the spirit of Pierrot, 'Clarkie'," George said. "Pierrot isn't only a thing of joy. Pierrot is a thing of sadness."

"That may be, but we shall present him with all the gladness that he does stand for," I replied.

"Pierrot is a creature who lives between the moon and the earth," said George, wild-eyed, with his Gerald du Maurier chin pushed forward and almost in a trance. "He's half man and half spirit."

"Right," I said. "We'll have the half that's man."

"All you think of is tempo, precision and applause," said George. And with that he went off to drown his sorrows in half-cans of beer.

A great musician, he persuaded me one season to provide him with an organ in addition to the piano. For some of our songs it was most effective. But it was a little disconcerting to hear *Yes, we have no bananas*, and *Onward, Christian Soldiers*, combined in a sort of voluntary.

An artiste who achieved great success in the show was Gwen Evans. She was not pretty, but she had tremendous *joie de vivre* and was a first-class dancer who loved dancing so much that I have seen her in tennis shorts, at six o'clock in the morning, rehearsing on the lawn. She danced with her whole body. Later she dropped this method and went in for a sophistication that curbed all her natural exuberance.

This season I tried an innovation. Hitherto I had handled the whole of the comedy myself. This year I had another comedian—Fred Wynne. I saw him first at the Coliseum, Portsmouth. I liked his rough good-humoured manner and neat and clean props.

On the first night of the season, after the opening chorus, Fred Wynne walked down to the footlights and, pointing at me, he said, "I know he's been the king-pin up to now, and I know that he's the guv'nor, but that's not going to worry me. I'm here to make you laugh." Then, turning to me, he said, "No offence, guv'nor. You go and have a rest, and leave them to me. You've been here a few seasons now and they'd like a change."

The sheer audacity of these homely remarks endeared him to the Westcliff audience, as indeed I knew that they would, and Fred Wynne made a tremendous success. He remained with me for several seasons, and apart from being an excellent trouper was my friend and snooker rival.

Many excellent people passed through the ranks of "Twinkle" in those early years. Among my first quartette of dancers was Renee Roberts, who afterwards married Ronald Frankau.

Rex (Tubby) Harold, the well-established London entertainer, the very image of Mr. Pickwick, urbane, loquacious and benevolent, gave me most excellent service in his Bognor seasons. He was a special favourite with the children.

Then there was Max Kirby, son of the West End revue favourite, Gerald Kirby. He had one god in his professional life, Jack Buchanan, and he went on to understudy Jack Buchanan in several shows.

After the "Twinkle" season I went into partnership with Harry Norris who, by this time, had ended his association with Herbert Clayton. Together we put on successful touring revues, notably "That's That" and "Carnival Time".

Our first venture was nearly our last. It was a show called "The Gay World". This opened at Wolverhampton Hippodrome, and in spite of my big local following I knew that it was doomed to failure. We took the show off after five or six weeks, and it was a nasty punch to take.

Christmas week at the Alhambra, Bradford, we produced "That's That". The cast included Olive Fox, Len Jackson and Charlie Rodney, and it was the nearest thing in pattern to "Happy Hours" that I could get. It was a success from the outset, and broke records at many theatres.

Len Jackson was an excellent natural comedian. A Jewish boy, he had all the race's instinct for grasping opportunity, and he was genuinely funny. His double-act with Charles Rodney was one of the high-spots of the show.

Following "That's That" came "Carnival Time". Sandy Powell was in a period of transition at that time, and we were fortunate in getting him as the other comedian, at a reasonable salary. He had just started to make gramophone records. These had a big vogue and were of immense publicity value to the show in each town.

In many places in the north, where they only just accepted me, Sandy Powell was an outstanding hit. His quiet, unobtrusive method is a tremendous asset to him. There is nothing an audience loves so much as the hapless, helpless fellow. Sandy Powell was this to perfection. He shot up to the big money like a meteor, and left us to run excellent shows of his own.

Sandy Powell's place in "Carnival Time" was taken by Joe Young. He was a bluff, hearty Jew, and one of the nicest-natured men I have ever met, with a tremendous sense of humour about himself. Joe and I had hardly a thing in common so far as tastes went. But we were grand companions, and had a very happy time.

The run of "Carnival Time" was marred by a great tragedy.

The head girl of the dancing troupe, Mae Harvey, had just married our musical-director, Hastings Mann. Mae was the petite, porcelain type and a lovely dancer. She was full of character, with rigid and definite ideas, and had been most carefully brought up.

One night at Nottingham Empire, just before the second house, we heard shrieks and rushed upstairs. A fire had broken out in the girls' dressing-room. Mae's clothes, of flimsy and gauze-like material, were on fire. Someone tried to pull them off her, but even in the midst of flames her rigid modesty tried to prevent this.

It may have been this modesty which caused her death. Another girl was similarly burned, but we got off her clothes. Both were taken to hospital. Mae died a few days later.

Olive and I had Hastings Mann with us in our 'digs' from then onwards. I used to sit up with him until the small hours because he would not go to bed and hated to be left alone. We did, however, turn out and publish some song successes, notably *The Bushes at the Bottom of the Garden*, which had a good vogue, both here and abroad.

The stark happening of death—in a theatrical company, surrounded by the tinsel and glitter of the stage, and with the hollowness and artificiality of everything—is poignant and frightening.

The unwritten law of our calling is that the curtain must go up. "Laugh, Punchinello, the people pay thee and want their laugh, you know."

In other professions and trades there are opportunities for quiet and reflection, at times of personal tragedy. Perhaps our profession is lucky in the fact that it cannot have these things?

In the effort of carrying on, hard though it may be, there are many compensations.

CHAPTER TWELVE

IN 1927, when I was appearing at the Alhambra, George Reynolds sent round to tell me that Philip Rodway, of the Theatre Royal, Birmingham, was in front and interested in my work. After the show Mr. Rodway came round to see me and said, "I want you to play dame in 'Robinson Crusoe' at the Theatre Royal, next Christmas."

From the artistes' viewpoint the Theatre Royal, Birmingham, in the Rodway regime, was the mecca of pantomime. In my opinion, his pantomimes as spectacles and stories have never been equalled, and certainly never surpassed, albeit that the Rodway rigidity may at times have weakened the comedy.

Many of his pantomimes, after the first run at Birmingham, were presented with success in other large provincial towns by Julian Wylie and James Tate. Rodway pantomimes were, in truth, the foundation of the Wylie-Tate pantomime combination.

Philip was a law unto himself. His theatre was run differently from any other theatre I have ever known—his pantomimes were almost his life. Being in a pantomime at the Theatre Royal was quite unlike being in a pantomime anywhere else. It was like going to a public school for the first time, and no matter what your status in the profession might be, you had to learn the rules of the Theatre Royal and abide by Mr. Rodway's customs.

He had his likes and dislikes, and with a few exceptions he never became on intimate terms of friendship with his artistes. I was told that "Wee Georgie" Wood, G. S. Melvin and myself were the only artistes ever known to be asked to his house at Edgbaston. I fitted in with him from the word "go"—learnt to love, respect and admire him—and finally—a sure sign of his trust and friendship—was even allowed to argue with him.

Mrs. Rodway and his daughters Phyllis and Lois shared his love of the theatre, but none of his family was ever seen back-stage. After his passing, his daughters wrote a book about their father, *A Tale of Two Theatres*. Reading it one realises how the whole family was bound up with him in his life, and the love of his life—the Theatre Royal, Birmingham, and the pantomimes.

After his casual remark to me, in my dressing-room at the Alhambra on the occasion of our first meeting, I said, "Well, Mr. Rodway, I don't have to tell you how honoured I am, but I have never played dame before except in songs and sketches, and dame at the Theatre Royal, Birmingham, is to me a terribly important thing."

I stopped. Mr. Rodway said, "Go on."

"You see, sir," I continued, "I have known the Theatre Royal almost as long as you have. As an office boy I have seen pantomimes there since the beginning of the century. When I think of the wonderful dames you have had there, especially the incomparable George Robey, I don't feel competent to undertake it."

Mr. Rodway blinked his eyes, drew a pipe from his pocket and asked my permission to smoke it. Then he said, "I understand all that you say, but I do not agree with you that you cannot play dame in my theatre. You speak the King's English, that is the type of speech that I want in my dame, and you are sufficiently a good actor to do the rest under my guidance."

Finally the matter was settled, and at Christmas I went to the Theatre Royal, Birmingham, to co-star with Robb Wilton in "Robinson Crusoe". It was a memorable engagement for me, not only because of the understanding that became established between Philip and myself, but also because it was the commencement of my great affection for Robb Wilton.

During rehearsals the comfort of the artistes was considered in every way. If the weather was exceptionally bad, Philip Rodway would many times ask his principals "not to go out into the cold air and risk getting a chill," and he would have hot food sent in from the famous Lisseter and Miller restaurant opposite the theatre.

The hospitality of the management during rehearsals was almost embarrassing. He liked to keep all his boys and girls under his roof all the time.

Rehearsals had been going on for a few days when Philip came to me and said, "I'm a bit worried about the script, Clarkson. I'd like to substitute a couple of new scenes for you and Robb. What can you suggest?"

Enthusiastically I replied, "Give me a day off rehearsals, Mr. Rodway, and I'll see what I can do."

I got a day off, and I wrote two scenes. When I showed them to the guv'nor the next day, he read them through slowly and methodically, and then said, "They're very good, Clarkson. But you've given most of the laughs to Robb."

"Well, Mr. Rodway," I said, "Robb is the chief star, and I felt that was the right thing to do."

"Well, my boy, I wish that more folks felt like that. I appreciate your unselfishness, and I shan't forget it," he said.

The two scenes proved very successful. I had fitted Robb and myself in just the right way, and we revelled in working them.

How lucky I was to have played my first dame co-starring with Robb Wilton. Although he was the chief star, no one could have been kinder and more co-operative, and, when I achieved success, he was so big that he could rejoice in it.

My first appearance as dame was of story value to the Press, and when I was successful in the part, it gave them a double opportunity to make a fuss of me, which they did. Robb Wilton was delighted, and actually handed me a newspaper and said, "Have you seen this? What does it feel like to be the hit of the show?"

Robb Wilton and I spent a lot of our time together, either he at my 'digs' or I at his. Philip Rodway likened our pantomime combination to the famous ones of John Humphries and Dan Rolyat, and George French and Tom Conway.

In his pantomimes Rodway would adhere rigidly to story, plot and period.   One of my vaudeville song successes at the time was *The Girls of the Old Brigade*, and I had banked on doing it in the pantomime.

"I've been thinking about it, Clarkson," said Philip one day, "and I'm afraid that you can't do it."

Dumbfounded, I asked, "But why, Mr. Rodway? It is absolutely made for pantomime."

"Yes, I admit that it's good.   But unfortunately you wear a Victorian bustle in it, and the 'Robinson Crusoe' dresses are a hundred years or so before that period."

"But surely, Mr. Rodway, in pantomime certain licences can be——?"

"Listen, Clarkson," he said.   "Don't talk to me about pantomime licences.   So many of them have taken licences—I know all the points that they advance.   But I will not do so."

That my song could not be in, depressed me very much.   Olive tried to comfort me and 'chivy' me out of worrying about it.   But it weighed heavily upon my outlook.

Before the first band rehearsal Philip Rodway sent for me and said, "I know just what you've been feeling about your song, Clarkson.   As you took it very well, and threw yourself into your work, I have given the matter further thought, and you can do the song in the Island scene. But you must first come on in your tattered garments from the shipwreck, and then one of the sailors can come and tell you that a trunk has been washed-up on the shore, and that he has opened it and found a lot of different kinds of dresses in it.   That can be a cue for you to say 'Dresses! Well, as I've hardly got a stitch to my back, I don't mind what kind they are.   Lead me to them and we'll sort them out.'   That will be a legitimate reason for you to go out and come back in your bustle dress."

I was overjoyed, and the number was the hit of the

pantomime. Philip was glad that he had found an excuse for its legitimate inclusion that satisfied himself.

A Rodway pantomime dress rehearsal was always played to a packed house and was a perfectly finished performance. A little, rickety bridge was built across the footlights from the auditorium, and once or twice Mr. Rodway would stop the proceedings, cross the bridge on to the stage and put something right, take something out, or put something in. It was one of his little vanities. Once the show had been passed at dress rehearsal not a syllable could be added to the pantomime by anybody.

One day during the run I couldn't resist putting in an impromptu. It was in the Island scene. Robb Wilton as Will Atkins had found me in a rather forlorn condition, and said, "Ah, there you are, Mrs. Crusoe. How are you?" My reply in the script was, "Don't ask me how I am, Mr. Atkins. I've been chased all over the island by cannibals and I'm starving." Instead of this I said, "How am I? You need ask me, Mr. Atkins. I haven't had a meal since the Villa won their last match."

Aston Villa were doing badly at the time, and the line, for its topicality, got a round of applause. Within a short time after leaving the stage John Roker, the assistant producer, was awaiting me with a note to go to the Board Room and see Mr. Rodway, after the performance. Robb Wilton also received a similar note.

In the Board Room after the matinée Mr. Rodway said, "Sit down, gentlemen." This was ominous, for he usually called us "boys". "I'm sorry to have to ask you up here," he continued, "but, as you know, I don't allow any liberties to be taken with the pantomime. This afternoon, when the pantomime was running its usual even course, my office door was open and I happened to hear a very big laugh and a round of applause. Now, which of you got it?"

Picture the situation. Robb Wilton, the great comedian, and a very high-salaried one, and myself, a near star, and also earning a large salary, were being put on the carpet for having got a big laugh! We looked at each other like naughty schoolboys, and Robb, in his hesitating and lugubrious way, said, "It wasn't me, Mr. Rodway."

Mr. Rodway's lips tightened. He turned to me and said, "It wasn't you, Clarkson, surely? Was it?"

I pulled myself together, and after some preamble admitted that it was I. The corners of Mr. Rodway's lips took a downward turn. "I am very surprised, Clarkson. I've always had implicit trust in you, and you know my rule. I presume, Robb, as you were on in the scene, you were a party to it?"

"No," said Robb, with his characteristic hand plucking at the side of his nose. "I said the right line, didn't I, 'Clarkie'?"

"He did, guv'nor," I answered. "It was all my fault."

"H'mm!" said Philip Rodway, pursing his lips. "Perhaps you would be good enough to tell me precisely what was said."

I then repeated the line. The large Rodway eyebrows beetled, his forehead creased and uncreased in a frown. Then he looked up and said, "I'm more than surprised at you. Do you realise, Clarkson, that if Aston Villa go in the second division, people in my audience will blame you for it?"

I tried, mildly, to remonstrate with him. "Surely, guv'nor," I said, "it's only a topical gag, and isn't it a comedian's job to do as W. S. Gilbert said—'Catch folly as it flies'?"

"That may or may not be," said Philip Rodway. "But not in this theatre!"

Robb Wilton is an inimitable off-stage raconteur. His telling of this story is a monologue of sheer joy. Never again during the run of the pantomime was any additional joke or gag inserted.

The customs and parties of the Theatre Royal were in keeping with the atmosphere. I can recall a night when we all gathered in the tea-room, and oysters from huge barrels were served, with champagne. On another occasion there was a trial by jury, the defendant was the pantomime itself. Counsel for the prosecution was the then famous agent, Ernest Edelsten, and counsel for the defence the equally famous pantomime producer, George M. Slater. Edelsten had a wicked and witty tongue, and although Slater was more suave and pedantic, he could be equally witty.

The well-being of his company always in his mind, Rodway did not go in for late night rehearsals. On one occasion, when Slater was helping in the production, Rodway crept down the stalls, lent over to him and said, "I don't want to interrupt you, George, but it is getting near midnight. I must dismiss."

George M. Slater, to whom time meant nothing, with his head in the clouds and intent on his ballet, just said, "Oh, Mr. Rodway, the fourth girl in the Grasshopper section is about seven months gone. I'm putting her in the Ladybirds to-morrow."

My first pantomime season at the Theatre Royal, Birmingham, was also memorable to me because, during the run, I received notification that I was one of the artistes chosen to appear in the Royal Command Performance at the London Coliseum, on 1st March 1928. The night before I had the official intimation Hannen Swaffer, at the Queen's Hotel, stopped me, and in his laconic way said, "You're in the Royal Show, Rose." I thought that he was 'kidding'.

Proudly I took Philip Rodway the letter, and waited for his congratulations. After reading it slowly, all he said was, "Ah, very nice, Clarkson. But we'll have to see."

"See, guv'nor? I don't understand."

"Well, I don't know whether I can let you go. It will mean you missing two shows, and I don't know whether that would be fair on my public."

It was an example of the Rodway mentality, just as it had been over the inclusion of my *Girls of the Old Brigade* song in the pantomime. But of course eventually he agreed to my going.

Several times during the run of the pantomime Rodway came into my dressing-room and studied the photograph of an old music-hall performer, Cliff Ryland, that was on the wall. When I asked him why he did so, he said, "Never mind, but keep your eye on it. I will tell you why one day."

During the last week he said, "Clarkson, I am going to pay you the biggest compliment that has ever been paid in this theatre. I want you to return here next year. No principal artiste has ever played two consecutive years in pantomime at the Theatre Royal, Birmingham, in the whole of its history. I want you to be the first." Then, pointing to the Cliff Ryland photograph, he continued, "That's something like the make-up I want you to use. You are going to play the title role in 'Old King Cole'."

Robb Wilton was the first to congratulate me, and when the news spread around, many letters and telegrams came from my friends. To be a principal comedian twice running during the Rodway regime was indeed an achievement.

The last night came with its speeches and its tears. Philip would not allow any 'mucking about'—as he called it—with his pantomime on the last night, but he did not mind an occasional departure from the book on this night, providing it was 'rehearsed'.

Robb Wilton and I had been singing the duet *Side by Side*. On the last night we changed places in this—Robb becoming Mrs. Crusoe and I Will Atkins. Robb as a dame was simply immense. I have often wondered why he has never 'had a go' at playing dame.

One of the great experiences of pantomime the following year was meeting and working with Fred Conquest. Fred played Fido, the dog, and I have never seen, nor do I expect to see, a finer animal performance.

He seemed to imbibe the very spirit, thought and outlook of a dog. At his every exit his wife, Kate, was waiting, with a little wire brush, to keep the dog's whiskers in trim.

CLARKSON ROSE AS THE LADY OF TUNBRIDGE WELLS

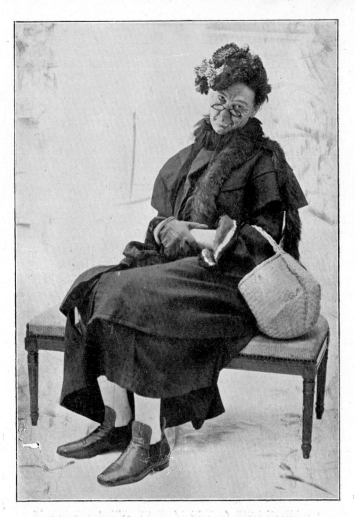

OLIVE FOX AS A LADY OF THE EMBANKMENT

We played in other pantomimes together afterwards, and I felt it a privilege to play dame to Fred Conquest's dog. Fred had worked with many famous dames, including Shaun Glenville and George Robey, but he told me that the best Mother Goose he'd ever been with, from the drama viewpoint, was Wilkie Bard.

Fred Conquest and I became great friends, and when he retired to the Isle of Wight it was fortunate for me that, with "Twinkle" playing a summer season at Shanklin, we were on each other's doorsteps. He had a lovely little cottage at Bembridge, and nothing gave us greater pleasure than to get into his boat and go off mackerel spinning.

It was an irretrievable loss to pantomime when he died. After his wife, Kate, passed on, his own end seemed inevitable. He gradually cracked up—and then they were reunited.

In "Old King Cole", Rodway, who never had much time for women, surprised me very much by engaging Olive for a specially written-in part, Quilini. Strangely enough, it was a better part than the Principal Boy's, and Olive was most successful in it.

The Principal Boy was a delightful Australian vocalist named Beryl Walkley. In her own country she had been playing leads in musical shows such as "Show Boat". Philip Rodway had brought her all the way from Australia, as he told me one day, "Because she has a magnificent voice, and I particularly want a Principal Boy this year with a real voice. I'm tired of voices that merely 'put over' numbers, as they call it."

Strangely enough the songs given Miss Walkley to exploit her beautiful voice were *Forty-seven Ginger-headed Sailors* and *Get out and get under the Moon*. She was obviously distressed at this waste of her considerable vocal abilities, but Philip was adamant. Later she was permitted to sing *Chloe* in one spot in the production, but still had to do the other two numbers.

"Old King Cole" was a magnificent pantomime, utterly unusual, full of fantasy, but lacking any robust

L

comedy. Mr. Rodway's attention to detail was stronger than ever.

For my character of King Cole I had to have a large ornate pipe. This was given to me before the dress rehearsal, and I was told to take great care of it as it had cost five guineas.

One night I was in the wings, about to make my entrance, when I realised to my horror that I had left my pipe in the dressing-room. "I've forgotten my pipe," I shouted. Almost before I had finished speaking, the assistant stage-manager handed me a duplicate from the prompt corner. Philip Rodway had anticipated just such a happening. I found that there was another duplicate in the O.P. corner also!

On the last night of "Old King Cole" the Theatre Royal, Birmingham, passed from Philip Rodway's control to Moss's Empires. All that day he went around like a lost soul.

Just before the curtain fell he came to me and said, "Clarkson, I can't go on with it. You must make the speech handing the old theatre over."

I tried to cheer him up as best I could. When I did what he had asked of me, I tried to lighten the proceedings. After giving impressions of certain theatrical managers singing their favourite songs, I ended with Rodway's, a parody on the Welsh National Anthem:

> "I leave the Theatre Royal,
>   My courage nearly fails,
> Good luck to my successors,
>   And God Bless the Prince of Wales."

The last line got a tremendous laugh, a laugh of relief that the tension was broken. Philip Rodway was, of course, merely moving up from New Street to Broad Street, where he controlled the destinies of the Prince of Wales Theatre until he died.

So the historic playhouse, the Theatre Royal, Birmingham, passed into the hands of a mammoth combine.

Tom D. Newell, one of the best dames in the profession, was the dame in "Old King Cole", but he was not happy at the Theatre Royal. His part was that of Dame Hubbard, but in the book and programmes it was "Winifred Hubbard"; according to Philip Rodway, Winifred Hubbard was a poor but genteel lady, and his idea of gentility in this instance demanded that Tom should wear a blonde wig instead of his usual harridan dame make-up.

Tom D. Newell hated it, and twice during rehearsals went to Philip Rodway and asked to be released from his contract. I made a friend of him, kept him there, and we worked happily together. We maintained a regular correspondence until his tragic death a few years afterwards.

He got married during the run of the pantomime. I was not only the best man, but made practically all the wedding arrangements—and very nearly had to answer "I will" for him, so nervous was he that day.

CHAPTER THIRTEEN

THE programme at the Royal Command Performance at the London Coliseum, on 1st March 1928,
included Larry Kemble with his comedy cycling act; A. C.
Astor, the ventriloquist; Lilian Burgess singing songs with
a nostalgic appeal; Stanelli and Douglas in their comedy
act with violins; Jack Hylton and his Band; eight of the
Victoria Palace girls; Anton Dolin; Noni and partner, the
famous clown; Will Hay, the schoolmaster comedian;
Gracie Fields, and myself.

We were in the theatre nearly all day, and most of us
admitted that we were very nervous. Gracie Fields was
quite frank about it, and said to me, "Eeh, Clarkson, I feel
as if I know nowt about owt."

One of the big hits of the programme was Noni. In the
course of his act he walked down to the footlights and, in
a pathetic way, said that he was only the "poor clown who
never got any flowers." During the interval Queen Mary
sent for him, and handed him a flower from her bouquet.
This, of course, received headline publicity in all the
national newspapers.

Of my own act, the newspapers said, "His Majesty
followed with interest Clarkson Rose's song *We always lay
the lino on the floor*. His Majesty must have known of the
intricacies of tenement furnishing."

Nerves were responsible for my making a hit by
accident. I was so nervous when I walked on for my
second song, *Girls of the Old Brigade*, that I slipped as I did
my usual jump round to waggle my bustle, and slid down
on to the footlights, disclosing my red flannel drawers.
The Queen was seen to rock backwards and forwards
with laughter at the incident, and at that very moment a
flashlight photograph was taken of the Royal Box, showing
Queen Mary given over to uncontrollable enjoyment.
Until then I did not think the actual words of my song

had been going over very well, but the moment the Queen laughed, the rest of the audience followed suit—and I finished to a big reception.

I appeared on the occasion of the twenty-fifth anniversary celebration of the Royal Automobile Club, when, at the Covent Garden Opera House, a wonderful programme was arranged, and the Prince of Wales was in the audience. The artistes, drawn from music-halls in and around London, included Harry Tate, Harry Weldon, Du Calion, Nellie Wallace, Tom Clare, Nelson Keys, Irene Russell. Several lesser acts had been asked to stand by in case there was any hitch in the programme, amongst them being a Jewish man and woman double-act, well-known in the profession, if not to the general public.

Stars kept arriving, "must get on and get away," and still this double-act kept waiting for the moment when they should appear. Finally Mr. Crocker, the stage-manager of the London Coliseum, who was in charge of the proceedings, told them that they were on next.

Just as they were about to go on, an equerry brought a message round to say that the Prince of Wales had to leave shortly, and particularly wished to see the acts of Nelson Keys and Harry Tate before he left. Mr. Crocker explained to the male partner of the double-act that the Prince of Wales was going early, and wished to see Mr. Keys and Mr. Tate, so other turns would have to wait.

"But we've been 'ere all the evening. That's all we're 'ere for, for the honour of appearing before the Prince of Wales," said the man.

"I'm sorry," said Crocker, who by then was shouting instructions to his staff about the change over in scenes, "but the Prince of Wales is going, and wishes to see Mr. Keys and Mr. Tate."

"Won't 'e be 'ere when we're on?" queried the double-act.

"No, he won't," replied the, by now, irate Crocker.

With that the male partner turned to the female section

of his act and said, "Gawd almighty, where's 'is bloody manners!"

I appeared at the People's Palace, Mile End, on an amazing programme arranged by the well-known Excelsior Club. In the front row of the stalls were the Prince of Wales, the Duke of Gloucester, the Duke of Kent, and various members of their entourages.

In addition to many music-hall stars, the programme included Carnera the heavyweight boxer, dear old Eugene Corri the famous boxing referee, and many well-known actors. There was a large ante-room plentifully supplied with liquor, but two fussy gentlemen, wearing their best suits with some sort of official badge thereon, would keep the bottles unopened.

"Aren't these refreshments intended for the artistes?" I asked one of the two.

"Yes, but the Prince of Wales, the Duke of Gloucester and the Duke of Kent are coming behind the scenes in the interval, and we can't have them opened until then."

"But some of the artistes have to go before the interval," I protested.

"Can't help that, nothing must be touched."

When Their Royal Highnesses came back-stage, the Prince of Wales walked up to the buffet and, turning to me, said, "It has apparently been a very dry party so far, Rose."

"Yes, Sir," I replied politely. "We were told that nothing could be touched until your Royal Highness came round."

"What a lot of rot," said the Prince of Wales. He reached for a bottle of Black Label, handed it to me, and I poured out drinks for the Royal party, one for Carnera, one for Corri, and one for myself.

The officious ushers were livid because they had been robbed of their job. But they couldn't do anything about it, and I returned to the Empire, Stratford, feeling " 'ighly delighted".

On this Excelsior Club programme I was working a

number of mine, *I had to go and draw another pound out.*
Music-hall audiences always repeated the catch-phrase
at the end of every verse, but on this occasion they did
not do so at first.   The Duke of Gloucester could see how
I was struggling to make them sing, and when the phrase
came round the next time, he and the Duke of Kent, and
later the Prince of Wales, led off the singing—and after
that it went with its usual swing.

CHAPTER FOURTEEN

BRITISH audiences have always taken kindly to good American acts. I first saw that dear character and nimble-footed genius, Eugene Stratton, playing Buttons in a "Cinderella" at the old Grand Theatre, Birmingham.

There was a forlorn quality about Stratton's work which had immense appeal. From the sympathetic viewpoint, I do not think the part could have been better cast. Many artistes have sung *Lily of Laguna*, and the whole world has sung it too, but no one has ever given the rendition of Gene Stratton, its creator.

R. G. Knowles was the prototype of present-day wise-crackers. His dissertations on women, husbands, fashions and so forth were masterpieces. I can picture him now, in the rather torn but always clean white trousers, the carefully buttoned but badly fitting frock coat, and the dilapidated opera hat, hear his husky voice, and see his arms going in and out like piston rods, emphasising points.

He was a highly intelligent man, a great philosopher, and, apart from his music-hall performances, lectured on many subjects in this and other countries. Towards the end, the throat affection from which he died became very troublesome and his voice became weaker, but he still kept his sense of humour.

At the New Cross Empire he had been on some little time and was gradually getting inaudible. From the gallery came one or two shouts of "Speak up!" and a few loud noises. Knowles stopped, looked up at the gallery, lifted one side of his frock coat, tapped his trouser pocket and said, "Thank you, boys, but you're too late."

The rest of the audience got the quick wit of the man, who was known to be very well-to-do. The retort got much applause.

Tom E. Murray was a different type. For an American

he was slow—but very, very pungent. I saw him play the Baron in "The Babes in the Wood" at the Prince of Wales Theatre, Birmingham. With all the other comedians dancing around him, he would stand like a rock, convulsing the audience with words spoken in a slow, nasal, vibrant twang, one hand up to the side of his face as though he were scratching some irritation. Murray never came out of character.

With the possible exception of Norah Bayes, I have never seen anyone who could handle a song like Sophie Tucker. She would take an ordinary song sometimes, and by the time that she, aided by her fine pianist, Ted Shapiro, had processed it, it became distilled perfection.

At the old Holborn Empire, with its large percentage of Jewish patrons in the audience, she was an idol. When she finished her act with *Yiddisher Momma* the applause was so great it was a well-nigh impossible task for any act to follow her. I had that unenviable position on two occasions. But "Soph" is not only a great artiste, but a great-hearted woman. I spoke to her at the band rehearsal on the Monday, and asked her to make it as easy as she could for me to follow her.

"Sure, Clarkson," she said. "Come in and tell me about your act."

I went to her dressing-room and told her that whereas I had been a great favourite at the Holborn Empire, I was very nervous about following her.

"Okay," she said. "Leave it to me."

That night, when she had finished her act, there was pandemonium with the audience clamouring and clamouring, and Sophie Tucker going backwards and forwards, taking call after call. I stood at the side of the stage in a frenzy of nervous tension.

After about a dozen calls, when some of the audience were starting to leave the theatre, Sophie went through and held up her hand. She then made her speech of thanks, and at the conclusion said, "And now, folks, I see that some of you are leaving the building. Listen to your old friend Soph. Get right back in your seats and stay there, because after me you've got one of your own favourites. Oh yes! I know that it's past eleven o'clock. But you don't have to hurry. This boy's got a grand act for you. I know, because he's been through it in the dressing-room with me." Then with an air of imparting a confidence, and a wink, "Between you and me, folks, I hope that it won't be the last time that he'll visit my dressing-room. We'd like an act like him over in the States. So stay right where you are—because here he is— your old friend and my pal—Clarkson Rose."

Sophie Tucker stood on the stage whilst I made my entrance and led the applause. During the *ad lib* of my song she walked to the proscenium, stood there for a second, and then shouted, "Go to it, Clarkson. Wham 'em!" After which she blew me a kiss and vanished.

It was a wonderful thing for me. Had not their own idol practically ordered them to enjoy my act? To make things even better, at the end, when I came through the tabs, Sophie came through with me, with that huge, loving expansive smile of triumph on her face, sort of "there-wasn't-I-right?"

When Norah Bayes made her first appearance at the London Coliseum I was on the programme.

I got to know her very well, and used to take refreshment in her dressing-room where she was always attended by her faithful negress dresser. One of the photographs I treasure in my collection is a portrait of Norah Bayes on which she has written, "To Clarkson Rose, from your loving son, Norah Bayes."

This was a humorous comment on the fact that, in discussing the act which she did on her first appearance in this country, which was not very successful, I told her that I was sure she had made a mistake in wearing a blonde wig. "You have glorious and abundant grey hair," I said, "it does not age you, but gives you dignity. A yellow wig makes it look as though you are trying to hide something."

When she performed at the London Palladium she discarded her wig, and appearing just as she was, she electrified audiences nightly. They refused to let her go, and she sang song after song.

Norah Bayes had dynamic personality—and tremendous authority. When she sang of Kentucky, you could see the grass and corn and new-mown hay.

When that great American duo, Burns and Allen, made their first appearance in this country at Brighton Hippodrome, I was on the programme. Val Parnell telephoned me and said, "Do me a favour, ' Clarkie ', watch the Burns and Allen act through, then get together with them and Anglicise any of their Americanisms that aren't understood."

I watched their act on the Monday and it did not go over too well. But it was obvious that the sweet dizziness of Gracie Allen had only to be exploited properly from a British angle, for the act to be a furore. I made one or two suggestions, for which Burns and Allen were grateful, and soon the act went on to its predestined success.

In 1928 I did not appear in my own show "Twinkle" for the summer season. I stayed upon the music-halls to cash in on the cachet of my Royal Command. How I missed the seaside!

Olive was running "Twinkle" for me at Bognor, and whenever I could, from whatever town I was playing, I slipped down to Bognor. I even managed it from Ayr, where I played a week for the delightful Popplewells.

Lily Morris and I had a most successful week at Ayr, and considering that our acts were typical London variety turns, and quite different from the humour that Scotland is supposed to like, we did very well at the Gaiety Theatre.

Lily Morris, with her songs *Don't have any more, Mrs. Moore,* and *Only a Working Man,* was of course definitely Cockney. But her husband, Archie McDougal, was very much on his native heath.

I played a number of weeks with José Collins, who was touring her own variety combination round the music-halls. José Collins was a woman of strong likes and dislikes, and I was fortunate to be one of her likes.

I found her splendid to work with and for. She was one of those lovely persons who do not count the cost of friend-ship and was quite without 'side'.

There was something of the team spirit of a summer show in this combination. In José Collins's own act were Kingsley Lark and "Buckie" Morris at the piano. Jimmy Hunter compered the bill. José's husband then, Lord Robert Innes Kerr, was also on tour with us.

In my last season at Westcliff-on-Sea I met Archie Pitt. At this time he was an important man in the theatrical world, he had many revues on tour—in his production, "Mr. Tower of London", he gave Gracie Fields her first chance, and he was the power behind the gun that shot her to stardom.

A modern manager, Mr. Archie Pitt observed many of the old-world courtesies. If he went to a show and saw an artiste that he would like to book, he would not com-municate with the artiste, as so many managers do to-day, until he had first contacted the artiste's employer. In several instances he booked artistes from "Twinkle", and always paid me this courtesy.

In management he had high ideals. He studied the welfare of his people quite outside the ordinary managerial spheres. He had a saving scheme for his companies, in which he encouraged thrift, and made tangible contri-butions to that thrift himself. His companies were run with discipline and law and order that was refreshing.

Alas, many of his ideals and schemes were shattered by the artistes themselves. Many managers have tried to run their companies as a family. There is much to be said for and against it, but the fecklessness of people in our profession makes it difficult.

Archie Pitt is dead now, and his name in many places is forgotten. But the world of entertainment can be grateful to him, not only because he discovered, trained and exploited the genius of Grace Fields, but also because of his gentleness and his general desire to play his part in show business in the highest possible manner.

In 1929 John Hart engaged me to play the title role in the "Queen of Hearts" pantomime at the Princes Theatre, Bristol. John Hart was a most lovable man, and one of the gentlemen of our profession. The Princes Theatre, Bristol, was an historic playhouse and a famous pantomime theatre.

From the time when, as an office boy, I had rushed down to the gallery of the Theatre Royal, Birmingham, to see George Robey give his memorable performance in the role, I had always wanted to play the Queen in "Queen of Hearts". Robey had been my boyhood idol, and I still thought him the embodiment of everything a pantomime comedian should be.

When I could not afford to go into the theatre I would glue myself to a crack in the dock doors to see him pass as he made his exit from the stage. Judge of my excitement then, when, on visiting Bristol to discuss wardrobe, I was handed one of the dresses actually worn by the great Robey himself.

Despite the protestations of the wardrobe mistress that she would make me a dress exactly like it, I begged, pleaded and cajoled, and finally persuaded the dear lady to alter Robey's dress, which was, of course, much too small for me. And I wore his dress in the pantomime.

As at the Theatre Royal, Birmingham, the Princes Theatre, Bristol, had many old customs. On the first day, the artistes met in the foyer of the theatre—dear Mrs. Shute would be present with the Bishop of Bristol and other notabilities—biscuits and champagne were served, and then the book was leisurely read through.

Another notable social function was the Peter Pan party held on Christmas night. The party had been run for years by the clergy of Bristol, prominent amongst them being Canon Norton, Canon Coles, and Jack Stancombe, who was the Actors' Church Union chaplain. Invitations were sent to everyone in the theatrical profession who was in Bristol on Christmas night.

In Fortt's Restaurant, long tables with shining white table-cloths, gleaming glass and silver were reserved for the various theatres and music-halls. There was an abundance of good food and drink, and an orchestra played during the meal, and for dancing afterwards.

There was a Christmas tree with presents for everyone and, behind all, the good companionship of those Bristol clergymen. For people in show business, away from home at the great family festival, the party was one of the loveliest ideas imaginable.

Another quaint old custom at Bristol was the New Year Church Service for Actors, held in the centuries' old Lord Mayor's Chapel in College Green. I was asked to read a Lesson, but instead of reading from Scripture I said that I would prefer to read the "Seven Ages" speech from "As You Like It".

The chaplain agreed. So when I mounted the lectern, instead of the formula "Here beginneth the first Lesson" I said, "I have taken for the lesson a famous philosophy from 'As You Like It', by William Shakespeare."

Tommy Hickson was Mr. Hart's manager at the Princes, Bristol. His good fellowship to all behind stage and in front was remarkable, and his tact was charming. His was an old and understanding head on young shoulders and great personal popularity did not spoil him.

I know what he must have felt when the Princes Theatre, Bristol, was destroyed in an air raid. Although he is now managing the old Theatre Royal, Bristol—one of this country's historic and traditional playhouses—as he walks past that empty gap in Park Street he must think of the old pantomime days in that lovely theatre, with its ample-sized dressing-rooms in which were large coal fires and great scuttles of coal, and where the dressers and stage-hands were quiet, dignified and courteous in the manner of old family retainers.

The cast included Athol Tier, an Australian comedian, tall and thin as a lath and very cadaverous-looking, with a lugubrious approach to his work that had its quaint moments; Eileen Fowler, who, with plenty of personality, made a hit as Principal Girl; Sheila Dexter, with a beautiful figure and graceful movements, was principal dancer; my old friend and "Twinkle" comedian, Fred Wynne, as the Knave of Hearts; Bryn Gwyn as the Joker; Jack Lennol as the King; and Olive Fox in a rather thankless Principal Boy's part.

In 1921 I had become a gramophone recording artiste, and I recorded regularly every month for Zonophone. After the Bristol pantomime I had several gramophone recording sessions to occupy me before returning to the music-halls.

When I first made records, it was by the old system of singing into a large horn. I had the interesting experience of recording all through the various changes in method up to and including the microphone and modern electric recording. I can still see Chaliapin and Sir Harry Lauder shaking their heads at the new "microphone contraption", as they called it, and saying it would not be so good. Financially and sentimentally I was sorry when my type of record was no longer required, and American ideas swept the recording market.

By this time each year I was engaged as the professional producer of the Metropolitan Police Minstrels. My old friend George Buck, then in the Press department of Scotland Yard, introduced me to this job, and I frankly admit now that I left most of the work to Olive. The Metropolitan Police Minstrels had been an institution for years, and Colonel Laurie, the Assistant Commissioner, wanted them taken out of the Minstrel groove.

I devised a show that was Minstrel in the first half, and all white in the second. What a fight I had to achieve the change, and how the old diehards who had been Minstrels for years disapproved and obstructed.

At the time, the Victoria Palace Girls were a much-publicised dancing troupe, and I conceived the idea of the Victoria Police Girls. A slim and good-looking young policeman sang the light-comedy song, and the Victoria Police Girls were the largest members of the Force—inspectors, sergeants and "coppers"—that I could find. They were magnificently dressed and made-up, and the turn was a sensation.

Each year the dress rehearsal took place on a Sunday at the Victoria Palace and many notable people would be in the audience. On two occasions the Queen of Spain came, and Olive and I were presented to her in the box. She was kindly and gracious and introduced us to the Infanta.

One night I was driving through Hyde Park when a dishevelled woman stopped me and said, "Please give me a lift, my husband is drunk and threatening me." Without thinking of possible consequences I said "Jump in," and off we went.

Almost immediately a policeman's torch flashed me to stop. "Don't you know that it's against the rules to stop and pick up a woman in Hyde Park?" said the "copper".

The woman jumped out of the car and dashed off into the night. Then it dawned on me that I was being accused of accosting a lady and 'picking her up' in Hyde Park.

At Marlborough Street, P.C. Wooster, one of my chief stalwarts in the Minstrel Troupe, roared with laughter when he heard the story, and a telephone call to George Buck put everything right. I never abused it, but contact with the police was useful in more ways than one.

It was a thrill, that summer, to return to the Isle of Wight where "Twinkle" had been born. I arranged with Terry Wood to present the show at Shanklin.

Terry Wood and I were great personal friends, and I found him splendid to work with. He was always on the

go, and in many ways had an able assistant in his wife, the
virile Sadie.

My cast included Winnie Goodwin, an excellent all-
round comedienne; her husband, Adrian Ross; Kathleen
Ellis, a sound hard-working soubrette; Peter Sinclair, now
the successful radio and music-hall comedian, but then a
baritone; Babs Mason; Leslie Cochran; an excellent
quartette of Rosebuds; myself—and an innovation for
Shanklin, an orchestra in the pit.

"Twinkle" did magnificent business and was a success
from the opening night, but I was not entirely satisfied
with it. Our opposition at my old friend Powis Pinder's
Summer Theatre included, playing his first season on the
Isle of Wight, the redoubtable Arthur Askey. "Twinkle"
stayed at Shanklin for three seasons before going to
Australia for a year, and then returned for the 1934
season.

I lived at the picturesque "Crab Inn" in the old village,
and was fortunate to have for my landlord Pete Marsh.
When the others had gone to bed, Pete and I would sit
pleasantly reminiscing until the small hours. His lounge
must have annoyed other theatrical visitors, for the only
pictures were photographs of myself and Olive in almost
every character that we had ever played.

That Christmas I played the Baroness in "Cinderella",
for John Hart, at the Opera House, Manchester. At the
Palace Theatre, Manchester, that year, Fay Compton
was making her first appearance as Principal Boy, and
the cast also included an act, the Hearne Duo. Young
Richard Hearne was appearing with his father, but his
work caught Fay Compton's eye, she introduced him to
several contacts in London, and from then he never looked
back.

Two pleasant events from this Manchester season
stand out in my memory. Fay Compton and I paid
a visit to Belle Vue Circus to christen two lion cubs.
One was to be called Fay and the other Clarkson. But
the mother was adamant that day, and refused to let

M

them out of her sight, and we left without performing the ceremony.

I appeared, with Fred Conquest, at the Free Trade Hall for a Charity Concert, and there met the idol of my youth, George Robey. Robey insisted that Fred Conquest and I should be photographed with him, and when the lights flashed out, it was indeed a great moment for me when I knew that I had had the honour of being photographed with the great George Robey.

Helen Fischer was producing the English Ballet in our pantomime, for Espinosa. She was born to dance and to teach dancing, and threw herself into everything with whole-hearted enthusiasm.

My secretary was taken ill, and Helen astounded me by proving that she was also a speedy stenographer. She did my secretarial work for a time, and this led to an association in which she was the producer of the Four Clarkson Rosebuds. Helen Fischer devised miniature ballets for the Rosebuds which, to this day, I have never seen equalled.

Her active association with me continued until the war broke out. It was useless to try to persuade her that the work she was doing was valuable work. She went back to her home at Camberley and threw herself into V.A.D. nursing, air-raid wardens' work, fire-watching and the like. Helen Fischer still pays us periodical visits, and on them always reinfuses her personality and ideas into the Rosebuds. She is a unique person judged by any standards.

The following Christmas I played the chief ugly sister in "Cinderella" at the Grand Theatre, Leeds. This was for John Hart's partner, J. E. B. Beaumont. Mr. Beaumont was another old-style manager, tall, courtly and gentle. His son, Jack Beaumont, was manager of the theatre, so it was very much a pleasant family affair.

The Grand Theatre, Leeds, is recognised as the County Theatre of Yorkshire. It is redolent of the old-fashioned theatre atmosphere and intimacy.

I was fortunate enough to achieve a big personal success; the other ugly sister, Fred Hastings, accompanied
me everywhere; Eileen Fowler was a delightful "Cinders",
and another success was the cheerful and cherubic
Babette O'Deal.

CHAPTER FIFTEEN

IN February, 1933, Olive Fox, May Goring Thomas, Bernardi, Hastings Mann, Ernest Arnley, Betty Kent, Helen Fischer, Geoffrey James, and myself—the nucleus of a "Twinkle" show—embarked on the *Strathaird* at Tilbury. "Twinkle" had been booked by the Williamson firm for a tour of Australia. Rosebuds and extras were to be chosen from Australian artistes when we arrived.

Olive had known the Trocadero Restaurant in London from the days when old Joe Lyons used to walk round greeting his guests and giving any children present a box of chocolates. From the time that I was able to afford it, the Trocadero grillroom had been a weekly meeting-place for us and our friends. The night before our departure the whole company, and many friends and relations, gathered for a farewell party at the Trocadero.

I chose the menu, and with a gourmet's pride I give it here: Colchester oysters or caviare; turtle soup with sherry; fillets of Dover sole Velasquez; suprême of chicken Trocadero, stuffed with foie gras; pêche Melba and lemon soufflé with Devonshire cream; angels on horseback or canape of mushrooms. With this meal went dry Mancilla Sherry, Chablis, Hock, and various liqueurs.

The guest of honour was Professor Albert Fox of the Guildhall School of Music, Olive's father.

After the meal we all went to the Comedy Theatre to see the revue "Razzle". Then some of us went back to the Trocadero for supper, and to watch a Cochran cabaret.

The *Strathaird* then, as it is now, was a lovely ship. My company were excellent 'mixers', and within a couple of days the ship was ours. I used to have two swims a day, one in the first-class, in which section Williamson's had put Olive and I, and one in the tourists' pool, in which class the company had excellent accommodation.

Our first stop was at Marseilles. We saw an excellent

revue at the Opera House, and a variety bill at the Alcazar Music Hall, on which every act seemed to sing songs of the same tempo. The male members of the cast and myself, as spectators only, also visited some of the less reputable places, including the notorious Madame Arlene's.

"Madame Arlene" was a big, cheerful-looking woman. After parading a number of girls before us, she insisted that we saw her "famous film", so down into the basement we went. It was all so obvious and so stupid that I roared with laughter, so much so that "Madame" thought that there was something wrong with my mentality.

We passed through the Mediterranean in glorious weather, tied up for a short time at Port Said, then off we went, down the Suez Canal. At Port Soudan I stood on the quayside and talked to one or two of the Soudanese police. For something to say, I asked one of them if he remembered Kitchener.

His eyes lit up, a broad grin spread across the large ebony mouth, he mumbled something that I did not understand, and turned to a grizzled-looking old man standing near him, who was not in uniform. This old man, wreathed in even larger smiles, and showing slightly yellower teeth, in comparatively good English launched into a tremendous reminiscence of Kitchener—a reminiscence touched with a reverence that it was pleasant to hear.

Aden, parched and shrivelled, I thought the dreariest and most unwholesome place I had ever seen. Yet there was a strange fascination about it, and I was intrigued by the little carts running about the streets from which fresh water was sold.

Olive, Hastings Mann, Ernie Arnley, Betty Kent and myself went by car to King Solomon's Wells—a tremendous engineering feat with such an air of tragedy about it, waiting for the water that never seems to come when it is wanted. The natives told us that we were not far from the site of the Garden of Eden. I have always pictured the

Garden of Eden as a far more beautiful place than this fœtid and dried-up spot.

The voyage continued, and I who love the sun did not listen to the advice of experienced travellers, but lay basking in the sunshine and alternatively popping into the swimming pool. "I feel fine," I used to tell Dr. Roberts, when he indicated in very non-medical language what he thought of me, "and look what a wonderful colour I am."

Starting with a slight irritation which I laughed at and scratched, and ending with excruciating agony, I got the most appalling blisters on my back, chest and abdomen. In the Red Sea, "Twinkle" gave a concert to the whole ship. The misery I suffered, getting on a stiff dress shirt over the burns, and performing, was a salutary lesson in behaviour in the future in such climates.

We arrived at Colombo one Sunday afternoon. With the handsome Galle Face Hotel glittering in the sun, it looked perfect. Natives rushed on board and offered to copy the dresses worn by the ladies, and the men's suits, in silks, in a few hours.

The Mount Lavinia Hotel was a modern place, right on the beach. The bathing-place was netted off from sharks, but there was an uncanny feeling that the natives, always casual, might have left one or two holes unrepaired and a shark could get in.

As I was swimming placidly something rushed past me which was, or so I imagined, a shark. I grabbed at a rock and attempted to climb on to it. This was a fatal mistake. The rock was spiky and sticky in a sinister sort of way, almost as though it was biting, attacking and tearing at one. I was glad to get back into the sea and wash the blood away.

With the technique of monkeys natives ran up coconut trees, brought us down coconuts, and gave us what was the coolest drink that we had had for some time. We had an excellent dinner in the Galle Face at night, with many strange dishes that intrigued us.

Ernie Arnley and I went for a ride in a rickshaw. We

had not gone far before the rickshaw man asked us if we wanted to see any of the 'naughty' places. When we indicated that we did, he took us to what looked like a small settlement with families or clans of people, and the most revolting women I have ever seen dancing round in circles.

There was certainly nothing 'naughty' about it, unless long sagging breasts flopping about are supposed to be 'naughty'.

At Bombay we were inoculated. On my arm this brought up a scab as big as a plum, which lasted for the rest of the voyage and a while after.

India has a charm and fascination all its own for many people. Not for me. I was disgusted by the dreadful ceremonies and rites that take place, and the commercialising of revolting disease.

One man followed me from the harbour, right up to the back of the hotel, with a carriage on which there was an object covered with a cloth. He kept asking me to pay him and lift the cloth. I vehemently refused. When one of my party paid him something, with great glee he lifted the cloth and disclosed a distorted piece of humanity, deformed in every way and eaten up with sores.

I am no prude, but the streets of native prostitutes appalled me. To see these women on their doorsteps, or seated in their porches, in varying stages of dress and undress, hawking their flesh and openly vaunting their prostitution, in the old-fashioned phrase, "gave me the willies."

At the Taj Mahal the waiter told us that we could have bottled Bass, and we were delighted, for it was something that we hadn't had for a long time. It was three shillings a bottle—a lot of money in those days—warm, and looked like porridge. We 'kidded' ourselves that we liked it.

On the way back to the ship a native persuaded us to see a fight between a snake and a mongoose. This episode, which earns the natives a lot of money, always ends in a victory for the mongoose.

It was a relief to me to get back to the clean decks and polished brass of the *Strathaird*, and to eat a meal from properly washed plates and dishes, using well-cleaned cutlery.

On the long journey from Bombay to Fremantle I learned a lot about the attitude of mind of the "Pukka Sahibs" and "high-up Wallahs", to whom a P. & O. ship is a second home. One chap was quite amusing.

He was a grizzled man with the sun-parched skin that is the heritage of years out East. He used to drink at least eight pink gins before lunch. At lunch he would have a bottle of red or white wine, followed by a couple of brandies. Before dinner he was back on the pink gins, which came up in a steady procession. At dinner he would have wine again, and then, in the Winter Garden, he would settle down to a steady two or three hours of Scotch-and-sodas. At half-past ten at night he would become a little talkative.

I gathered that his whole life had been spent soldiering, and he had the reputation of being a very fine fellow. He was in an important administrative post at the time. How he held this, and could have any judgment at all, I do not know.

Sir William Firth was on the ship. He obviously intended to forget all about steel until he landed in Australia, and was a grand and hospitable companion to us.

At Fremantle an emissary from the Williamson firm met us, and told us that we had to travel overland by train the following day, instead of going round to Sydney in the ship, as plans were changed, and we were to open at Melbourne.

He showed us the pretty town of Perth with its glorious Swan River. And we saw the old Cremorne Theatre, home at one time of Jack Waller and his concert-party, long before the days of "No, No Nanette".

At the Savoy Hotel, Perth, instructions were given us for our trip across the Continent. Just as we were on our way back to the ship to collect the baggage, a message came through that we were to stay on the ship and adhere to our original plan of opening at Sydney.

I was to learn that this was typical of Australian show business. Everything was haphazard and casual, and no one seemed to worry about the expenditure of money through alterations of plans from time to time.

After a very bumpy voyage round from Fremantle we stopped at Adelaide. It is a really beautiful city, and its King William Street ranks for me with Princes Street, Edinburgh, as one of the finest thoroughfares in the world.

The charm of Australian beaches is very over-rated. But the bathing at Adelaide's Glenelg I really enjoyed. Mrs. Dixon—sister of that excellent Principal Boy, Violet Field—and her husband gave us fine hospitality in the atmosphere of an English home.

At Melbourne we presented our credentials to the Williamson office. Melbourne is one of the loveliest cities in the world, and has about it an air of breeding and background. One is impressed with the definite character of Melbourne, and Menzies's Hotel really makes one think of London.

In a music-hall we saw replicas of many acts and sketches that were the property of British performers. We knew that much of the material was from current London shows.

For some reason the taking of other people's material has never been looked upon with the same seriousness as other forms of thieving. If a burglar comes into your house and takes your silver, he is a thief, the law is on your side, and you get redress. But when it comes to material, all sorts of complications ensue, and even respectable artistes have been known to 'pinch' other people's property in this direction.

At Sydney the Australian sun was absent, and the place resembled nothing so much as Manchester. I take off my hat to the Commonwealth publicity organisation. No sooner had we arrived before the Press were on the ship, photographers were at work, and we were whisked off to a broadcasting studio to talk to Australia about ourselves, our work and our show.

The Williamson organisation was known throughout Australia as "the Firm", and had for years represented all that was best in show business. In many ways I do not think I have seen a better organisation. Their stores, their wardrobes, and many of their theatres could teach the United Kingdom much.

It was amazing to go round the Williamson outfit with John Tait. In one department one would find a complete production of "The Maid of the Mountains", with the most expensive sets of dresses and scenery, and down to the smallest props. Then, just across the alleyway in another section, would be just as complete a production of "Hamlet" or "Macbeth". The law and order of these productions was tremendous, and in strange contrast to some of their other methods.

In England I had already met Nevin Tait. He was a gentle person, entirely suitable to handle the Williamson interests in this country. In Australia I liked John Tait immensely. He was tall, blunt, with a good sense of humour and a rather quaint prim-and-properness which appealed to me. Frank Tait was a different type—pleasant, suave, but very much on the *qui vive*.

At that time the firm were importing English and American successes. These were not always a success in Australia. But at a minute's notice they could always shut down a flop, and open the following week with a magnificent revue, a musical-comedy, or Gladys Moncrieff in "The Maid of the Mountains", which they often revived.

Olive and I stayed at the Australia Hotel, recognised as the leading hotel in Sydney. Personally, however, I always had a preference for Usher's.

After many more preliminary difficulties than one would have expected, "Twinkle" made its début in Australia, at the Theatre Royal, Sydney. Dante, the famous illusionist, had been put into the theatre as a stop-gap, and as often happens with shows in such circumstances, had hit the public taste and was playing to colossal business. It was unfortunate that we had to displace him, but when, on his final Friday, Olive and I watched his show from a box, he gave us a magnificent introduction and build-up to the Sydney audience.

Our first night was an unqualified success. It was not that we were offering Australia a new form of entertainment, for Australia can almost be called "the home of resident shows". Our pattern, individuality and intimacy, however, were something new to Australian audiences.

Olive Fox was the outstanding success of the show. The *Sydney Bulletin* described her as the greatest British comedienne seen in Australia since Marie Lloyd.

A delightful unrehearsed incident marked the close of her act. Geoffrey James, who was Olive's son, was our youthful compere. Olive had finished her act with Hastings Mann at the piano, the tabs had closed, and Geoffrey went forward to announce the next item.

The Theatre Royal audience would have none of this. I had always trained him never to let an audience master him, but young and inexperienced, the noisy and insistent demand was something he had never had to face. In vain he tried to get on with his announcement. They kept on shouting, "We want Olive Fox."

Finally his nerve collapsed and, turning in a very despairing way to the wings, he entirely forgot his professional status and called out, "Mother!"

Olive by this time had gone to her dressing-room, which was through some double doors and quite a distance from the stage. She had removed her dress and was in a dressing-gown tidying her make-up with a grease cloth. The stage-hands fetched her, and she came on to the stage just as she was, and her reception was deafening.

Olive tried to pull Geoffrey forward, but the audience would have none of him. Hastings Mann had to jump down over the footlights, go to the piano in the orchestra pit, and play some more songs for Olive.

After our Sydney season, our next place was Brisbane. We travelled in compartments in which a bed lets down at night, and which, except for slight confinement of space, is comfortable.

On this route meals are not eaten on the train. The porter takes orders for meals at the next stop, and as the train pulls into the station one walks into a large airy restaurant pavilion carrying a numbered ticket, and everything ordered is soon on the table. The whole proceeding does not take half an hour, and is splendidly organised.

Brisbane had a pleasant, intimate air about it, and the people were exceptionally friendly. "Twinkle" was an immediate success at His Majesty's Theatre, and we settled down to a happy run.

The Australian stage-folk are a grand lot of people. When I was out there, their star performer was Gus Bluett, a first-class comedian in musical-comedy parts created in London by such other star comedians as Leslie Henson and W. H. Berry.

The only artiste I saw there with claims to originality was Roy Rene, known throughout the Commonwealth as "Mo". His outrageous make-up consisted of a very pale face on which a crude beard was painted, and rather sloppy clothes. He had great humour with a definite Rabelasian touch, a remarkably quick wit, and a complete disregard for the conventions.

"Mo" was a natural comedian, with a technique that was refreshing.

He was so definitely individual that it is difficult to liken him to any performer in this country. He had a touch of Bud Flanagan, without Bud's pathos, and at his best, a flash of George Robey.

He was crude and could be dirty. But there was a guileless innocence in his handling of questionable gags that softened them.

Jim Gerald was a great Australian favourite. By English standards he could be described as "just another good revue comedian". He came to London in an ill-fated show at the Garrick Theatre.

George Wallis had moments of greatness in his shows. Gladys Moncrieff had an electric quality in her voice which made it compelling, and it was easy to see why she had reigned supreme as the queen of Australian musical shows. Dorothy Brunton was a capable actress.

Albert Whelan came from Australia long years ago and, hitting London as a young man, immediately became a star. His suave polish, and the gentle under-statement of his work, is a delight to watch.

When I first saw Madge Elliot in "Lady Luck" I thought her one of the loveliest girls I had ever seen. The lissom grace of her tall figure was exquisite, and despite her height, her dancing was sheer poetic rhythm. She and Cyril Ritchard left Australia early on, and have achieved great heights in musical comedy, revue, and the legitimate theatre.

Our own Sylvia Welling arrived in Australia when we were there, to star in "Music in the Air". She was indeed "the rage", and could have stayed in Australia as long as she liked.

CHAPTER SIXTEEN

AUSTRALIANS will come miles from outlandish places to see a live show. They are lavish with their gifts, and one gentleman so liked "Twinkle" that he came back from the Bush the following week-end with a whole sheep, which he wanted to hand up over the footlights.

The success of "Twinkle" was so great in Brisbane that it seemed we would stay indefinitely. Then the Taits made one of their sudden switches, and we were booked to go to New Zealand. We all wanted to see New Zealand, but the nearest we got to it was having our passage booked, for there was another switch.

The Ernest C. Rolls revue at the Princes Theatre, Melbourne, had finished, and the Taits wanted "Twinkle" to be the nucleus of another big production. At this time Rolls had established himself as the Cochran of Australia. The new revue, "Tout Paris", was to be his reply to the big film musicals.

"Twinkle" cast were the principals of the show, augmented by the excellent double-act, Ambrose Barker and Peggy Wynne; Jack and Sylvia Kellaway, who had returned to Australia from "Casanova" at the London Coliseum; and Pat Nelson, a striking American blonde, who startled all Melbourne by walking down the main street wearing slacks—something that had not been seen in Australia before.

The dress rehearsal of "Tout Paris" started on a Friday morning at ten o'clock, and went right through until half-past ten on the Saturday morning. The show was lavish to a degree, and the finale to the first half, "The Birth of Melody", was one of the most beautiful production scenes I have ever seen.

"Tout Paris" was an outstanding success and ran for eleven weeks in Melbourne. "Twinkle" cast fitted naturally into this gigantic show of one hundred and fifty people, and the social side of life was delightful.

The Australian minister Roger Casey's mother, a grand hostess who was known to everyone as "Lady" Casey, was particularly kind and hospitable to us. She even cabled to Weinberg's for cigarettes because some of the Australian brands did not suit my palate.

It was a delightful experience to leave the heat of Melbourne for the mountains at Healsville, snowy and wintry although in bright sunshine. We went to Madame Melba's house at Lillidale, and the old gardener who showed us round allowed us to peep into the bedroom, which, he told us, was exactly the same as when the famous prima donna was alive.

From Melbourne "Tout Paris" went to the Theatre Royal, Adelaide, where it was again a success. A somewhat smaller edition was devised, which went first to Brisbane— where the nakedness came in for criticism from the clergy —and then to the delightful Criterion Theatre, Sydney.

Olive and I had a flat in Darlinghurst, overlooking the harbour. To show how far Australia was ahead of the Old Country in 1933, it is interesting to note that this beautiful modern furnished flat, with refrigerator, radio and various other electric gadgets, was only two guineas a week.

We were also fortunate in having the services of an excellent dresser-cum-housekeeper called Jenner. She had dressed many famous people, knew all their faults and virtues, and was no respecter of persons.

When "Tout Paris" was at the Criterion Theatre, Sydney, I wrote a new sketch which visualised the arrival of various people in Hades, one of whom was Hitler. I played His Satanic Majesty, and Bernardi, in an excellent make-up, was Hitler. In the course of the sketch, when I allotted him his duties, he said, "Which way do I go?" My answer was, "Turn to the right, straight through the Polish Corridor."

This brought a vehement protest from the German

Consulate, and I had a visit from a red-faced very guttural gentleman, who completely lost control of himself and threatened me with all sorts of dire penalties unless I cut it out. The management were perturbed and were quite prepared for the sketch to be deleted. But I refused, and in this I was backed up by producer Ernest C. Rolls.

Walking up Darlinghurst one morning and turning into Macleay Street, I met Ada Reeve. In these days of film stars and radio personalities, and all the publicity and adulation that goes with them, idols are made overnight and sometimes topple in a few weeks. Ada Reeve was of a different and sturdier generation.

After many years of success in England she became an idol in Australia. I have yet to see a finer comedienne, and every person whose knowledge and experience enables them to recall former pantomimes agrees that she was the finest Aladdin ever known.

I fell in love with her when I was a clerk in Birmingham, and I used to send her a sixpenny postal order every week to buy herself some chocolates. I got replies and photographs, and I was happy. I would haunt the theatre just to watch her go in and out of the stage door, and I could sing now every word of her songs in that production of "Aladdin", in which Harry Tate played Abanazar.

When I was appearing with Shirley Kellogg in "Happy Hours" I went one Sunday night to a party at Harry Norris's house at West Hampstead. I was introduced to a lady wearing rather thick-lensed glasses—it was Ada Reeve.

"Clarkson Rose," she said, with that unforgettable trill in her voice. "How strange I've just told my manager, Tommy Holt, to book you up. I'm taking 'Spangles' out to Australia, and I want you to play the George Clarke part."

I started to tell her about the office-boy correspondence. With a toss of her head and in charming staccato tone she said, "I can tell you all about it. He was a most faithful admirer. Used to send me postal orders. I've

E FINAL CURTAIN OF THE LAST PANTOMIME AT THE LONDON LYCEUM. THE
THOR AS "QUEEN OF HEARTS" MAKING THE FINAL SPEECH. In the background
ARE DAVE AND JOE O'GORMAN, BERNARD ANSELL, AND ANNE LESLIE

SIX FAMOUS DAMES.   DENNIS LAWES, SHAUN GLENVILLE, THE AUTHOR, DOUGLAS BY
SONNIE HALE, AND BOBBY HOWES

JANICE ADAIR, THE AUTHOR, AND JOYCE GIFFORD WHEN THEY APPEARED IN " J
AND THE BEANSTALK " AT THE KING'S THEATRE, HAMMERSMITH, IN 1948

still got 'em." When she found that I was the person, she said, "That settles it. You simply must come to Australia." But at the time that was impossible, for I could not get out of various contracts.

Now I had met her again, in Darlinghurst. I invited her to see the show. When she appeared in the box that night she got a great reception. We could do with a few more Ada Reeve's to-day. She was a star in whatever line of business she undertook—variety, musical comedy, pantomime. Now, in her old age, she is appearing in the legitimate theatre, and giving every character that she plays the sure, deft touch of the born actress.

Just before Christmas Ernest Rolls asked us to remain for a pantomime. But I was really homesick, longing for a shower of gentle English rain—or even a London fog—and we refused.

Rolls did not give up easily, and finally brought up the Taits, who made a most attractive offer to us to remain in Australia for another two years, with a guaranteed run of forty weeks a year, which is excellent for Australia, taking into account the time required for long journeys and rehearsals.

The snag was that I had given my word to Terry Wood to return and play the 1934 season for him on Shanklin Pier. No contract had been issued and no details arranged—it was just a question of our word. I cabled Terry Wood, told him the position, and that I was prepared to return if he wished it. The reply was that he did so wish. So Olive and I started to say our good-byes, and soon we were on the *Strathaird* on our way home.

Australian food always looks very nice, but never tastes as good as it looks. Salads and fruit look wonderful, but I am told by a world-famous scientist that the Australian soil does not give the fruit and vegetables the same flavour or nutriment value as English soil. It is the same with the meat, and I had commented on this to various people.

N

At a wonderful party which "Lady" Casey gave us when the ship called at Melbourne on the way home, there was a most luscious-looking saddle of lamb. The dear old soul had got this lamb from a special breeding farm, and fed and looked after it for several months. It was perfect in every way—very different from the usual Australian meat. "Lady" Casey said, "I have heard so much from 'Clarkie' about Australian mutton in comparison with his Southdown mutton, that I was determined to show him what we could do. From the first moment he made remarks about our meat I decided to give him this surprise."

At every port of call in Australia on our way home our cabins were full of flowers—flowers from friends, flowers from the Williamson management, and although I did not work under his management there, flowers from Sir Benjamin Fuller.

A wonderful feeling of relaxation came over me on the ship going home, and I did nothing but rest until we got to Colombo. We were taken to Kandy by one of the most irresponsible drivers I have ever known, and who appeared to be quite oblivious to ravines and precipices.

The Holy Elephants did not look different to me from any other elephants, and not nearly so well groomed as those I used to ride on in Wombwell's Circus.

We lined up with a lot of other visitors and natives, including some crippled and infirm, to see the Buddha's Tooth. A wily priest spotted us, and we were soon taken out of the queue.

After we had seen the exhibition he led us through to a private room, and wrote out a verse on a palm leaf for each of us. He was obviously an educated man, but I should think a wily one, for when I asked him what we owed for all this, he shrugged his shoulders, went to a little drawer and opened it, and showed us that it was full of notes of every description and value from many countries. I duly added mine.

When we got to Suez we hired cars to drive us across

the Libyan Desert to Cairo. This was an exciting experience because we ran into a sand-storm.

The sun was going down as we approached Cairo. The many colours of the various buildings of this ancient Egyptian capital seemed reflected in a million shades of dancing light.

We thought that we were sensing the atmosphere of the mysterious East and the mighty Pharaohs when, on an ancient wall, we saw a poster of the Ezibekieh Theatre advertising A. C. Astor the ventriloquist, and the double-act Kimberley and Page. Somehow we all felt relief that we were in contact with our own profession.

The theatre manager's office was a sumptuous apartment, rather like the rest-room in a Turkish bath. It would not have surprised me to see beautiful Eastern harem girls walk in.

At Shepheard's, the outstanding feature of the meal was the largest tray of hors d'œuvre that I have ever seen in my life. It contained such delicacies as whole quails in aspic, and the special part of a frog that was very toothsome.

The ladies' gauntlets, thousands of years old, in Tutankhamen's Tomb, arrested my attention. And I was intrigued with the wig block used by one of the Pharaohs that was in every particular like one from Gustave's in Long Acre, to-day.

There used to be a song, *I wonder what the old Sphinx thinks*. Our guide to this enormous piece of masonry had no time for philosophical reflections, his outlook was completely commercial, and he wanted to do his job properly and get it over as quickly as possible.

When Olive corrected him on some detail in his story of the Pyramids, he merely shrugged his shoulders, went back to his formula, adding the piece that he had previously omitted. We were, of course, on camels.

My camel turned very nasty and went for us when I was dismounting. It rejoiced in the name of Agnes, and had a crafty look, like Claude Dampier in a temper. Not that I can imagine Claude in a temper.

The Citadel was a wonderful building. When the architect had completed the roof, the Caliph for whom he was working had his eyes put out so that he could never devise a similar roof for any other person.

The train to Port Said was hot and dirty. But on it a wonderful meal was served. Port Said is not my idea of an ideal watering-place. Yet it seemed a veritable spa after the fœtid atmosphere of Cairo.

Despite the fact that I had a large carbuncle on my toe which had been lanced, I had to remove both my shoes before we could enter the mosque. The old boy at the door was not prepared to let me keep one shoe on, the one on my bandaged foot.

The 'dives' cater for every depraved appetite. The 'dirty' postcards are just primitive muck unrelieved by any flash of wit.

Getting back on the *Strathaird* was like opening a window and letting a draught of clean, fresh air into a hot, stale room. At Marseilles, Ernie Arnley developed ear trouble, so we decided to travel by the Blue Train overland, taking him with us. We had a glimpse of Paris, and almost immediately we were at Calais, and on the packet homeward bound.

Many people have rhapsodised about their feelings when they first sighted the White Cliffs of Dover coming home. Although there was a nasty wet mist around Dover, and it was raining heavily, the fact remains that I stood on the deck, oblivious to the elements, and I just cannot explain the suppressed excitement that tingled all over me as we sailed into the harbour.

As the train took us to Victoria it was dark, and it seemed wonderful to see the lights of the suburbs. There was a little fog about, and I have never welcomed fog with such joy. For was it not a London fog?

At Victoria old friends met us, including the ever-faithful George Thomas and my secretary, Millie Solomon. In our little house at Golders Green we were welcomed by our good old Cockney housekeeper, Peggy, with,

"There now, you're nearly an hour late. The dinner will be spoilt. I've got Mr. Rose some braised leeks, knowing his weakness for them, and they'll be in rags."

Not poetic, perhaps, but intrinsically a fine welcome home.

CHAPTER SEVENTEEN

I WAS eager to get back to work. I had not been back two days when Val Parnell put me into the Palladium, and just to make sure that I was getting back into harness, Miss Leddington of the Syndicate Theatres asked me to play at the Metropolitan the same week.

One of my brand-new comedy songs was a burlesque of a Principal Boy of the 'nineties in which I wore large padded tights. The times of my performance at the Palladium and the Met. were cut so fine there was no time for me to remove these tights.

Any evening I could be seen emerging from the Palladium stage door with a towel around my head and a dressing-gown over my tights, laboriously getting into a taxi whilst my dresser saw that I did not bump the padding out of shape. It was touch and go whether I made it each night.

There are always vintage years in shows like "Twinkle", and 1934 was one of them. The cast included Ernest Arnley, Michael Cole, Milton Stanley, Cicely Compton, Hastings Mann, Diana Grafton, Madge Villiers, Olive Fox, four outstanding Rosebuds, and myself.

Murray King and theatrical Eastbourne were almost synonymous. What an amazing man he is! Ask him his age, and he'll reply, "God knows." His bald pate, twinkling eyes and Peter Pan outlook, plus a great sense of humour, make him a composite of W. C. Fields, Micawber and Grock. Whatever your mood, you always feel better after meeting him.

He has been identified with Eastbourne pantomimes for countless years, and ranked one of the best 'dames' in our profession. He will laughingly tell you that no one has ever done more farewell performances than himself.

We commenced our 1934 "Twinkle" at the Devonshire Park Theatre, Eastbourne, for Murray King. It was here that the foundations were laid for what was to be the long association of "Twinkle" with Eastbourne. Murray King's enthusiasm for "Twinkle" could not have been greater had it been his own show.

The tour that followed extended as far north as Darlington, and as far south as Portsmouth. Then we returned to Shanklin Pier to keep our promise to Terry Wood.

Our opposition, Powis Pinder's "Sunshine", had an enormously powerful cast, including Arthur Askey, Webster Booth, Rupert Rogers and Mario de Pietro. But "Twinkle" was outstandingly successful, and indeed, to use the theatrical expression, "cleaned up" on the island.

During that season we paid the last of many visits to Parkhurst Prison. The Governor and Major Froggatt demurred about my taking my Rosebuds. They thought that bare legs and sex appeal might be bad for the men. But I was adamant, and they gave in.

On this last visit, as we passed the Borstal Institution, many faces were pressed against the windows and hands beckoned us through the bars. I asked Mr. Clayton, the Governor, if we could give them a show, and he replied that there were no facilities, not even a piano.

"Never mind about that. We'll do them a show without a piano," I said. The boys were herded into a corner of a large room, a space was cleared, and without any musical accompaniment we gave them an hour's entertainment.

At the finish it was almost as though they were going to mob us. The atmosphere was full of the odour that clings to all prisons, and the smell of hot bodies.

"Twinkle" was proud of its Parkhurst record. Wilfred Macartney, in his book *Walls have Mouths*, writes: "I think it was in 1932 that we experienced our first professional party. Clarkson Rose and Olive Fox were appearing at one of the seaside resorts, and Froggatt asked them to give us a performance. I shall never forget it. To listen, after nearly five years, to a sophisticated London production! Clarkson cut none of his stuff. He abolished the vile prison air of restraint, and never once did he play down to us. He treated us as if we were paying stall prices in a West End house. His stuff was witty and clever, and he took no notice of the parson. Olive Fox was an experienced and polished performer. The troupe was capable and well handled. The singing was fine, and the girls smart and pretty. And did he go! He nearly lifted the roof off, and the reciprocal effect was electrical. The stimulus given to performers by an appreciative audience, by people who got the joke immediately, whose applause was a thunder-clap at the right moment—these are the dreams of every artiste, and in that prison chapel, from men whose lives had been spent behind prison walls, starved, beaten, brutalised, helpless, shapeless, these dreams were made true.

"Clarkson told us, in an address that was a model of suave, easy *savoir-faire*, slightly coloured by the effect of the terrific reception, what a wonderful audience we were. He compared us to those at Huddersfield, who sat on their hands and wagered their tripe suppers that the pro. could not make old Murgatroyd laugh. Clarkson Rose and Olive Fox came in succeeding years, missing out only the year they went to Australia. It was from Olive Fox that I first heard *Little Man You've had a Busy Day*. Whatever may be the artistic merit of that song, Olive Fox had ninety-five per cent. of Parkhurst prison with swimmy eyes, myself included."

Clayton, or "old One Lug" as they used to call him, was an ideal governor. We used to have tea with him in his private quarters and were waited on by good-conduct prisoners, and another prisoner made special cakes and things.

"What excellent servants these men are," I said to him. "And they appear to be very happy."

"Unfortunately they are."

"Why unfortunately?" I asked.

"Well," Clayton said, "when their time is up they beg and entreat me not to let them go. Two of the men who

waited on you to-day, and the man I allotted you for
stage-manager, cried like babies when they were let out a
short time ago, and assured me they would commit some
crime in order to get back. As you can see, here they are."

"Is the discipline very strict?" I asked.

"It all depends," Clayton said. "But the best discipline
I know is to tell them that 'Twinkle' is coming to Parkhurst on such and such a Sunday, and that anybody who
makes trouble will not be allowed to come to the concert.
I can assure you the good conduct a couple of weeks before
your visit is one hundred per cent."

One night during the season Owen Taylor and the
Directors of the Pier at Eastbourne paid "Twinkle" a
visit. At Daish's afterwards they put their proposition in
front of me, and it did not take me long to make up my
mind. Much to Terry Wood's regret, and despite his
definite further attractive inducements to stay, I decided
to move to Eastbourne the following summer.

Back on the music-halls in the autumn, one night at
Birmingham Hippodrome, "Mickie" Fraser, the well-
known Midlands journalist and publicity man, came
back-stage and asked me if I would be interested in
playing pantomime at the Alexandra Theatre, Birmingham. As he left he said, "By the way, we can count on
you to appear at the Rockets on Saturday night, can't
we?" and I replied, "Of course."

The Rockets are a Bohemian and Benevolent Club who
hold smoking concerts periodically at the White Horse,
Birmingham. They are a grand lot of fellows, sound,
honest-to-goodness Brummagem Boys, who do a tremendous lot of known and unknown charitable work.

There is hardly a star of repute who has not made one or
more appearances at the Rockets. If you can "get them"
at a Rockets concert, it is safe to say that you "have got
something".

The Rockets pantomime visit is noted. They will book
out the theatre, and are quite capable of altering the book
and evolving other odd stunts for that night.

Bert Brown, their secretary, was a distinct personality. He had white hair with a tinge of yellow in it, always carefully parted, and a baby-like complexion. He was dapper in dress and gallant in manner. I once called him "Birmingham's Platinum Blonde", and that appellation stuck to him until he died.

Leon Salberg was a Polish Jew, a good Jew in every sense of the word. They don't come much better than Leon Salberg in any walk of life. At the Alexandra Theatre he had made Birmingham theatrical history. No greater tribute to his remarkable personality can be given than by saying that, despite his origin, and the fact that he never mastered the English language very success-fully, he became one of the best loved of Birmingham men.

I received a note from Leon Salberg asking me to call on him at the Alexandra Theatre. He became a great personal friend of mine. At that first interview was forged not only a business link, but an affection which I shall always cherish.

When Philip Rodway left the Theatre Royal, I promised him that if ever I had an offer to return to Birmingham in pantomime, I would give him the first refusal. Just before his death I had discussed with him the possibility of my going to the Alexandra if ever I got the offer. He said, "Clarkson, as long as you don't go back to the Royal whilst I am at the Prince of Wales, I don't mind. In fact I should like you to go to the Alexandra. You will find Mr. Salberg a gentleman."

"I vant you to come into my pantomime next Christmas. I like your vork. I know you were at the Royal with Mr. Rodway, and I know your salary. I can't pay that salary, but I give you a guarantee of fourteen weeks' work," Leon Salberg said when I met him. After a minute or two I asked him the pantomime subject.

"Dick Vittington."

"I'm afraid that I'm not a very good Idle Jack."

"Don't vant you for Idle Jack. I've got the best Idle Jack in the business—Hal Bryan."

"Well the dame part in Whittington is not a very good one. It would have to be built up."

"Don't vant you for dame. I've got the best dame in the business—Jack Villiams."

"Well," I said, frankly disappointed.

"Then I can't see why you sent for me, Mr. Salberg."

"Vot about Fitzvarren?" said Leon.

"Fitzwarren!" I almost shouted. "Why, that's only a small feeding part. He's just on in the first scene, then in the shop scene, and then he doesn't appear again until the Cheapside scene at the end of the pantomime. All the other principals embark on the ship and go to Morocco, but not Fitzwarren."

"He goes to Morocco at your salary," Leon Salberg retorted in a flash.

To cut a long story short, Fitzwarren did.

Dear old David Cochran was commissioned to write the book and make Fitzwarren the principal part. It was a magnificent part that I was able to play on character comedy lines, and act as a sort of liaison between Jack Williams as the cook and Hal Bryan as Idle Jack. So successful a combination were we that several other managements made us offers as a trio for revues and pantomimes. The pantomime still ranks as one of the best the Alexandra Theatre has ever had.

That grand woman Lily Lapidus was the Principal Boy, but her role was rather overshadowed by a fine strapping girl with much glamour, Hannah Watt, in a specially written part, The Prince of Morocco.

Renee North was a dainty Alice, and with Sam Linfield's knockabout troupe to help things along, and an excellent chorus, the whole show was pantomime at its best.

This was the last pantomime at the old Alexandra Theatre, and at the sumptuous dinner which Leon Salberg always gave on the stage on the last Sunday there were many sad hearts and damp eyes. We all had to make speeches at this dinner, and I took refuge, as I did at subsequent dinners, in writing special doggerel for the occasion. This always gave Leon Salberg great joy, and copies had to be made and sent to all his managerial friends.

It fell to my lot to speak the last words that were spoken in the old Alexandra Theatre, and to write the first words that were spoken in the new.

During the last week of "Dick Whittington" Leon Salberg asked me if I would appear in the first pantomime in the new theatre, the following year. He told me that "Wee Georgie" Wood was already booked to return to the theatre and had to have the star billing. "It's a toss-up whether you or he is more popular in Birmingham," Leon said, "but that is my contract with him."

"Nonsense," I said, "if I were running a pantomime myself I should, of course, head the cast with 'Wee Georgie' Wood."

In 1935 Eastbourne stood practically alone as a seaside resort that still retained its dignity and exclusiveness. Eastbourne Pier still retained its Victorian atmosphere, and, to my mind, was all the better for it.

Owen Taylor, the manager, was rigid in his rule and his sense of the fitness of things. Under his regime the Pier was a serene and dignified pleasure parade and not, as so many piers are, a rough shambles of mediocre amusements and cheap-jack showmen.

"Twinkle", in the Music Pavilion, was following a popular show that had been there for ten years—Felgate King and Elsie Mayfair with their "Pier Revels". At the Winter Garden my friend Rex Newman had been established some years with a "Fol-de-Rols" company that, the year of our début, included the Western Brothers and Marriott Edgar.

The form and pattern of "Twinkle" was an innovation for Eastbourne, and the fact that we had an orchestra was an added novelty. The success of "Twinkle" was instantaneous.

During my association with "Teddy" Taylor he allowed me to do his Sunday Guest Night bookings. For eight years we jointly presented such famous artistes as Layton and Johnstone, Elsie and Doris Waters, Flotsam and Jetsam, Clapham and Dwyer, Flanagan and Allen, Max Miller, Sandy Powell, Muriel George and Ernest Butcher, Peter Dawson, Will Hay, Bransby Williams, Albert Whelan, "Wee Georgie" Wood, Arthur Prince, Stanley Holloway, Arthur Askey, and many others.

The business association between Owen Taylor and myself was a good one, and our personal friendship better still. To this day I miss the nights when "Teddy" would 'phone down from his office and say, "What about one for the road, after the show?"

In a letter he wrote recently he said, "I miss the little gatherings and the 'gettings together' that we used to have. One of my proudest moments was when 'Twinkle' made its début on Eastbourne Pier, and it is difficult to realise that it's over ten years ago that we had to make our hurried exit from the pier on Empire Day, 1940."

CHAPTER EIGHTEEN

JUST before the production of "Cinderella" at the New Alexandra Theatre, Birmingham, the following Christmas, I lost my voice, and did not recover it until eighteen months later. It was an agonising experience and utterly frightening.

Doctors and specialists prescribed and diagnosed, but nothing would do any good. Occasionally my voice would recover its power for a few minutes, and then seemed to muffle itself in a blanket in my chest.

I had the reputation of having one of the biggest and clearest voices in our business. Since most people of repute in the theatre world—managers, agents and artistes —all made a point of seeing the pantomime, it can readily be imagined what I went through.

The sympathy of artistes who, hearing me from the front, came round to enquire what was wrong, was the biggest torture of all to bear. The whispers that went round that my voice was gone, and that I was finished, almost drove me to suicide.

A delightful moment of relief came one afternoon when dear, kind Laddie Cliff came round to see me. My voice had been particularly bad, and when he came into my dressing-room I waited for the usual "Blimey, what's the matter with you?"

Instead, Laddie smiled, peered at me through his huge spectacles, and said, "A magnificent performance, Clarkie. That's my idea of an ugly sister." My dressing-room held an array of bottles, gargles and sprays, and Laddie blinked at them and said, "Yes—you're going through what I went through for a year. But don't worry, it'll come back."

Then I opened my heart to him. "You don't have to tell me," he said. "It's the most terrifying experience for anybody. But when one's bread and butter depends on it, it sometimes brings you mentally very near the abyss."

After that he changed the subject, and by the time he left the dressing-room the call-boy was calling beginners for the evening show. I felt calmer, went on with more confidence, my voice was slightly better that night, and I put much of this down to Laddie Cliff's soothing influence.

Right through 1936 I struggled under the handicap of this loss of voice. I used to go to bed with a burning throat, wake up with a burning throat, and whatever I did made no difference.

My voice seemed to settle down into a permanent husk. In my second season at Eastbourne the Press said: "Mr. Clarkson Rose has developed a fascinating husk in his voice which is most realistic in those peppery colonel parts in which he excels."

On the stage I tried to make capital of the husk. Mentally I suffered more and more as the voice got worse and worse.

Occasionally it would come through in normal strength, and I would be on top of the world and glorying in the use of it. Then the throat would close up, and nothing would come.

My doctor at Eastbourne gave me some measure of relief from the burning in the throat. But he always insisted that nothing was wrong, and that it arose from something to do with nerves.

Frederick Melville sent for me to see him at the Lyceum Theatre. By that time my voice was so bad that even in ordinary conversation I was sometimes inaudible.

With half an hour to spare before the appointment I went into the Concert Artistes' Association Club. There I met an old artiste of mine, and a very old friend, May Goring Thomas.

"How's the voice, Clarkie?"

"Oh, getting on nicely, May, thank you."

"It sounds better, but it hasn't got the old 'Clarkie'

resonance. I have often thought about you, and worried about your voice. I'm going to be direct and say that I have sometimes wondered if it might not be a syphilitic throat."

I turned it off lightly, but I was in such a state of nerves and fear that I began to wonder if that might be the reason. I would add that I had run no risk of such infection.

"I want you to be dame at the Lyceum," said Fred Melville.

Calling every reserve of will-power and resilience to my aid, I tried to conduct the conversation in as normal a tone as possible. When we had settled terms I asked him why he had sent for me and where he had seen me.

"I saw you at the Theatre Royal, Birmingham, some years ago, and I marked you down as a suitable dame for the Lyceum, because you have got a big voice and the Lyceum's a big theatre. You have a bit of a cold now, haven't you?"

"Yes," I replied. And as quickly as possible I terminated the interview, and left him.

By the big columns in front of the theatre I stood trembling. "He picked me because I've got a big voice—and my voice is getting worse and worse. He thinks I've got a cold, and I haven't got a cold at all. May Goring Thomas thought that it might be a syphilitic throat. It can't be. But I can't go back to Eastbourne until I do something about it."

Panic-stricken I rushed off to the Lock Hospital and demanded a blood test. The doctor asked me one or two personal questions and seemed amused at my answers.

Back in Eastbourne I hardly slept for nights. Every time the postman came I jumped to see if he had brought the report.

Finally it came . . . negative!

I rushed off to my doctor. He roared with laughter.

"TWINKLE" PLAYS EASTBOURNE AT CRICKET AT SAFFRONS. THE GROUP SHOWS THE AUTHOR NEXT TO H. D. SWAN, THE FORMER M.C.C. MANAGER. AMONG THE "TWINKLE" ELEVEN ARE: JOHN WHITEHEAD, RUPERT ROGERS, EDDIE HENDERSON, GORDON HOLDOM, ERNEST ARNLEY, AND ISAAC STEWART

THE AUTHOR WITH GEORGIE WOOD. ALEXANDRA THEATRE, BIRMINGHA
1935-36

TOMMY FIELDS, GRACIE FIELDS AND THE AUTHOR IN HIS DRESSING ROOM, EASTBOUR
PIER, MAY, 1940

As the weeks dragged on I became almost resigned to the fact that my voice would always be bad.

Pantomime rehearsals at the Lyceum were not strenuous. My voice was rested, and on the opening day, for my first entrance, was almost normal.

Two nights later it went again. The band struck up my music, and on I went shivering with fear. I managed to get through the number somehow, and on going upstairs to my room was greeted by Dave O'Gorman with, "What happened to your Hobson's, Clarkie?"

I was in the depths of despair. Here I had a big chance at the Lyceum Theatre, London, had made a big hit, had a wonderful Press—and now my voice had gone again.

I prayed, I cried, and went back to my little house at Golders Green feeling that the end of everything had come. I had not touched whisky for several years, but this night I gave way, and drank myself silly. Olive disapproved, but was very tolerant.

In desperation I telephoned a Christian Science practitioner at Bognor. Mr. Sanderson was a great character. I had met him, not in connection with Christian Science but socially, and I must admit that I telephoned him not with a very good grace, but in a "I'll try anything once" spirit.

He came to my dressing-room as a matinée was finishing. He saw my array of bottles, gargles and sprays, and roared with laughter.

"Do go on using them if you feel that they help you," he said.

"But they haven't done me any good," I said impatiently.

Then I told him the whole story. He did not seem to pay much attention, and rather annoyed me by eating numbers of sugar buns from a paper bag that he had brought with him.

After I had finished my tale of woe, he sat quietly for about five minutes with his eyes closed. I waited for

o

some word from him, a reading from the Bible, or a quotation from the Christian Science text-book. Instead, he began asking me questions about the pantomime, and asked if he could see the evening performance.

"Of course you can," I said. "But I have called you here to set my case before you, and to hear if you can do anything about it."

"I know that," he answered. "But I would like to see the pantomime."

I got him a seat. "Thanks very much. I'll call in and see you before I go back to Bognor. Now sing well, because I'm looking forward to it. I've never seen a Lyceum pantomime," he said, and then went out.

There was about three-quarters of an hour to spare before I had to get ready. I lay down, and promptly went to sleep.

At night my voice started groggily, but in a few moments I felt it strengthen, and somehow I forgot to think about it at all. When it came to my chorus song, I looked down at the audience and saw the beaming face of Mr. Sanderson. He looked just like a happy schoolboy.

He sang at the top of his voice. So did I. For the rest of that pantomime my voice was as right as rain.

He popped into my dressing-room at the end of the show and said, "I *did* enjoy it, but I must rush away now." He did not mention my voice, but as he was leaving he noticed that there was one more bun. "Oh, I must have that," he said, grabbed it, and went out.

About a week later I received an account for an infinitesimal sum. I have not seen nor heard of Mr. Sanderson since!

The year of "Twinkle's" début at Eastbourne I had a second company at Shanklin. The cast included Cecil Johnson, who has since become the proprietor of an excellent summer show himself; Jack Murray, who for years had been an established summer show comedian; Gordon Whelan, son of Albert Whelan, with his partner Billie Lockwood, a first-class comedienne; an experienced soubrette, Beth O'Dare; Frank Webster, a virile baritone; and a quartette of Rosebuds.

This show was not successful. The fault was probably mine in that I was so engrossed in establishing "Twinkle" in its first Eastbourne season.

Hastings Mann, my musical-director, obtained his release from me and went to Shanklin, where for several seasons he presented for Terry Wood an ideal unit for Shanklin Pier, "After Dinner". Terry Wood spared no expense in dressing and staging these shows, and artistes in the "After Dinner" casts have included Babette O'Deal, George Doonan, and Tommy Trinder.

Now to Birmingham, and my joyful anticipation of working with Georgie Wood, let me digress a moment, on my tenth birthday I was given a watch. I stole from my home in Dudley one day, pawned this watch for eight shillings and sixpence, and with that money decided to take myself to the Birmingham pantomime.

I caught the tram from Dudley because it was cheaper than the train. One could get off at Oldbury, walk two miles, thus saving three ha'pence, and then get another tram.

I was first in the gallery queue at the Prince of Wales Theatre. There was an old acrobat who did hand-springs and overs to entertain the queue, and I gave him a penny. There was an old lady who sold whelks and cockles and thick slices of bread. From these I made my midday meal. She shook a bottle of vinegar vigorously until the plate was swimming, and some of the vinegar even went over me.

There was another old woman who, from a barrow, sold boiled sweets at four ounces for a penny. I had a pennyworth of these.

A raucous-voiced man walked up and down the queue selling Felix McGlennon's Song Sheets. "All the pantomime songs," he shouted, "*Good-bye, Dolly, I must leave you, The Soldiers of the Queen.*" I bought a song sheet.

When the doors opened we surged forward, up and up and round and round the stone steps. In the gallery I took a short-cut over the benches and got myself into the front row.

Everybody in the gallery sang songs from the song sheets whilst we waited. There was a wonderful buzz when the gentlemen of the orchestra came into the pit, with the conductor, a man with long hair and an imperial beard, last. He waved his baton, there was a crash on the cymbals, a roll on the timpani, and the overture commenced. We sang the choruses as they were played.

The lights were lowered, there was a momentary hush, and the huge curtain rose slowly. The Demon King came on and told us all the evil things he was going to do. Then the Fairy Queen made her entrance, put the Demon King in his place, and reassured us.

Then we were transported to a wonderful village with a windwill and an inviting-looking public-house. Crowds of villagers, boys and girls and children, came on and danced and sang. They had wooden buckets, which they turned upside down and danced on.

I forgot all about the world outside as I gazed, entranced, at the stage. When the interval came, and the ponies had taken Cinderella to the ball, I was in a perspiration of excitement, and I would not leave my seat in case I could not get to it again in time for the second half.

At the ball the Demon did something to the clock, and in a moment it was twelve o'clock, and Cinderella, shorn of her beautiful ball dress, was seen rushing across in her rags.

It all ended very happily, and a regular army of girls came down carrying flags. Some of them were dressed as C.I.V. troops in the Boer War, and we all went nearly mad at this.

When I came out it was dark, and the old woman with the cockles, the old woman with the sweets, and the man

with the song sheets were still there. There was a queue
for the evening performance, so I joined this, and went in
and saw the wonderful show all over again.

When I got home my punishment was severe. But the
experience was worth it.

With memories such as these, and with the other
Birmingham pantomime experiences that I have recorded,
it will be apparent how I was looking forward to co-
starring with "Wee Georgie" Wood in the first pantomime
in the new Alexandra Theatre. Unfortunately it was not
a happy experience.

After the pantomime was over, George Wood wrote to
me from abroad and promptly put his finger right on the
crux of the matter. "The trouble was, there were two
leaders in the orchestra, which doesn't always make for
harmony."

This "Cinderella" was a sumptuous production. Leon
Salberg had gone all out to open the new theatre with
éclat, and neither trouble nor expense was spared.
"Wee Georgie" Wood played Buttons; myself, the chief
Ugly Sister; mercurial Eddy Henderson, the other one;
forthright George Betton, Baron; that brilliant pair of
pantomime comedians, Rich and Galvin, the Brokers'
Men; clear-voiced Muriel Cronshaw, Prince; compact
and competent Kitty Prince, Dandini; Avril Angers,
Cinderella; and dear, sweet Marie Shaw as the Fairy
Queen.

The pantomime had many great moments, but it lacked
good teamwork.

In spite of the clash of temperaments, George Wood and
I remain firm and understanding friends. There is no one
in our profession in whose company I would rather be
than George's. He is a remarkable man, and a genius
in his own right. His amazing intellect, quick wit and
uncanny discernment of human nature, his personality
and charm, make him a law unto himself, and if I had his
brains and ability, so would *I* be!

"Twinkle" completed its second successful season at

Eastbourne, and soon I was assembling with Jack Barty, the O'Gorman Brothers, Marjorie Sandford, Polly Ward, Molly Vivian, and the army of small-part people and old pantomime performers for whom Fred Melville always found work, for the Lyceum Theatre pantomime.

CHAPTER NINETEEN

I NEVER knew Walter Melville well. But I got to know Fred Melville very well, and the better I knew him the more I liked him.

After his passing, as I stood in the little church at Shoreham with his family, and many of the famous people who had worked under his banner, I felt hushed and grieved, not only for the loss of a friend, but for what I felt sure would be the end of a pantomime era.

There has been no one in our profession quite like the Melvilles. All of the family—June, who is an excellent actress; Andy, who was Andrew Melville's son, and still carrying on at the Palace Theatre, Watford—had a charm, inconsequence and lovable quality entirely their own.

Walter was immaculate and imperious, Fred untidy, easy-going and stubborn. They both knew their job, and knew exactly what to set before a Lyceum Theatre audience.

A Lyceum pantomime was like a packet of liquorice all-sorts. In addition to a strong team of comedians and outstanding speciality acts, there was always a Melville "gang" who played all sorts of parts, back and front legs of animals, harlequins, and eccentric parts which I always looked upon as being Fred's own inventions. There were always some half-dozen dwarfs running about all over the place, and you had to step carefully unless one trod on them.

The whole conglomeration was right for the Lyceum, and Fred never changed his formula. He took a liking to me and went so far as to honour me by asking my advice on occasions, and trusting in my judgment.

Rehearsals would, on the surface, seem casual and most unbusinesslike. "What have you boys got?" Fred would ask. And one by one the comedians would produce their "one horse wires" and "tried and trusteds", and Fred would listen and say "Yes" and "No".

Every so often the rehearsal would stop and Molly Vivian would make tea. Tea was an institution at the Lyceum.

Fred Melville was an astute manager and producer. He would let the comedians put everything in at the public dress rehearsals, and would watch audiences' reactions. When it came to cutting to proper dimensions, he had an excellent line to go on.

I did not have a lot to do as Dame Tickle in "Puss in Boots", but what I had was well placed, and I was lucky enough to be a hit. The O'Gorman Brothers, Dave and Joe, Jack Barty and myself were friends, and we were a happy team.

Her Majesty Queen Elizabeth brought Princess Elizabeth and Princess Margaret to a matinée. In my chorus song the audience were somewhat subdued and looking towards Her Majesty's box. Perhaps somewhat cheekily I turned to the Royal box and said, "Won't you please sing my chorus?"

Immediately the Queen whispered to the two Princesses. In a moment they were leading the singing, and the whole audience joined them lustily.

Towards the end of the run Fred asked me if I would like to come back. "Of course," I said. "But what about a bit more money?"

A look of pain passed over his face. "Can't do that. Things are very difficult," he said.

Next day I made him walk through the pass door on to the stage and face the empty auditorium. "How many seats are there in this theatre, Mr. Fred?" I asked.

Puzzled, he said, "We can hold over three thousand."

"Do you think that my return here next year would be responsible for, say, fifty people a week wanting to see me again?"

"I should think so," was his somewhat unguarded reply.

"Then don't you think I'm worth an extra ten pounds
a week?"

With a twinkle in his eye, he said, "All right. You
win."

The pantomime the following year was "Beauty and the
Beast". Under Fred Melville's treatment it resembled
"Cinderella" with a zoological angle.

I had a magnificent part as the chief sister. It was a
joy to work with Johnny Kavanagh as the lesser sister, and
with his personality and inconsequent Tyneside humour,
he gave an outstanding performance.

Jill Esmond was playing Principal Boy for the first time
in her career. Her rendition of the character was somewhat like a martial Peter Pan, faithful and artistic in the
extreme, and her obvious enjoyment in playing the part
came over at once.

Anne Leslie, a protégée of mine whom Fred had booked,
played Beauty. She was just right for the part and looked
lovely. Fred said that of all the Principal Girls he had
ever seen, Anne was his favourite, because, as he put it,
she was "as sweet and dainty as a dew-kissed rose".

The popular North-Country comedian Albert Burdon
joined the comedy team. I don't think, however, that this
excellent comedian was quite happy at the Lyceum.

During the summer Fred Melville came to see
"Twinkle" at Eastbourne. "I like that orchestra, and
I like that conductor of yours, Conrad Leonard," he
said.

"Oh, I'm so glad," I replied.

"I'm thinking of making a change at the Lyceum. They
tell me that my band is old-fashioned."

The Lyceum orchestra had served its era very well.
In the light of modern methods and orchestration, and
different idioms in light music, it was, however, old-
fashioned.

Reluctantly Fred allowed me to fix up with Conrad
Leonard to go to the Lyceum, and he allowed us to
select the new musicians. I shall not readily forget Fred's

face when he heard the new and modern orchestra at the first band rehearsal.

"Do you like it?" Conrad Leonard and I asked him eagerly.

"Yes—it's very nice. But I do miss my strings."

Nevertheless the new orchestra stayed until the last of the Lyceum Theatre pantomimes.

During the run of "Beauty and the Beast" Fred said, "Clarkie, you know the B.B.C. Get us a broadcast."

I went and saw Harry Pepper and between us we conceived the idea of Lionel Gamlin, as one of the chorus, walking around with a hand-microphone commenting on everything. Lionel enjoyed it—and so did the listeners.

Harry Pepper was in my dressing-room one day with Doris Arnold when Fred came in. I introduced them, and, gazing at the lovely Doris, Fred said, "You're just the girl I want for my Principal Boy next year." Harry Pepper roared with laughter. But Fred was quite serious.

"Beauty and the Beast" was a great success, and one day, towards the end of the run, Fred said, in his laconic way, "You can stay here as long as you like. Do you want to?"

"Yes."

"All right. I suppose you want some more money?"

"Yes, Mr. Fred."

"Then leave it to me to treat you properly."

"Yes, Mr. Fred."

The next day, on his personal notepaper, he gave me a contract for five years, with regular increases of salary each year. Within a week or two I was attending his funeral.

There was to be one more pantomime at the Lyceum Theatre. Bert Hammond, schooled so long in the Melville method, took over the reins, and engaged me to play the Queen in "The Queen of Hearts". I was in luck's way, for the Queen, in addition to being the title role, was a magnificent part. The same team of comics were engaged, including the stalwarts Dave and Joe O'Gorman, and Albert Burdon was better suited as the Knave of Hearts than he had been in his role the previous year.

Nancy Fraser, daughter of those grand old troupers Walter Passmore and Agnes Fraser, was an outstanding Principal Boy; Anne Leslie was again Principal Girl; that excellent actor, Arnold Bell, played the Yellow Dwarf; and the specialities included the breath-taking Colleano Family. One wonders if young Bonar Colleano thought that one day he would change from acrobatics to "A Street Car Named Desire"?

My pantomime husband, the King, was Bernard Ansell, trained in my own school of pierrots. He was a lovely foil, and dithered delightfully to my bombastic bullying.

Macqueen-Pope, the theatre historian, and one of the finest publicity experts in the profession, left nothing undone to "put me over". I have never had a more wonderful national Press. "Popie" and I are kindred souls in our great respect for the traditions of the Edwardian theatre.

I am moved by the fact that I was the last artiste to speak on the stage of the old Lyceum Theatre. I treasure the flashlight photograph that was taken in the theatre on the last night showing me fully dressed in my court regalia and jewelled crown, in the centre of the entire company, presiding as Queen over a court whose time had come. There were many tears that night, in the auditorium and on the stage.

With the end of the run of the "Queen of Hearts" came the end of the reign of King Pantomime at the most famous of all pantomime theatres. When I write "the most famous" I do not except Drury Lane, for famous as Drury Lane pantomime was, the Lyceum had a wider and more democratic appeal.

When I was appearing in one of my own pantomimes at Torquay a parcel was handed to me across the footlights. It contained a large Christmas cracker, and written on a card: "To our Queen of Hearts, from the person who caught this, the last bon-bon thrown from the Lyceum stage by the Clown in the Harlequinade."

It hangs in my study, a poignant reminder of all the fun and frolic, the glitter and gaiety, the love and laughter of those great days that will never come again.

CHAPTER TWENTY

ONG-WRITING is a heterogeneous job, and collaboration is not always easy, but I found it smooth-
going with Conrad Leonard. He married his tunes to
my lyrics in a splendid way, and, like myself, was a
quick worker.

We wrote together for many years, and the "Twinkle"
theme songs always received immediate publication. It
seemed, however, that we were never going to write a big
winner.

One day at Bournemouth I wrote the lyric of what I
would term a "sloppy ballad". When I took it to the
theatre I apologised to Con for the 'mushiness'. He gave
one of his quaint little shrugs, accompanied by his high-
pitched laugh, and said, "Well, when we've got these
present programmes done, I'll set it."

Some years later Conrad Leonard became the professional manager of the famous music publishing firm,
Lawrence Wright. Lawrie was stuck for a ballad, Con
showed him my lyric, and *My Love is Only for You* was
published. It became an exceptionally popular song, and
was advertised with Lawrence Wright's usual flamboyance
as "the world's greatest ballad".

It has had an extraordinarily long life, and even the
week in which I write these words has been broadcast on
three different radio programmes. It has been something
of a menace to me because every soprano who gives me an
audition starts by saying, "I'll sing your own lovely song,
Mr. Rose."

How different was Conrad Leonard in method from a
former collaborator and great friend, Tommy Sterndale-
Bennett. Whereas with Con the whole thing would be
complete in a few hours, with Tommy it was a case of
endless correspondence, alterations and revisions.

We had a very successful collaboration with both comic

songs and ballads. Our *Sing Ho, for the Days of Drinking* was sung by Leslie Henson and Davy Burnaby at the Winter Garden Theatre in "A Night Out".

Writing kept me very busy. I had my weekly column in *The Stage* and a big list of artistes always waiting for material.

Elsie and Doris Waters were amongst my earliest and best clients. I know of no two people for whom I have greater admiration. Once in their early days, they were at the Victoria Palace as first turn and not doing very well. They advertised in a theatrical paper: "Elsie and Doris Waters, first turn at the Victoria Palace, thus proving it is possible to die more than once!" There's resilience for you. Later they proved that they could not only "take it" but also "make it".

The work that Elsie and Doris Waters did for ENSA was wonderful. And never did they throw their weight about or demand the red carpet.

Harry Champion took one of my early songs and sang it for a long time. It was called *Don't get the Wind up, Walter*. Whenever he saw me, he would yell from the other side of the road, "Wotcher, Walter, when am I going to have another wind up?"

I count myself fortunate that David Day, of Francis, Day and Hunter, liked my work. David was a grand man, and his influence on the catalogue of his firm was remarkable. He was of another generation when there was dignity in the music publishing business.

As a youngster I first saw Charles Whittle at the old His Majesty's Music Hall at Walsall. He was singing *I'm Billy Muggins*. I wrote some doggerel on the same lines, called *I'm Bertie Knowall,* and sent it to him. He sent it back, and having looked at it since, I can't blame him. Eventually Charles Whittle sang my *Tails Up Every Time*.

That brilliant piano entertainer, Ernest Hastings, was a careful and cautious client. I had to take my songs to his house at Willesden and almost act them to him.

Some years later, when I was on the bill with him at Shepherd's Bush Empire and preceding his act with my

topical song *Rule, Britannia,* he said to me in his Lancashire
way, "Mai word, that's a bonny song. You never sell me
any like that." My reply was, "I submitted this song to
you three years ago. It was exactly the same as I sing it
now except for a slight topical alteration. You told me it
was too long and not funny enough."

"Then I was a proper bloody fool," he said; "it's the
best song I've heard in years."

Norman Long was a good judge of material. I sold him
a song for eight guineas which, he told me, lifted him from
comparative obscurity to an established position on the
music-halls. It was called *The Drage Way,* and had the
recurring phrase, *We always lay the lino on the floor.*

When I had a number of return dates at the London
Coliseum and needed some new material for myself,
Norman, after a lot of persuasion, allowed me to buy the
song back for use on the Stoll tour. Its reception was
electrical, and in the newspaper space given to music-hall
reports, hit the headlines. In his last years Norman Long
did not bother about songs, unless some of his clients at
the hospitable Bolt Head Hotel at Salcombe prevailed
upon him to give "one of his old 'uns". Norman died
in 1950.

Ernie Lotinga and Julian Rose were difficult to please.
They both paid me deposits down, and I kept sending
them sketches and songs, but I never suited them. The
material they rejected was always eventually sold.

Julian Wylie was the most business-like person I dealt
with regarding material. I wrote two revues for him for
his Isle of Man seasons, and in both instances it was a
happy experience.

I would take him my scripts and suggestions, go through
them with him, and he would "okay" this and reject that.
Then would come a meeting at his office where he would
have his stage-manager, producer and wardrobe mistress.
He would sit at one end of a long table and I would sit at
the other and read the script. Notes were made of require-
ments as we went along, and that would be the last I

would hear of the matter until I received my weekly
royalties, punctually every Tuesday morning.

There was the same business-like routine when I produced the Julian Wylie Pierrots for him at Douglas. This
was a grand company, including Archie Glen, Betty
Jumel, Irene North, Roy Barbour, Sylvia Welling and
May Clapham. I went over to Douglas, laid the programmes out, and the whole thing was done in five days.

Davy Burnaby wanted me to supply some material
when "The Co-optimists" were going to do a revival at
His Majesty's. But there was so much dillying and dally-
ing that nothing ever came of it. I could never get used
to Davy Burnaby being a big, portly gentleman, because
he was slim and debonair when I first met him in 1912,
when "The March Hares" did a short summer season
at the Liverpool Repertory Theatre. He was a big
"Twinkle" fan, and I miss him now every time we go
to Cheltenham.

This is the era of the free song and publishers paid
stars to sing their numbers. The music-hall stars of the
past had their own songs. If you wanted to hear those
songs, then you had to go and hear the original singers.
The popularity of old music-hall songs, when they are
revived to-day, lies not only in their nostalgic appeal, but
because in their times they were never hackneyed.

In show business the wheel always turns, and history
repeats itself. One lives in hope that the time will come
when the music-halls will produce and present again
artistes whose identities are bound-up with the songs and
material that they offer.

Then we shall have again the thrill not only of seeing
the number of a music-hall favourite go up in the frame
on the side of the proscenium, but the buzz of whispered
anticipation that went through the auditorium when the
orchestra struck-up the introduction of *I love a lassie*, for
Harry Lauder, or *Oh, oh, Antonio*, for Florrie Forde.

The method to-day is for a song to emerge on the air,
and if it is what is known as a "plug song", to be featured

SHIRLEY KELLOGG AT THE EMPIRE

HARRY RANDALL COLLIE KNOX

THE AUTHOR AS DANDINI, EDDIE WALKER AS THE PAGE, AND OLIVE
FOX AS THE PRINCE IN THE FAMOUS ROBERT COURTNEIDGE "WHITE
CINDERELLA" PANTOMIME AT THE OPERA HOUSE, LEICESTER, 1919

in nearly every programme on the air, and to be sung and played by all and sundry. Commercially I suppose it is successful, but in reality it is quite artificial. Programmes with the title "Somebody's Choice" are laughable. They have no choice except to choose from what they hear, and what they hear is what other people choose for them.

P

EXCEPT for a cinema in Wales, the Pier Pavilion at Eastbourne was the first place of entertainment to reopen after the closure of all theatres and cinemas on the outbreak of war in 1939. It was a glass pavilion, and my company and myself, with paints and brushes, assisted the Pier staff to black it out, so that "Twinkle" could ring up again. At the end of the season we departed for our first appearance at Torquay.

Although his business interests are wide and varied it is as the director and moving spirit of the famous Malvern Festival that Roy Limbert will go down in theatre history. I had known Roy for many years, and had it not been for him it is possible that "Twinkle" would never have played Torquay.

Roy Limbert's office at the Malvern Theatre is indicative of his whole character. It is crammed with trinkets, toys and souvenirs of every description; photographs of the great and not so great are everywhere, and the inscriptions on them reveal the love, affection and respect that all who know him feel for him.

His association with Bernard Shaw must be unique. His private files contain many an amusing letter, drawing and postcard in the well-known upright caligraphy of the master.

There is a wide gulf between the G.B.S. classics and "Twinkle". But Roy Limbert has been at the booking helm of "Twinkle" for ten years, and since he still takes every opportunity of dashing in his wayward Wolsey in all sorts of weathers and to every type of place to see my show, one can assume that he still approves of us. For years I have called him "Uncle Roy", and that is the best description of him.

Talking of G.B.S., here is a typical experience in connection with "Twinkle".

He had been staying at Eastbourne for his annual visit
to the Glyndebourne Festival, and one morning, during a
break in rehearsals, I strolled from the theatre on to the
Pier to get a bit of fresh air. Mr. Shaw was whiling away
his time playing with the slot machines. He took particular interest in that rather lurid one where there is a
hangman and an execution. I had the temerity to go up
to him and say, "I wonder if you remember me, Mr.
Shaw? I was Arthur C. Rose at the Liverpool Repertory
Theatre, and I played Schutzmacher in your 'Doctor's
Dilemma'."

His penetrating eyes examined me, and then, in those
gentle, high tones, he said, "Yes, I do. You were an
excellent Schutzmacher. What are you doing now?"

I told him about "Twinkle", and that we were rehearsing, and he asked if he might come in to watch us.

A bit flustered, but very honoured, I took him inside.
I showed him our tiny stage and, knowing he was interested in lighting, proudly displayed the excellent
effects we could get with our cyclorama. He watched very
attentively for a few minutes as we brought the lights
from 'dawn' to 'sunset', then with a twinkle in his eye,
he said, "It is very beautiful, and it is a shame to think
the theatre cat could walk on in the midst of it and spoil
the whole effect!"

Afterwards, at the Burlington Hotel, I reminded him
of a photograph I had asked for all that time ago, and the
next day I got it.

And now back to Roy Limbert.

For years I had been trying to book Torquay and had
never succeeded. Finally "Uncle Roy" booked us in
there.

The black-out made Torquay at night as much like the
Torbay Riviera as Stoke-on-Trent or Ashton-under-Lyne.
"Twinkle" opened to a small and apprehensive gathering
in the Pavilion Theatre, but gradually people became a
little less nervous, and came in better numbers, especially
to the matinées. "Twinkle" was doing its famous

'digging-in', and indeed we were laying the foundations of what was to become one of our strongholds.

For the first Christmas of the war I returned to the Theatre Royal, Birmingham, in the "Babes in the Wood" pantomime. It was the Drury Lane production of the previous year, and I was booked to play Nurse Merry-weather, the part created by G. S. Melvin. It was Philip Rodway who had first put G. S. Melvin and myself into skirts, and both of us, I feel that I may claim, justified his judgment.

Helen Breen, one of the finest Principal Boys I have ever known, with face, figure, voice and glamour, was in the cast. She is Tom Arnold's wife, and it is a pity that she does not come out from her present happy retirement and let the public see a first-class Principal Boy again.

Ethel Revnell and Gracie West were the completely successful "Babes". Ethel Revnell, a supreme low comedy woman, was so much the gamin that one forgot her height and forgot that she was an adult—and Gracie was the ideal foil as the rather brow-beaten brother.

Despite her gaucherie, her contortions and her grimaces, every now and then the sweetness and softness of Ethel Revnell's nature comes through in her gentle, velvet-like eyes. Her smile is one of the most beautiful that I have ever seen.

Revnell and West were unselfishness itself to me in the nursery scene. I had to put them to bed, and then undress myself, and I pride myself on having an undressing scene that is full of "belly-laughs". It would have been natural of Ethel Revnell to say, "I am not going to lie in bed for nine minutes whilst you get all the laughs." But she sank herself entirely, did lie quiet in bed, and helped in every possible direction.

When the time came for the pantomime to be broadcast, it was Ethel Revnell who insisted emphatically that my undressing scene should be included. The management and the B.B.C. demurred, saying that it was visual comedy. "Never mind," said Ethel, "the listeners will hear the biggest laughs they have ever heard in any theatre, and you can give a commentary on what 'Clarkie' is doing." And that is exactly what happened.

My old friend Billy Danvers was playing Jack o' the Green; those grand drolls the Chevalier Brothers were the robbers; Bert Platt, a most excellent all-round comic actor, was outstanding as the Baron; Anne Bolt was Maid Marian; and Vincent Tyldesley's Master Singers vigorous and vocal as Robin Hood's merry men.

Through war conditions all the principal artistes were on a percentage basis. Some weeks it worked out better than one's salary, and sometimes not so good. To my mind, in abnormal conditions, it is a very fair way of arranging things.

Despite the war, pantomime was very much alive in Birmingham. Arthur Askey, Billy Bennett, Cora Goffin, and the O'Gorman Brothers were in Emile Littler's "Jack and Jill" at the Prince of Wales Theatre; Dorothy Ward, Shaun Glenville, and "Wee Georgie" Wood were the stars at the Alexandra.

With so many friends in the town it was natural that there would be lots of convivial meetings, and indeed there were. Shaun and Glenville had taken a house in the Bristol Road, and entertained lavishly. George Wood and I lived in the Queen's Hotel, not in this instance from choice, but because the fuel shortage made the 'digs' so cold, we were compelled to move into the hotel.

Saturday night in the Queen's Hotel was a provincial edition of the Savoy Grill Room, for the members of our profession in Birmingham made it their rendezvous on that night.

For the 1940 season at Eastbourne I had assembled one of the strongest "Twinkle" casts that we had had to date—Olive Fox, Cynthia Rawson, Audrey Acland, Sybil Summers, Rupert Rogers, Gracie Field's brother Tommy Fields, Petre Julian, Murray Stewart, Rex Korda, Four Rosebuds and myself. It was a record opening night, and for the next ten days business went up and up.

Impressed by his good looks, his wonderful smile, and the clarity of his delivery, I had picked Tommy Fields after he had given me a public audition. Gracie Fields came to visit us twice in the early season to see how he was getting on.

Naturally, when Gracie Fields came to visit us the whole of Eastbourne knew. In typical Gracie Fields's style she stood up in the audience one night, gave a speech, and ended up by saying, "As you know, I've knocked about a bit, and I've seen a lot of shows, but I've never seen a better than our old 'Clarkie's' 'Twinkle'."

She came back-stage and was photographed with Tommy and myself, in my dressing-room. Little did we think, as we posed, wreathed in smiles for the picture, that in a few days the dressing-room would be stripped of its trappings, and that the grease-paint, wigs, and props. would have to be packed into baskets and removed hurriedly.

A few days later, after the evening performance, in the entrance hall I saw a tall, be-ribboned, be-medalled officer, who greeted me.

"Good evening," I said, then cracking a nervous joke, I went on, "When do we finish?"

Quite unemotionally he replied, "You have."

The War Office had taken over, the Pier was to be mined, and we were given a few hours in which to get out. Early in the morning the company and myself got cracking, and very soon all that was left of "Twinkle" on the Pier were the posters, almost new, which advertised that "Twinkle" would appear "from Whitsuntide until October, nightly at 8.15."

At the other end of the Pier, at the Pier Theatre, where Godfrey Tearle and his company were due to appear, Mr. Tearle was taking the sun by the stage-door.

"What are you going to do about it?" I asked.

"What can I do?" he replied, "but leave my scenery here and see what happens."

When I am in doubt as to what to do, I have always

been a great believer in the Asquith adage, "Wait and
see." So I said to the company, "All contracts are finished,
as you know, but if you like to hang on here for a week,
I'll see what can be arranged. Meet me every day at the
Queen's Hotel at midday, and I'll let you know when
anything tangible happens."

The lessees of the Devonshire Park Theatre, Albert
Donn and Sir John Hammerton, proposed that I took the
company into their theatre. At that time the experienced
repertory actor Forbes Russell was running a repertory
season there, and Olive said, "I'm not going in there to
throw another company out of work."

In vain I protested that it was quite legal for Mr.
Russell's contract to be terminated, and that we had a
company out of work.

"That may be," said Olive. "I know that it is all
above board, but there's something more to it so far as
I am concerned, and there should be so far as you are
concerned. Things are not normal; they can't go and get
another job in the state that show business is in."

Then a telephone call came from Percy Dunsford at
Exeter, with the suggestion that "Twinkle" went into the
Theatre Royal. "Exeter is full of troops, and business
should be good," he said.

This was tentatively arranged when Alderman Rush,
the Mayor of Eastbourne, sent for me, and said, "Look
here, Clarkson. 'Twinkle' has been on the Pier a number
of years, and is as much a part of Eastbourne as Beachy
Head. Will you stay and take the company into the
Winter Garden, and help us all to keep going, and
maintain the town's morale?"

The only financial arrangement he could offer was
60 per cent. with a guarantee of £100 a week. Our
salary list was around £270 and the current production
had cost over £2,000, so it was a gamble. But since
Eastbourne had been very good to me, I felt that I must
take it.

The next day the Exeter contract arrived. Had I gone

in there with the city full of troops, and freedom from raids until the Baedecker raids of later on, I think that I would have made a small fortune. I do not think that Percy Dunsford ever forgave me for returning the Exeter contract, and I regret sincerely that, through his death, I was never able to explain to him what I felt about my owing it to Eastbourne to remain there.

With the company on cut salaries we went into the Winter Garden, Eastbourne, a big rambling glass building, never intended for anything else but a concert orchestra. No visitors came to the town, and we were entirely dependent on residents, but they supported us tolerably well until they decreased in numbers as people were evacuated.

Cynthia Rawson, the soprano, who has since married Tommy Fields, did excellently. Audrey Acland, too, proved a magnificent trouper. The Rosebuds, Hilda Beardmore, Margaret Goodchild, Renee Lovell and Barbara Lewis, no matter what was happening in the skies above, would go to their glass-covered dressing-room and put on their make-ups quite unperturbed.

Murray Stewart, the Scottish tenor, was another who more than pulled his weight. He was a quaint chap who, winter and summer, always wore a number of pull-overs and waistcoats, for he feared his chest. It sometimes gets very hot in the greenhouse-like Winter Garden, and at one matinée, when I noticed the perspiration pouring from Murray, I said, "Why not lie in a tepid bath when you get home?"

"Noo," said Murray, "I never immairse."

Night after night I had to warn the audience that the sirens had gone. Night after night when we came out flares had been dropped, and the drone of planes overhead meant another night without sleep, for it was generally daylight before the "all clear". We had to put on programme after programme because, of course, we were playing to the same residents each week.

Emile Littler and Egerton Killick, in a luncheon meeting

at the "Ivy", suggested that "Twinkle" might go into the
Comedy Theatre. Sir Oswald Stoll sent for me and discussed my producing a show for him at the London
Coliseum, with the "Twinkle" cast as the nucleus of the
production. My title was "Carry on, London".

Neither of these schemes came to fruition. In the meantime we carried on at Eastbourne, audiences dwindled as
the town emptied, but always we had the faithful few.

There was a queue one day when a dog-fight took place
overhead. Not a soul moved. I was, quite frankly,
terrified as I sat with Mr. Dennis, the Winter Garden
manager, but I felt that I had to go out and talk to that
queue.

As Corporation Entertainments Manager, Mr. Dennis,
like other public officials, had his detractors. In difficult
circumstances I enjoyed every minute of my association
with him. He was a good manager, and, what is more, a
good companion.

When "Twinkle" was opposition to him on the Pier I
met him one day, and he said, "I hear that you were
packed to suffocation on Bank Holiday, 'Clarkie'?"

"Yes, it was a marvellous house. How did you do,
Mr. Dennis?"

"I think our show played to fourteen pounds," he said,
his face wreathed in smiles.

"But that's dreadful, and on a Bank Holiday too."

"Ah well," said Dennis, quite seriously, "it doesn't
matter. I had a record day with the ladies' lavatories
on the front. We took over eighty-seven pounds."

Despite conditions, our Farewell Night in September
was sold out in advance. On the Monday night prior to
it, Arthur Rush sent for me and said, "Sorry, 'Clarkie',
but we've got to evacuate you." Shortly afterwards there
were a couple of unexploded bombs on the lawn outside
my dressing-room.

We were due to open at Torquay in a few weeks' time,
and my first thought was to save the scenery and wardrobe
and get the production to Torquay. This was quite a

problem. Carriers would not come near the place because of the unexploded bombs.

Some of the company, with the wardrobe mistress, Millie Solomon, my secretary, and Geoffrey Cawardine, my stage-manager, did all the packing and superintended the removal, whilst Olive and I went on to Bristol, which was then the headquarters of the B.B.C., to try to arrange some broadcasts. This hurried exit was the end of a season that had opened with such promise and to record business.

The first letter that I opened when I got to Torquay was from my bank telling me how much I was overdrawn, for I had lost a lot of money. Financial loss, however, was nothing to the heartbreak I felt at being forced out of my beloved Eastbourne, where "Twinkle" had been raised to such prestige, and where, in spite of the dreadful conditions, every seat had been sold in advance for a Farewell Night that, for all the public knew, might have been spent in an air raid.

CHAPTER TWENTY-TWO

AT Torquay, despite the fact that people were chary of coming out at night in the black-out, business with "Twinkle" grew and grew. A supposedly safe area, the town was very full.

At Christmas I was under contract to return to the Lyceum Theatre, which Tom Arnold and Harry Foster were going to reopen. Intensified air raids on London, however, made this reopening impossible.

"I'll send you to Newcastle, 'Clarkie', if you like," Tom Arnold said on the telephone. But I refused, and I was out of work for the pantomime season when Ernest Goss suggested that I did my own pantomime at Torquay.

Sir Henry Wood once told me that, as an all-round orchestral conductor, Ernest Goss stood alone. Personally I have never known more sage counsel and advice than that proffered in the deep bass tone that comes, so surprisingly, from Ernest Goss's spare, dapper figure.

I went home and started to write the book of "Forty Thieves". I also sent a cheque to a firm who advertised that they could supply scenery of every description.

Emile Littler who, with his wife, Cora Goffin, was staying at the Imperial Hotel, said, "Don't do the 'Forty Thieves', Clarkie, it's most unlucky." But I refused to listen.

When the scenery arrived it was appalling. Then I contacted Harry Drury at Brighton, and from him I hired an excellent production of "Chu Chin Chow", and in that decor my first pantomime production was played.

It was a great success, and the forerunner of several Christmas pantomimes that I have produced for the Torquay Corporation.

After Christmas, "Twinkle" stayed on for another twelve weeks and doing another twelve programmes. I booked guest artistes each week, and amongst them that fine character actor Bransby Williams, and the man who is one of the greatest humorists we have ever had, Gillie Potter.

At a somewhat desultory matinée, Gillie Potter commented from the stage, "We have a very exclusive audience this afternoon. There are, I think, some people from Bovey Tracey here. I know they're from Bovey Tracey because I saw a plough in the cloakroom."

"Twinkle" finished its season by doing a full-scale revue in connection with War Weapons Week, which was called "Half a Million". I wrote an original book and lyrics, and Conrad Leonard provided some sparkling music.

The success of this production was crowned by a visit from the First Sea Lord, A. V. Alexander. He rocked with laughter like a schoolboy, and afterwards asked me for a copy of one of the lyrics.

From Torquay "Twinkle" went to Llandudno, another safe area, where it was a great success. From Llandudno we went to the New Theatre, Hull.

Hull was entirely the reverse of a safe area. I took my secretary and some of the Rosebuds to their 'digs' the first night, only to find that the house was on the ground. Petre Julian, another member of the company, was greeted with, "Here's your bedroom, you'll have your meals with us, Anderson shelter's next door, closet's in yard and the antiseptics on shelf in scullery."

Olive and I, with several members of the company, were living at a country club at Cottingham, four miles out. For all the rest we got we might have lived in Hull. It was a fortnight of raids of every type and description. On our last Friday night Hull resembled nothing so much as one vast bonfire.

From Hull we went to one of England's fine old playhouses, the Theatre Royal, Newcastle. A bomb on Gateshead Empire just prior to our opening hardly encouraged audiences passing a gaping, gutted theatre, to visit the entertainment in another theatre, but a short distance away.

Olive and I were in 'digs' next to an aircraft battery. "Gives you a sense of security," said the landlady. Personally the only thing it gave me was a sense of being shot out of bed every night by vibration. On the Sunday morning, as we left Newcastle by car, we were machine-gunned from the air.

From Newcastle to Harrogate. The spa was full of Government offices, and so business was good.

At Harrogate it was good to meet again an old friend, John Wiltshire. Tall, handsome, what a wonderful personality he had, and an invaluable quality of making everyone feel that they were important.

From Harrogate we went to make our first appearance at the Arts Theatre, Cambridge, where, despite a heat-wave, business was excellent, and from there, through my old friend Rex Newman, to the Opera House, Tunbridge Wells.

This was a small theatre which, for the greater part of the year, showed films. "Twinkle" was soon playing to capacity for nine shows a week and stayed for eleven weeks. We returned to Tunbridge Wells many times afterwards.

"Miss Gracie Fields to speak to you on the telephone," said the porter at my hotel in Tunbridge Wells, at three o'clock one morning. She had come back from America on a brief trip to England, and had travelled all the way from Folkestone to Tunbridge Wells on an army lorry.

"Ee, I'm sorry to fetch you out of bed, luv. I'm at the Wellington Hotel. I've no idea where Tommy lives, and I want to get hold of him. I'm only here for a few hours, and I'm on my way to do some more troop concerts. Can you help me?"

So I got up, collected Tommy Fields in the car, and delivered him to his internationally famous sister. Gracie Fields wrote me a lovely letter, and taking back to America one of Conrad Leonard and my songs, took the trouble to cable me about its success when she sang it.

We went to Torquay for an autumn season. My second

pantomime, "Sleeping Beauty", broke all records for the Pavilion Theatre. It was work all the year round now, because we wanted to keep the company together for "Twinkle" and for pantomime.

We had a contract to fulfil for Emile Littler at the Prince of Wales Theatre, Birmingham. "Call for your contract at our house in Henley-in-Arden," said Emile, who knew that we would be passing that way on tour. We called one Sunday night, and collected the contract. It was never played, for a short time afterwards the Prince of Wales Theatre, Birmingham, was bombed.

For our first summer season at Llandudno, Tommy Fields had left the cast and been replaced by Eddie Childs. By the careful exploitation of his great comic abilities, and their right placing in our programmes, Eddie Childs became one of the greatest favourites "Twinkle" has ever had.

In all our programmes Eddie Childs and I did a double-act just before the finale. It was a high spot in "Twinkle", and Val Parnell and Prince Littler wanted to make this double-act a headline attraction on the music-halls.

Eddie Childs was very excited about this. But the idea had to be abandoned when Eddie, poor lad, had to leave the "Twinkle" cast and enter hospital with chest trouble.

At Llandudno, where "Twinkle" was an outstanding success for its first and three more summer seasons, it was a thrill to me to see my name across the pier, where thirty-five years previously I had been turned down at an audition. Arthur Sutcliffe did give me an audition, and apparently so amusing did he find it that he gathered all the rest of the company together and asked me to do it again. I realised that they were pulling my leg, and felt the ignominy terribly. Kennedy Allen, an excellent comedian and a good fellow, said, "Take no notice, you'll be all right."

At Llandudno I was fortunate enough to take up the threads of an old friendship with Bert Lee, probably the greatest domestic comic song-writer we have ever had.

Bert Lee approved of "Twinkle" and liked writing for it. In his later years he did not bother to write comic songs.

"Eeh, lad," he would say in his Lancashire way, "they don't want comic songs to-day. All they want is a feller to go on in a lounge suit and white hat, put his foot across the orchestra rail, and cheek the audience."

In my early days of song-writing Bert Lee, who at that time was supplying practically every star in the business, often paid me the compliment of sending me clients that he could not cope with himself. The last comic song that he ever wrote was in collaboration with me, an anticipatory song of what would happen at the end of the war, called, *It's going to take a lot of getting used to*.

What a happy town is Llandudno! The County Club made the male members of the cast very welcome. Sumner's Restaurant in Mostyn Street, presided over by quiet and gentle "Uncle" Hughie Williams and his sister, "Aunt" Fanny, with the lads from the B.B.C. there, and visiting artistes from the various programmes, was like any famous West End of London theatrical bar.

There were lots of interesting personalities in Llandudno at the time. Tom Webster was there, and some of his best cartoons of County Club members adorn the Club's walls. Marie Kendall was there, looking the youngest grand-mother of all time, and "just like the ivy", clinging to any opportunity of mixing with members of the profession in which she was so long a star.

It was a pleasure for "Twinkle" to spend three long seasons in this safe area, and to produce shows in the Pier Pavilion, under the quiet, efficient Tom Turner Pilling and admirable Arnold Macara. Moreover, with the B.B.C. at Llandudno and Bangor, we were on the spot to do any radio work that came our way.

Ernest Longstaffe found me a spot on many occasions in "Happidrome". Reggie Smith devised a programme called "Pierrot Remembers", based on a song I had written for "Twinkle", called *Once Upon a Time*.

The following Christmas saw us once again at Torquay,

this time to produce "Aladdin". It was a fine pantomime, but a trying season, for by this time Torquay had sampled an air-raid, and there were several hit-and-run affairs. Long immunity from attack had lulled the residents into a false sense of security. Consequently, when the trouble did come, it assumed magnified proportions in the public mind.

A tour followed, and an enjoyable short season of six weeks at the White Rock Pavilion, Hastings. Then we had to do our period of National Service on ENSA.

Greatorex Newman, then an important executive at Drury Lane, said, "Where do you want to go, 'Clarkie'? Do you want a good time? Or do you want to do import-ant and very necessary work, in places where they do not often get a show of 'Twinkle's' calibre?"

"That's exactly what I will do," I replied. So "Twinkle" toured the less glamorous spots of ENSA. It was a joy to see and hear the appreciation of Forces audiences for a show in which everything was immaculate, and where the production was as near as circumstances would permit to the staging in a proper theatre.

Some of the theatres that we played were excellent. In others, the stage was but a platform. Some had tip-top pianos, and others had dreadful instruments that were the bane of my meticulous musical-director Charles Tovey's life.

The waste of money and petrol over ENSA transport seemed ridiculous. But I have nothing but praise for the hostels, where the accommodation and fare provided for thirty-five shillings a week were alike excellent. The matrons were efficient and particular, and the NAAFI staff seemed to enjoy looking after the artistes.

Some strange specimens of humanity held jobs as ENSA managers. For many of them, whose chief interest seemed to lie in alcohol in the messes, it must have been a lovely war.

Most of us enjoyed a short visit to a mess after the show. But it always seemed all wrong to me that the officers,

THE AUTHOR AS THE OLD TIME PRINCIPAL BOY AND JILL ESMOND AS THE MODERN
EXAMPLE IN " BEAUTY AND THE BEAST " AT THE LYCEUM

ANOTHER STUDY OF THE AUTHOR WITH JILL ESMOND AT THE LYCEUM

many of whom could not afford it, should have to entertain
the artistes, who had no way of returning the hospitality.

I shall not readily forget one ENSA manager's face
when, on a return visit to one of the camps where we had
been entertained, I said, "Please give my compliments to
the Colonel and say that we'd like to accept his hospitality.
But on this occasion we should like to be the hosts."

In the main, ENSA did a wonderful job of work, not
only for the troops and the workers in the factories, but
for a great number of artistes, some of whom had reached
a stage, pre-war, when jobs for them were practically
non-existent. ENSA gave them long, consecutive work.

Very many people connected with ENSA were worthy
of their jobs. There were "jobs for the boys", of course,
and I can think of many people connected with ENSA
who must have been sorry when the war was over.

After the ENSA tour it was pantomime time again,
and I took my "Aladdin" pantomime to the Coliseum
Theatre, Harrow, for Alfred Denville. The Coliseum
Theatre was converted from a cinema, and has a fine large
stage.

Alfred Denville is an actor-manager of wide experience
and repute. My interview with him, when arrangements
were completed, took place at the House of Commons,
where he was M.P. for Newcastle-on-Tyne. It followed a
strange routine: he showed me over interesting parts of the
House, then left me to listen to some rather dull debates,
and ended up by introducing me to the late Ernest Bevin
and James Maxton.

The pantomime, originally booked for four weeks, was
so successful that the run was extended to eight. This,
despite bad air raids and the black-out. Mr. Denville
issued a contract for me to return the following year, but
I did not do so because he could not see eye to eye with me
about the provision of front-of-the-house limes.

Politicians may like the limelight. But one, at least,
did not want to provide me with any.

In the tour that followed pantomime, "Twinkle" had

Q

the unique experience of playing for the first time at the
Memorial Theatre, Stratford-on-Avon. "Twinkle" was
honoured in being the light entertainment chosen to go into
this august theatre, to follow the famous Shakespearean
Festival.

We opened on a very foggy Monday, in the black-out,
and for the first two or three performances business was
not good. On the Friday the dramatic critic in the local
paper—who has since departed—gave clear indication of
his dislike for our type of entertainment.

I did what is for me a most unusual thing—I replied to
him from the stage. The audience were entirely with me,
and for the next two weeks business increased nightly.
Perhaps the best answer lies in the fact that "Twinkle"
has, every year since, played at the Memorial Theatre.

Sir Archibald Flower, although very ill, was fond of us,
and later his son, Fordham Flower, went out of his way
to make us welcome. Harry Tossell and I became firm
friends.

When a change of regime came at Stratford, Harry
Tossell and his lieutenant, Alice Crowhurst, were pensioned
off. Dear Harry took this very badly and never entered
the theatre again. But that wonderful woman Alice
Crowhurst remained an inveterate theatre-lover, and
weekly can be seen in her usual seat watching the show.

At Christmas 1945 I took my "Aladdin" pantomime to
the Arts Theatre, Cambridge. Norman Higgins is a most
enthusiastic theatre-director, and one who really tries to
help the touring manager to put on a show properly.

The Arts Theatre, Cambridge, is an exclusive theatre,
and many fine productions have first been seen there.
Everyone connected with the theatre, at pantomime time,
really gets the Christmas spirit, and my robust version
of "Aladdin" played to capacity for the whole of its five
weeks' run.

Rosamund Belmore was the Aladdin, and she had many
great moments in the part; glamorous red-headed Marjorie
Cormack was the Princess; Cliff Weir, an old colleague

who is just right in pantomime, was Wishee-Washee; and Claude Chandler had his first chance in pantomime in the important role of Abanazar. Olive, who produced the pantomime, took immense pains with him, and he was outstanding in the part.

Gilbert Brown, on a scouting mission for Jack Buchanan, came down and saw the show. The result was that I fixed-up to take "Aladdin" the following year into the King's Theatre, Hammersmith, for Jack Buchanan.

On my variety tour that followed pantomime I had with me my Four Rosebuds. I was apprehensive whether they'd be tough enough for the music-halls, venues used to the high-powered, regimented work of Tiller Troupes and Rodney Hudson Girls. But their fragile daintiness made an instant appeal, their "Twinkle" training had made them meticulous and careful in and out of the theatre, and it was a joy to hear stage-managers, on our return visits, say, "Here come four of the best-behaved girls in the business."

Betty Goode, with her cheeky prettiness, joined me when she was barely fifteen. She seemed typical of the "couldn't say boo to a goose" type of girl. But when it was necessary for me to find another head-girl, I took the chance with Betty, and the responsibility thus given brought out her many excellent qualities.

"Twinkle" made its first appearance at the Theatre Royal, Brighton, in 1934, when tall, dignified Lawson Lambert was in charge. Edwardian in tradition and outlook, Lawson Lambert was a great stickler for the proprieties. One night during the week Charles Austin came over to see our show with his wife, Ruby, and a party, straight from the beach at Shoreham. Charlie was in an open-necked shirt, and as he passed through to the stalls Lawson Lambert noticed his dishevelled appearance.

"I'm sorry, but you can't go into my stalls dressed like that," said Lawson Lambert.

"Cor blimey," said Charlie, "I've come to see my old pals Olive and 'Clarkie'. I've just come off the beach."

"So I see," said Mr. Lambert acidly. And Charlie had to repair to the cloakroom and tidy up before he was permitted to pass into the stalls.

Olive was on the stage, playing in a sketch in which she appeared as the Empress Josephine, as Charlie passed the orchestra rail. In a very audible whisper he said, "Wotcher, Olive. Not to-night, Josephine, eh?" I think that Mr. Lawson Lambert always regarded me with some suspicion after Charles Austin's visit. In the early part of the war Baxter Somerville came to Worthing to see "Twinkle" and booked us for the Theatre Royal, Brighton, again.

It is a gracious, intimate theatre, and under the present management is one of the most prosperous playhouses in the country. For the greater part of the year, important prior to London productions with West End casts occupy its boards. "Twinkle" is honoured to appear between these fine shows.

Baxter Somerville is a big-boyish type of chap, with a nice sense of humour and an astute outlook. Jack Keates, his manager, has Brighton in general, and the Theatre Royal in particular, right into his system.

There is an old-world courtesy about Baxter Somerville and Jack Keates which is very refreshing. Gracious customs, such as putting flowers in all the ladies' dressing-rooms, irrespective of their status, indicate the essential niceness of the management.

The Board of Directors are not mere figure-heads. If ever I have a theatre, I hope that Charles Smith will be one of my directors.

The artistes' bar at the Theatre Royal, Brighton—aptly known as "The Single Gulp"—is unique. Signatures of the famous adorn its walls, and the whole atmosphere is one of Bohemian hospitality. It was in this genial place that we found ourselves when the end of World War II. came.

We had already celebrated V-Day at the Knightstone Theatre, Weston-super-Mare. The word 'celebrated' does not apply to myself, because I felt exactly the same as I did on Armistice Day, 1918, and I felt it too poignant for celebrations.

In November 1918 Olive and I were in dingy 'digs' at Kilburn. Olive need not have been there, but she insisted on sharing them. When the maroons went off, Olive burst into my room and found me writing a song.

Olive and I had four lucrative engagements that night, two of them booked that very morning for peace festivities. One was at Anderton's Hotel; one at the Great Eastern, Liverpool Street; one at the Criterion, Piccadilly; and the other at the Great Central, Marylebone.

How we made them I do not know. By the time we made our final engagement, there was very little of Olive's evening attire left intact.

At the King's Theatre, Hammersmith, I found my old friend Tommy Piggott not in active management at the theatre, but a trustee of the Mulholland estate. Jack Buchanan with Coral Brown and Elsie Randolph came down on Christmas Eve to give my "Aladdin" pantomime a send-off.

"Aladdin" was very successful at the King's Theatre and was the foundation of other pantomime associations for me there. It was good to see the business grow year by year.

The following year I made "Jack and the Beanstalk" my subject. I had hired a production, the scenery of which was first-class, but the dresses were in an appalling condition.

Many friends came to my aid. Francis Laidler of the Alhambra, Bradford, although in the throes of his own famous pantomimes, came to my help with lots of dresses; Roy Limbert, at Malvern, let me ransack his wardrobe for a further supply; and Reg Maddox of Bath let me hire from him.

Jack Buchanan's verdict was that "Jack and the Bean-stalk" was even better than "Aladdin".

In this pantomime I gave the first big chance of her

career to a girl named Janice Adair. This remarkable girl had given me an audition a year previously. It was an unusual audition because she was punctual, absolutely clear-cut in what she wished to do, had engaged her own pianist, rehearsed with him, and prepared a special act for the audition.

At this time her name was Dorothea Orbell. After the audition, when I booked her at once for "Twinkle", she said, "I'm worried about my name for stage purposes. I haven't yet decided what to call myself." She signed her contract in the name of Orbell, and then, after a series of telephone calls and much correspondence, we hit on the name of Janice Adair. She had the most roguish smile, the frankest eyes I have ever seen, and great personality.

The following year, at the King's Theatre, Hammersmith, my pantomime subject was "Goody Two-Shoes". I decided to play Janice in the title role. Successful as she was in "Jack and the Beanstalk," her "Goody" was even more so. She gave the best performance of a Principal Girl's part that I have ever seen.

Henry Hall saw her in this pantomime and booked her for his summer show at the Grand Theatre, Blackpool. Soon after she opened there, our dear, sweet Janice was stricken down with an internal illness. She never recovered, and soon this young and beautiful girl, so obviously destined for stardom, was buried at Brighton, in the presence of her broken-hearted family, two of her intimate friends, and myself.

Janice Adair was twenty-two. She had done some great war work. Despite her success, and the adulation of many men, she always kept her balance and sense of values. Losses like this are irreplaceable.

Another notable success in the pantomime was Frank Formby, who, as Pickles, was beloved of the children. "Goody Two-Shoes" eclipsed its predecessors easily, and ran for nine weeks, a record at the King's.

Jack Buchanan had to relinquish his interests in the King's Theatre, but the new management took my contract over. In my final year I did "Cinderella". Personally, I am not enamoured of this favourite Christmas story, because I have to play either an ugly sister or a baroness. The ugly sister can be funny, but is unsympathetic, and the baroness has none of the human appeal of the other pantomime dame parts.

With the help of Dan Leno, Junr., who wrote some of the book, I fashioned a "Cinderella" which I really began to like. Owing to prior bookings, the pantomime could run only seven weeks and some odd days, but the business even exceeded my previous productions at the King's.

I said good-bye to the King's Theatre, Hammersmith, with regret. My associations with everyone there had been happy ones.

Arthur Camp, the stage-manager, knows his job from A to Z, and has a sense of humour that always helps things along. Mr. Willard, the dignified stage door-keeper, eminent as an actor in his day, though well over seventy is sprightly and upright, and he gave me the feeling of comradeship that one gets from an old family servant.

The domestic comfort of my regime at Hammersmith was blessed by the wonderful kindness and hospitality of Joe Myers, the landlord at the "Rose and Crown" opposite. Joe in former days had been a well-known manager for Sir Oswald Stoll at the Middlesex Music Hall, now the Winter Garden Theatre.

Prior to that, Joe had been a musical-director, and once occupied the chair for a tour of the United States and Africa, of the D'Oyly Carte Opera Company. Consequently the "Rose and Crown" is more than a pub, it is a real pros. rendezvous. Joe Myers's saloon bar has what is possibly the finest collection of Victorian and Edwardian music-hall stars' photographs to be found. Although he has left me this collection in his will, much as I like it, I hope that it will be a long time before it comes my way.

The kindness and care which Joe Myers, and Frances, and the whole of his staff showed me was wonderful. Every day, during all my pantomime runs at Hammer-

smith, I had lunch in his private sanctum. Not content
with that, he was always sending little delicacies over to
me at the theatre.

We had much in common, for he, like myself, has met
most people in our profession. Sometimes we would sit up
reminiscing in his sitting-room until the small hours.

He was proud of the fact that I, through his sponsorship,
became, like him, a Freeman of the City of London. I
felt honoured that I became a Freeman on the same day
as Sir Laurence Olivier.

The King's Theatre, Hammersmith, was a theatre in
the full Edwardian sense of the word. It has a spacious
stage, and a large yet intimate auditorium, free from
chromium fittings and stucco decorations. It is redolent
of the days when a theatre was a comfortable and sump-
tuously furnished building. Maybe it is my imagination,
but the aroma of oranges still seems to cling to it.

In my regime at the King's I presented four successful
pantomimes in a theatre where I once used to watch the
pantomimes from the gallery, and where twice I was
turned down for jobs. And all within the shadow of
near-by Rowton House, where once I stayed, wearing
threadbare clothes and with but coppers in my pocket.

CHAPTER TWENTY-THREE

ONE of my most memorable experiences was the night on which Charlie Chaplin was made a member of the Grand Order of Water Rats. He arrived for his initiation very late, brought along by Charles Austin.

As if to compensate for his lateness, after the ceremony Chaplin gave a one-man cabaret which still lives in my mind, as I am sure it does in the minds of many famous entertainers who were present. It is almost impossible for me to give an adequate description of it.

He mimed, he talked, he 'mugged', he clowned. It was an impromptu show that scintillated with artistry and genius. It is safe to say that there was not one person in the audience who was not spellbound.

The effect on me, when I see a genius like Chaplin, is to make me feel that I must go and destroy my props. and find another way of earning a living. That is only momentary. When the balance of thought is restored, one remembers that even the Chaplins of our profession cannot appear in every theatre, and therefore we lesser lights serve our purpose.

Agents have been much maligned in their time, occasionally with justice. But I have found some nice folk amongst them, and some were definite characters.

Fred Peel is a remarkable man amongst agents. He could have stepped out from any of Dickens's books. Quiet, cultured and courteous, he is, nevertheless, very astute. If he did not want to do business with you, he could shake you cordially by the hand, whilst gradually pushing you through the door of his office.

Another character was George Millett, for so long the provincial booker in the Ernest Edelsten office. He was forthright in his speech and no respecter of persons.

Amongst agents, Herbert Blackmore was an autocrat for many years, and knew it. His office in Garrick Street was always a heartbreak to go into, and see the rows of people waiting for jobs.

George Slater was a very knowledgeable and informed man of the theatre. He was not a man who made many friends. Arthur Rigby was one and Fred Melville another. I consider that Olive and I were honoured in that we were often invited to his house in Cleveland Square.

He had an immense wardrobe of suits for every occasion, many of them duplicated and triplicated, and the largest collection of hats and boots that I have ever seen. He was the man who told me always to write "account payee" across cheques. "You never know," he would say pedantically, "all sorts of people can cash cheques, but not with 'account payee only' on them."

I have known Miriam Warner for forty years, and from a young girl, "Mims" (as she is known to everybody) has had her whole life bound up in show business. A long time ago I wondered why she ever went into agency, because I know many a young actor or actress from whom Miriam Warner has refused commission, and to whom in addition she has lent money to tide them over bad times.

Harry Norris was another great character, and the best straight-faced leg-puller I have ever met. His son-in-law, Elkan Symons, has imbibed some of his humour, and a happy-go-lucky approach that overcomes obstacles.

Professional landladies of a few years ago had amongst them many characters. There was the fussy but attentive Mrs. Fram, of Pershore Road, Birmingham. Her rooms were like a new pin, and she was almost finicky in her personal appearance. When I made my first entrance in my first Lyceum pantomime, Dave O'Gorman turned round to me and said, in an undertone, "Good God, it's Mrs. Fram!"

Mr. and Mrs. Hodge, of Llanbeddian Gardens, Cardiff, were famous amongst pros. They had, I believe, been in the service of a peer. When one arrived on the Sunday, Mr. Hodge would bring in a meal, beautifully cooked by Mrs. Hodge. When it was over, he would bring into the room a string of chickens' wishbones. For more years than he could remember, he had saved the wishbone of every bird eaten by his favourite boarders.

He would then light a candle, draw the curtains, and, holding the bones aloft, recite an incantation. He did this once to David Poole and myself, and I'm afraid that we rather upset him by our irreverence.

A dour appearance absolutely belied the kind and humorous nature of Miss Paterson of Glasgow, and she had a remarkable memory for the dishes one liked. Once when I told her that I was trying to slim, she said, "Och, I'll gi'e ye what Mr. Albert Whelan has. Ye'll just ha'e a plain fillet steak wi' some green vegetables and noo potatoes, and afterwards ye'll ha'e some stewed prunes wi' noo custard. Mr. Whelan lakes that ivery dee, and look at his lovely figure."

Sophie and Hannah Ogbourne of Edinburgh, two sisters, were possibly the most famous of all landladies. What a sense of humour they had, and great tolerance. They lived for the profession.

Once when I was ill in their house, Sophie, although a confirmed spinster, was putting a poultice on my chest. My pyjama jacket broke loose, and since I am sensitive to the ministrations of women when they have to nurse me, I pulled up the sheet.

"Och, dinnae fash yersel'," said Sophie. "Ah dinnae wan' tae see yer pairson."

Madame Pettit, of Lovaine Place, Newcastle-on-Tyne, liked to have people from the music-hall in one of her sets of rooms, and people from the legitimate theatre in the other. I had the happy experience of staying in her perfect 'digs' when Fred Terry and Julia Neilson occupied her other set on one occasion, and Sybil Thorndyke and Lewis Casson on another.

She prided herself on her cooking, the bulk of which was done in Pyrex cookers when they were practically a new invention. An attractive woman with a mass of auburn hair, she looked as though she had never seen a kitchen, and her clothes could have been worn in a mannequin parade.

Jay Laurier, Billy Bennett and I once spent a Christmas season in the house of Mrs. Mitchell in Bristol Road. She had teeth which, when she talked, sounded like a busy typist. Her cooking was very good, but she was expensive and extravagant with her etceteras.

"Halibut, ten shillings?" I queried on one occasion.

"Yesh," click-click, "Mishter Roshe," click-click. "There wash oyshter shaushe," click-click, "and I put half a doshen oyshters in."

The Misses Watson of Birmingham were rigid spinsters, and, I think, always suspected actors of being wicked people. When Lily Lapidus stayed with them, I often used to have supper with her. If I wasn't out of Lily's sitting-room well before midnight, one Miss Watson would shout upstairs, "Now, Mr. Rose, you know my rules. It's time Miss Lapidus was in bed, and you too."

Even during the war, when hers was the only hotel open, Hilda Clemmons, at the "Swan's Nest" at Stratford-on-Avon, always reserved some of her rooms for members of our calling. The "Swan's Nest" is like a big country house, with the expansive personality of Hilda permeating it all.

I know of no finer hotelier in the whole world than Mr. Paul, at the Grand Hotel, Torquay. "Twinkle" has had the good fortune to spend many anniversary dates at Torquay, and the hospitality of Mr. Paul and his wife Eileen, to my company, has been lavish.

At Torquay also are George and Nora Gillin, who in a few short years have transformed the small Royal Hotel into a most successful concern. It is very near the Pavilion Theatre, and we always stay there at rehearsal times. George and Nora Gillin love the profession and cater especially for them.

I have been fortunate in my own home with many grand housekeepers. Old Mrs. Veasey was always ready to serve us at any hour of the day or night.

There was another, old Peggy, always attentive and ready to murder the King's English. On one occasion I gave her a cantaloupe, told her to put it on ice, and slice it ready for lunch. When we were ready she brought it in, and said, "'Ere's the hantelope, Mr. Rose. Hi never knew it was pink."

At the time Peggy was with us I was in the habit of using a spot of ammonia in my bath. One morning she knocked frantically at the door of the bathroom and said, "Oh, Mr. Rose, I've forgotten to put your harmonium in the bathroom."

Alice Kinnaird, who believed she could trace her ancestry to Bruce of Scotland, was more indifferent to bombs than anyone I have seen. She was a good soul, and terribly worried if, when cooking a meal, the lights had to be lowered.

Our present Ada is unique in every way. Brought up in a strict Yorkshire home there is nothing in the domestic line to which she cannot turn her hand expertly. In the W.R.N.S. during the war her wonderful cooking was noticed at once, and officers took good care that she was kept in their respective galleys. She is the most competent person that I have ever met, and her care and attention is something quite out of the ordinary.

"Do you want any pog for your tea?" Ada will say laconically. Pog, I learnt from her, is, in the Navy, anything in the paste or galantine line that comes out of a tin.

"Don't know why you want to buy those tins," she will go on. "I can make better pog than that." The next day the pog will be something that Ada has made herself, that tastes like a first-class *pâté de maison*.

When times were very bad, I can recall my father saying to us, "Well, my boys, you may have to go short of clothes—you may even have to wear your elder brother's —but as long as it's humanly possible, you'll always have a good table." My parents kept this up as long as they could. Even when we were reduced to very frugal fare, it was served in the correct manner, and with the right sauce.

There is a trend of thought to-day that it is wrong to pay too much attention to food. I do not share it. Although the war has been responsible for many curtailments, in my submission, it will be a good thing when restrictions are lifted and restaurants can worthily maintain their characters again.

Simpson's in the Strand was a rendezvous of ours for many years. It was an eating-house typical of London of long ago. Joints were wheeled round on wagons—the carvers had intimate knowledge of their regular clients' likes and dislikes, and the whole atmosphere was club-like.

Freddy Heck, the manager, once said to me when I looked in during the war, "If you like to go into the bar and have a drink, in about twenty minutes I might find you a piece of meat." A search for meat in Simpson's, the restaurant of the well-to-do middle classes!

When I was an office-boy in Birmingham, Bank's Restaurant in Needless Alley—where no dish cost more than sixpence, vegetables were a penny, and boiled pudding bulging with fruit cost twopence—provided meals impossible, even in the most expensive restaurant to-day. Beef, mutton, veal, pork, boiled beef, boiled pork and steak pudding were always on the menu. Cream was a penny, and a hunk of household bread with a large pat of butter was the same price. If you gave the sturdy waitresses in their spotless white aprons more than a penny tip, you were regarded as a snob.

Once at the old Hippodrome, Newcastle-on-Tyne, I was appearing on the same programme as a marvellous animal act, Troubka and his lions, tigers and bears. Although Troubka handled animals expertly, there was practically no part of his body which had not been bitten and torn in the course of years.

My act preceded this performance, and I had to sing my final song in front of the curtains so that the big cage could be set. One night something went wrong in this fitting up.

In a moment the stage resembled and sounded like the jungle. The animals came off their pedestals and went for each other, and as they charged round, the cage kept bumping me in the back.

As I came to the end of my song Mr. Alexander, the manager, put his head round the prompt corner and said, "Clarkie, for God's sake do some more."

I was terror-stricken. Trembling all over, through parched lips I stammered to the conductor, "Turn to number nine."

The audience, realising that something serious was wrong, were getting restless. By staying before them and singing a comic song I averted a panic.

I had a tremendous local and national Press the following day, with headlines such as "Comedian's Bravery", and so on. George Black and Val Parnell wrote me wonderful letters about my 'heroism', and Mr. Black went so far as to say, "Wherever the George Black banner flies, be it a Bank Holiday or a Boxing Day, you have the right of free entry into my theatres."

"Heroism!" I just did what I was told because I was afraid to move from the spot!

Following on one of my pantomime engagements at the Gaiety Theatre, Dublin, I was booked to play a week in variety at the Theatre Royal. The management insisted that I sang my song, *Dear Old Dirty Dublin*.

On the first night, just as I reached the end of the refrain with the words "Dear Old Dirty Dublin", a drunken man made his way to the back of the conductor, pointed a revolver, and shouted, "How dare you call Dublin dairty, yer bloody Saxon?" I went on singing.

A member of the audience and an attendant got hold of him and put him out. Once again I was eulogised for my 'bravery' in the Press.

Once again I had gone on singing because I was afraid to move!

CHAPTER TWENTY-FOUR

IN comparison with artistes in series shows, broadcasting at the same hour on the same day every week for long periods, I cannot claim to be a radio artiste in the full sense of the term. But in view of the fact that the first comic song ever to be broadcast was written by me, *Down in our Village in Zummerzet,* sung by Norman Long, and of the fact that my own broadcasts started in the 2LO days, I can advance a tentative claim.

From Savoy Hill, in 2LO days I did two broadcasts. I found them frightening affairs. A gentleman named Fryer was in charge, and I can remember much discussion about a golfing medley that I was doing.

With all the present-day discussion in the Press about whether there should or should not be studio audiences, it is interesting to note that there was an audience for those 2LO broadcasts. I remember that I was surprised to find them there.

In 1925 my Show "Twinkle" did the first full hour's broadcast from any seaside place. The producer was very worried because he wanted to create over the air the effect of a show coming virtually from the edge of the sea, complete with the sound of the waves, and Shorefields Pavilion, at Westcliff, backed on to the mixture of shingle and mud, euphemistically known locally as "the sands". On that occasion I put in some good work with a brush on a drum, and everyone was satisfied with the extremely consistent waves! The following year "Twinkle" did another hour's broadcast from the same place.

In 1935 "Twinkle" did an hour's show from Broadcasting House, and this became an annual event for the next couple of years. These broadcasts were in charge of my old friend Harry Pepper, and for the first two the orchestra was conducted by another old friend, Kneale Kelly.

For the final year Charles Shadwell took over from Kneale Kelly. "Twinkle" was the first show that Charles of the laugh handled for the B.B.C.

Relays of pantomimes in which I broadcast came from the Alexandra Theatre, Birmingham, in 1936, and the Theatre Royal, Birmingham, in 1940. "Twinkle" broadcast many times in the Summer Series, from East-bourne Pier.

These season broadcasts from seaside places were handled by a regular platoon of producers and com-mentators. On one occasion I entertained Harry Pepper, John Watt and Davy Burnaby to lunch at the Grand Hotel, Eastbourne.

It was the season of grouse—if not, in those happy days, of grouses—and a whole grouse was served to everybody present. Screams of delight went up from the party when Davy Burnaby had two.

"Twinkle" broadcast regularly from seaside places, and from Knightstone Pavilion, Weston-super-Mare, did a special programme for V-day. Elsewhere in this record I have commented on the broadcasts in various programmes that we did from Llandudno, when the B.B.C. functioned in the war years from that happy Welsh resort, and pleasant Bangor.

A programme I recall with pleasure was my appearance in "King-pins of Comedy". It was done from Manchester, and a very nervous Wilfred Pickles came round to inter-view me in my hotel bedroom and, doubtless because of that venue, apologised for having his wife with him.

Richard North handled us twice from Harrogate. He was one of the swiftest and most direct producers I have ever encountered. I can picture him now, yelling from the control room, "Clarkie, for heaven's sake stop your compere from introducing every artiste with 'And now'. Let's think of something else." We did!

An outstanding memory is a broadcast I did with Albert Whelan, Blaney and Farrar, Ivy St. Helier, and other notable artistes, called "The Story of the London

R

Coliseum". It was a magnificently handled programme, and Mark Lubbock surprised me with an expert handling of comic songs. It was broadcast from Bedford, and since we were all in the same hotel, it was a night of pleasant reminiscing until the small hours.

The broadcast from St. George's Hall of the Grand Order of Water Rats was another notable programme. Either individually or in ensembles all the prominent Rats of the time were included, and listeners heard Will Fyffe, Charles Austin, Claude Dampier, Will Hay, "Wee Georgie" Wood, Bud Flanagan, Talbot O'Farrell, and Fred Russell amongst them.

I was fortunate enough to be given an individual spot, and had chosen one of my own songs. During rehearsal Fred Malcolm and Nat Mills came along, and said that they had written a song, would I hear it, and, if I liked it, broadcast it? I took out my own song, and thus created *Nice People with Nice Manners*, which became one of the most popular songs of the year. Later I used it in a Lyceum pantomime.

One of my saddest experiences in broadcasting was when doing a "Palace of Varieties" from the King's Theatre, Hammersmith. Just before we went on the air we heard of Tommy Handley's death.

It had a particularly damping effect on Nosmo King, who, strangely enough, passed on himself a few days later. This broadcast did not go out until it had been re-recorded with a different chairman.

The rich "rortiness" of "Palace of Varieties" appeals to me. My friend Ernest Longstaffe enjoys the programmes so much himself that he conveys that enjoyment to his artistes.

Henry Hall's Guest Night programmes are always happy experiences. On one occasion at Blackpool there was a tremendous hou-ha about my appearing on Sunday night dressed as a 'dame'. I did so appear, with the full backing of the B.B.C. legal department.

Collie Knox wrote in the *Daily Mail*: "Along with 698

other members of the studio audience at last Sunday's recording of the Henry Hall Guest Night, which you will hear broadcast on Saturday, film star Robert Beatty and I witnessed a whacking smack in the eye to this ridiculous antiquated law that bans Sunday performances with artistes in 'make-up'. Already Wilfred Pickles and others had been forced to cancel bookings. Clarkson Rose who, with Olive Fox, is the permanent 'Twinkle' in Eastbourne's eye, was booked as guest artiste.

"He said, 'I shall appear in full "Dame" costume.' B.B.C. North Regional lost its nerve and banned him. Before the recording, Clarkson Rose told me that the B.B.C. in London upheld him, and had said, 'Go ahead, wear the kitchen stove if you like, we will take full responsibility.' So before our delighted gaze on he strode—looking a Dame to end all Dames.

"The Law could not do a thing about it because the audience did not pay to come in. Mr. Rose's defiant action should prove once and for all the utter fatuity of a law which, while allowing an Abbott and Costello film on Sundays at the local cinema, debars artistes from giving Sunday shows should they wear a hat or a false moustache."

Broadcasting will always be nerve-racking work to me. But producers like Brian Johnson and John Ellison make it very pleasant. On one occasion when I broadcast in a relay from the Empire, Hackney, London, Brian not only announced but was a most enthusiastic member of the audience. He led the applause when I made a slip, and said, "Oh dear, I've put a bit in that was cut."

I have a completely open mind about the value of commercial broadcasting. The several programmes I did in Australia, sponsored by various firms, were useful publicity both for my show and myself, and I think had a happy spontaneity perhaps missing from the less haphazard B.B.C. shows. The high standard and probity of the B.B.C. is, however, acknowledged throughout the world.

After forty years in show business, with present-day taxation, I, like many others, still have to keep at it. As I sit in the garden of my Eastbourne home, looking at the evening sky over the Downs—a sky that has the colour of a dish of damsons and custard—I am glad that I can still continue my work.

I have passing regrets.

I am sorry that I was unable to take the four weeks' engagement that Henry Sherek secured for me at the Palace Theatre, New York, back in the '20's.

I am sorry that I was unable to accept C. B. Cochran's offer to play the comedy part in "Paganini" with Evelyn Laye.

I am sorry that, when Stanley Lupino dropped out of "Better Days" at the London Hippodrome, that I could not take his place, a booking which Ernest Edelsten offered me.

I am sorry that I could not take the South African tour with Harry Lauder.

I am sorry that I could not accept "Uncle" Roy Limbert's suggestion that I played in the Malvern Festival one year.

I am sorry that, when Shaw's "Pygmalion" was first produced at His Majesty's Theatre, London, my colleague Algernon Greig, of the Liverpool Repertory Theatre, was chosen for the part of Freddy, and not myself.

I am sorry that I had to refuse Robert Atkins's invitation to play comedy parts in a Shakespearean season at Stratford-on-Avon. One day I hope to do this.

I am sorry that I could not book Tommy Handley and Jack Hylton in 1919 at Bognor, when I had the opportunity. "Handley and Hylton" were a double-act, they wanted eight or nine pounds and Wallis Arthur offered them a pound less, and whilst they were considering it, they had a better offer from elsewhere.

Years previously, when I ran Saturday night "Pops" at the St. Anne's Hall, Aigburth, Liverpool, Tommy Handley was amongst the artistes I booked. His fee was seven shillings and sixpence, later increased to ten shillings!

As Barry Lupino has written, "The stage is an ancient institution founded upon one of the most irrepressible instincts of humanity." It is a full-time job, with no five-day week, nor double pay at week-ends. It carries no superannuation nor pension, and it is always subject to the changes and fluctuations in taste of its employer—the public. For established star or young beginner, the stage means work—work—and then more work.

On a Sunday night recently, at the Redoubt Bandstand at Eastbourne, I sat and watched my old friend George Buck performing on the bandstand, and sometimes jumping down into the audience for a chat. My mind went back forty years, and once again I was on a small alfresco stage at Pwllheli, Burnham-on-Sea, or Laxey Glen in the Isle of Man.

I felt again the sea breeze blowing up my pierrot trousers or disarranging my ruffle. I pictured myself once again stepping down from the stage, proffering my hat and saying, "Patronise the pierrots, madam—thank you—did you? I'm so glad—that song? *Out in the Open.* Yes, of course, we'll sing it to-morrow afternoon. What's that? You've just given. I'm sorry, madam, but I'm sure as you're enjoying it so much, you'll give again. Thank you, sir, you've been here every day for some time now, haven't you? A sovereign!—thank you, sir, you are kind. I shall tell Mr. Smith; I won't put it in with the coppers."

I envied George Buck, and I was proud that I had been a pierrot.

Back in my Eastbourne garden, my pierette, Olive Fox, shouts from the window, "Haven't you finished that book yet? It's getting late and we've got to get to the show."

"Just on the end now, dear, I shan't be a minute."

"Darling, do you know the time?"

"No. What is it?"

"It's half-past seven."

"Blimey, we ring up at eight. Freeman will be getting frantic."

Freeman has been my "Man Friday" for many years, and is one of the few "Men Fridays" who does not put the thought of Friday first!

Then off we go, Olive and I, middle-aged Pierette and Pierrot, on our bicycles—for petrol is short—to the Devonshire Park Theatre, Eastbourne. When I get to the stage-door, somehow my bicycle wants to take me to the pier and the bandstand, where Wallis Arthur's Pierrots appear twice daily in my memories.

Wallis himself is in charge and greeting the patrons. Presently an important-looking clerical gentleman wearing ecclesiastical gaiters moves up from a back row and seats himself in a front-row deck chair that has a "Reserved" card on it. Wallis steps forward.

"Excuse me, sir, but that seat is reserved."

"Yes, yes, I know. But the show's been on about twenty minutes and nobody has occupied it, so I thought I'd take it."

"I'm sorry, it's reserved; you can't do that."

"But Mr. Wallis Arthur, surely you know me? I'm the Dean of Chichester."

"Quite so, sir," says Wallis politely. "But for all I know that seat may have been reserved for the Archbishop of Canterbury."

It is a soft warm night, and I would like to get into my pierrot suit and join George Buck on the Redoubt Bandstand. There is hardly any breeze, and Dorothy Atlee at the piano will be all smiles, for no one will have to hold her music on the stand. It is indeed a pierrot's night.

I know of no greater thrill than seeing a vast auditorium crowded with happy holidaymakers. They've had their dinner or their high tea, and they're waiting eagerly for Pierrot and Pierrette.

The festoons of coloured lights are twinkling. Attendants with stentorian voices are shouting, "Programmes, threepence."

As the time for starting approaches there is a general buzz. Dorothy walks through the little curtain with a bundle of music.

A burst of applause welcomes her. She crashes out a cascade of chords, and the show goes on.

INDEX

A

Acland, Audrey, 229, 232
Adair, Janice, 246
Adams, Blake, 77
Adelaide, 185, 191
Aden, 81
"Aladdin", 106, 240, 241, 242, 243, 245
Alexandra Theatre, Birmingham, 201–203, 213
Alhambra, The, 110, 116, 121, 132, 140, 153
"Ali Baba and the Forty Thieves", 235
Allen, Chesney, 59
Allgood, Sara, 61
Anderson, Millar, 65
Angers, Avril, 213
Ansell, Bernard, 219
Arbuthnot, Archie, 101
Argyle Theatre, Birkenhead, 63
Armstrong, Billy, 63, 67
Arnley, Ernest, 180, 181, 182, 196, 198
Arnold, Doris, 218
Arthur, Wallis, 80, 81, 82, 83, 88, 90, 96, 102, 103, 110, 111, 119, 260
Arts Theatre, Cambridge, 237, 242
Ashford, Murray, 115
Askey, Arthur, 177, 199, 205, 229
Asquith, Lord Oxford and, 79
Astor, A. C., 164, 195
Austin, Charles, 116, 119, 243, 244, 249, 258
Aylmer, Felix, 72, 73

B

"Babes in the Wood", 228
Barbour, Roy, 224
Bard, Wilkie, 64, 116, 134, 161
Barker, Ambrose, 190
Barker, Granville, 54
Barnard, Ivor, 72, 73
Barnum and Bailey Circus, 29
Barrett, Wilson, 26
Barty, Jack, 214, 216
Bassano, Vera (Yvette), 73, 75, 76, 77
Bayes, Norah, 169, 170, 171
Beardmore, Hilda, 232
Beaumont, J. E. B., 178
"Beauty and the Beast", 217
Bell, Arnold, 219
Belmore, Rosamund, 242
Benefit nights, 105, 107, 126
Bennett, Billy, 132, 133, 229, 252
Bernardi, 180, 191
Bernhardt, Sarah, 134
Bertram, Hilda, 81
Betton, George, 213
Birmingham Repertory Theatre, 71–75
Black, George, 255
Blackmore, George, 80, 81, 83, 103
Blackmore, Herbert, 69, 249
Blain, Kenneth, 81, 84, 87, 88
Blaney and Farrar, 257
Blaney, Norah, 95
Bluett, Gus, 188
Bobs, The Two, 95
Bode, Milton, 69, 70, 93, 98
Boer War, 22
Bognor Pavilion, The, 83
Bolt, Anne, 229

264